Raising Your Jewish/Christian Child

RAISING YOUR JEWISH CHRISTIAN CHILD

Wise Choices for Interfaith Parents

Lee F. Gruzen

An Eric Weber Book

DODD, MEAD & COMPANY   New York

Copyright © 1987 by Lee F. Gruzen and Eric Weber
All rights reserved
No part of this book may be reproduced in any form
without permission in writing from the publisher.
Published by Dodd, Mead & Company, Inc.
71 Fifth Avenue, New York, N.Y. 10003
Manufactured in the United States of America
Designed by Mark Bergeron
First Edition
1 2 3 4 5 6 7 8 9 10

Library of Congress Cataloging-in-Publication Data
Gruzen, Lee F.
   Raising your Jewish-Christian child.
   Bibliography: p. 257.
   1. Interfaith marriage—United States.   2. Children of
interfaith marriage—United States.   3. Family—United
States—Religious life.   4. Family—United States—
Religious life (Judaism)   I. Title.
HQ1031.G78   1987   306.8′43   87-9257
ISBN 0-396-08551-2

For Rachel, Georgia, Alex,
and their grandparents, with love.

CONTENTS

ACKNOWLEDGEMENTS

My deepest thanks go to Kathryn Watterson whose friendship, great spirit, and savvy were a miracle to me. From the heart, I also wish to thank Eric Weber, Reverend Daniel Heischman, Egon Mayer, Robin Elliott, Sheila Gordon, Robin Margolis, Leslie Goodman-Malamuth, and my editor, Jerry Gross, for their support and contributions throughout the entire process of this book.

I am deeply indebted to the community of Trinity School and its former headmaster, Robin Lester, as well as to The American Jewish Committee, especially Cyma Horowitz and Steven Bayme, for making their resources and considerable experience on this subject available to me.

To the many members of the clergy who responded to my requests for information, I'm appreciative of the readiness with which each of them tried to help and explore these issues with me. No one refused an interview or turned away my questions. My special thanks go to Reverend Richard Spalding and Rabbis Lavey Derby, David Greenberg, Edwin H. Friedman, and Barry Friedman.

I was influenced a great deal by Marie Sabin, Amanda Houston Hamilton, Carla Hall, Virginia Blacker, Sue and Richard Bender, Sylvia and David Nelson, Judith Mac-Donald, Miriam and Milton Handler, Jane and Ira Silverman, Hilde and Rabbi Joachim Prinz, Zachary Dand, Ilana Friedman, and Thomas Lehrecke, a supremely generous and wise human being.

What a pleasure it is to thank, as well, my friends and allies who were patient and full of advice, good humor, and willingness to help over an unexpectedly long stretch of time. My love and appreciation go to Mel Berger, Violette Jean, Laurie Scott, Theodora Sklover, Ryl Norquist, Ann and Clive Cummis, Lynn Butler, Dr. Lois Berman, Rose Kolberg, Eva Golinski, Dr. Alvin Blaustein, Blossom and Saul Krawcheck, Cara Aisha Campbell, K. C. Cole, Adele Brody, Jon Surgal, Linda Wolfe, Doe Lang, Ray O'Leary, Karen Crane, Rita Lord, John Brumfield, Heather Shepherd, Arlene Gross, and Sara and Philip Chasin. I will be grateful forever to Phyllis and Mel Heiko, George Shimamoto, Joanna Weber, Doris and Alex Weber, Ellyn Peister, and Jacki Jackson for providing wonderful places to work.

I thank Benjamin Gruzen, Jeanette Shrago, Bruce Garfield, Gar Ferguson, and my parents, Eleanor and Clinton Ferguson, for their enthusiasm, mounds of clippings, family histories, and coffee.

And to my husband Jordan, my love always for supporting me through the aggravations as well as the great pleasures that have resulted from writing this book, and for adding, as he always does, a calm, wise way of enjoying and handling life.

A NOTE TO THE READER

A word about the names that appear in this book. Because many of the people I interviewed didn't want to be identified, I have fictionalized their names and substituted ones that easily could have been theirs based on the ethnic and religious characteristics. The exceptions are those individuals who are clearly identified by their professional titles, affiliations, or family ties. Relatives, clergy, professors, and other consultants fall into this category; their names are their own.

INTRODUCTION

Early in my interfaith marriage I started fielding questions from relatives about how my husband and I were planning to raise our children. "Will you bring them up as Christians? As Jews?" relatives would ask, trying not to be too intrusive. I wrote this book, in part, to learn how to answer their questions. Seven years of awkward responses seemed more than enough.

Every time my husband Jordan and I went to a niece's christening or a nephew's bar mitzvah, a funeral in the synagogue or a wedding in the church, there was always one, sometimes two members of the family who came over and asked the discreet question. Like us, they'd been moved by the opening chords on the organ, the glow and soft jingle of a Torah scroll held high, a phrase in the liturgy, or a memory from family history, and they would ask if—and how—our daughters would have that same continuity and tradition to call upon. I suspect they also wondered how our daughters could assure them of their own continuity and carry on the great traditions by experiencing what they loved.

In fact, Jordan and I both valued our own backgrounds and treasured what we were learning about the other's religious and ethnic heritage. Jordan is Jewish, the product of four decades in a Conservative synagogue in New Jersey. I'm Protestant and equally bound to the traditions of a New England Congregational church and, since college, the moody rituals of Episcopal services. When Jordan and I married in 1976 in a beautiful spot overlooking the ocean, we avoided any conflict by having a justice of the peace preside. And when our daughters Rachel and Georgia were born in 1977 and 1981, we stayed clear of religious ceremonies once again.

But now we had to face the real question. How *were* we raising Rachel and Georgia? Jordan and I usually mumbled something about "Episcopal kindergarten and Jewish summer camp . . . the menorah and the Christmas tree . . . seders in New Jersey and Easter on Cape Cod."

"A little bit of both," we would say to each other, adding our final defense that "Rachel and Georgia are still young after all."

The answer was an apt reflection of what we knew about honoring our Jewish and Christian roots—that each was important, and we were unwilling to forfeit either of them. What we knew even more keenly, however, was that our answer was too superficial and unexamined to be anything more than an introduction to more serious questions that we needed to ask ourselves about our marriage and spirituality, the nature of the complicated bonds of family and faith guiding all our choices, and our dreams for our children and ourselves. We'd stuttered our way through one relative's challenge too many about the religious background we were going to give our children. It was time to know where we stood about an important part of our lives.

Once I decided to write the book, I found many other people who wanted answers to the same questions. I found that we were pioneers exploring uncharted territory. Even though several people said my project was fifty years too late and others asked, "What's the big deal about interfaith children?" I realized that essentially our generation is the first to struggle openly with the question of how to raise our Jewish/Christian children. The truth is that America's interfaith marriages have only recently become commonplace and socially accepted events, and many churches and synagogues are welcoming interfaith families for the first time. Moreover, Jewish/Christian children offer opportunities for growth and harmony that are unprecedented. In our interfaith family's search for greater understanding about how best to integrate two powerful and rich traditions into our lives, there are many new and important questions to ask and new ground to explore.

As you will see when you read this book, I've found some answers to our relatives' questions. The process has been confusing at times, but always provocative and challenging. It's a process, however, that continues. We're still learning to celebrate and deal wisely with aspects of our religions that we can blend into our lives and with the choices that work for us.

Lee F. Gruzen
October 1986

Raising Your Jewish/Christian Child

CHAPTER

1

FINDING MY WAY

A fellow parent in an interfaith marriage once said something that haunted me through most of my research on this book. At a time when I felt totally awash in conflicting notions about how to help my daughters get the most of their dual heritages, she sighed and said, "You know, if we didn't have so many preconceptions about what we're supposed to be and do, the matter wouldn't be half so difficult." She was right, but it took months of confusion and self-doubt to understand the meaning of her words.

The subject of Jewish/Christian families has undergone a transformation. By the very fact that there are approximately three-quarters of a million adults who are part of (or until divorce were part of) interfaith marriages and probably at least that many interfaith children today, it's clear that times have changed dramatically. The widely accepted statistics, which are, in fact, "guesstimates" based on a number of nationwide demographic studies conducted by Jewish organizations, indicate that in 1960 fewer than 6 percent of Jews getting married chose a non-Jewish partner. By 1985, however, the percentage rose to over 30 percent in most American cities and to 60 percent or more in others.

According to Dr. Egon Mayer, professor of sociology at Brooklyn College, who has conducted three major studies on interfaith marriage for the American Jewish Committee, there are a handful of reasons for the dramatic upsurge. "Firstly, the sheer movement of Jews away from densely Jewish areas to places where they've encountered larger numbers of non-Jews has led to more intermarriage. This is a demographic factor. Secondly, the non-Jewish world became more accepting of Jews, so as Jews moved in—to residential, educational, and professional environments— non-Jews were more hospitable. This is a factor of social climate. Thirdly, the increase in divorce has been a very important factor. It's hard to put a number on it, but it's apparent that second marriages are more likely to be in- termarriages than first ones. It's been suggested by soci- ologists, in fact, that a previous divorce is one of the strongest predicters of intermarriage."

The skyrocketing increase has led researchers like Dr. Mayer to conclude, as well, that the number of interfaith children will have a major impact on American society in the not-too-distant future. "If current statistical population trends continue, it is not inconceivable that by the year 2050, the descendants of Jewish-Gentile intermarriages will constitute a major group of American Jews," said Mayer. Even more immediately for Jewish and Christian families, it means that increasing numbers of grandparents, in-laws, stepchildren, cousins, and friends are intimately tied to those, like my husband and me, who are dealing with intermarriage on a day-to-day basis. Unfortunately, the insights into the dilem- mas, triumphs, and everyday revelations that are part of Jewish/Christian lives haven't kept as up-to-date as the care- fully gathered numbers.

My daughter Rachel was the first to introduce me to the legacy of outmoded thinking and ignorance that complicated my own attempts to deal with this subject. One Saturday morning when she was five years old, our family was sitting around the kitchen table for breakfast, and my mind was miles away, thinking about this book. Offhandedly I asked Rachel, "What religion is Daddy?"

"Resligen?" she asked; it was obviously a word that hadn't been used in our house too much.

"Religion, Rachel," Jordan said matter-of-factly.

"I don't know," she answered, whereupon Jordan said, "Daddy is Jewish."

I reminded her that Mommy's Christian.

"Chrisligen?" Rachel asked, having caught on to the new game. But then she pointed to herself with both hands, and her face clouded over. Looking back and forth between us, she asked slowly, "So what am I, Rachel?"

I heard Jordan say, "Both," and I held my breath. "Both" was supposed to be the terrible word, the choice that parents make when they're avoiding responsibility and settling for a superficial religious education that makes for an ignorant, confused, and totally neurotic child. Children need clarity and concreteness, don't they? They need to belong to one group and have one religious identity, don't they? Actually, I didn't have a clue what children needed in order to be well-adjusted and comfortably sure of themselves. Rachel seemed happy enough with Jordan's answer as she went on eating her eggs, but I decided it was time to reach out to the experts and see what they had to say to help parents be more confident and spontaneous in these typical situations at home. I assumed the supposed experts would have wise words to offer on this matter and that my own understanding would develop very logically and calmly after hearing or reading their comments. The process didn't quite work out that way.

The literature in the library became my first source of information about interfaith families, and reviewing those depressing surveys often felt like sifting through a pile of gray stones to get to an occasional fleck of gold. Time and again, the writings conflicted dramatically with my own sense of the gifts I was giving my children.

Because Jordan and I were raising Rachel and Georgia in an environment that was animated by friends, relatives, and celebrations from two different cultures and religions, we felt we were giving them such an abundant, joyous introduction to life's possibilities. We were proud that we offered them a stable home with parents who loved each other and valued each other's differences, and though we'd never sat down and carefully worked out our plans for raising them religiously, we assumed we'd handle the matter as it developed. At the moment, we welcomed any and all Jewish and Christian experiences that seemed to come our way. We expected our daughters to grow up to become resilient, happy, well-adjusted, and much richer and wiser for having been raised with our Jewish/Christian duality.

The observations on interfaith marriages and children, written mostly in the period between the late 1950s and the early 1970s when intermarriage started its sudden and steady increase, were relentlessly gloomy. I wondered where the sociologists and clergy found such an array of troubled families. When I looked around at the interfaith families I knew, I saw couples getting along much like any other, and the children seemed as lively as their religiously homogeneous peers. But the twenty-or-so-year-old books and articles never seemed to come across anyone who was reasonably well-adjusted. They specialized in the interfaith marriages that were marked by conflict and irreconcilable differences, and though they didn't write as much about the children (because the population was still relatively small at that time), they were unanimous in their insistence that "mixed marriages are not well adapted to rearing children."

What happened to them, supposedly, were a rash of identity problems and other disturbances, such as alienation, anxiety, marginality, and low self-esteem. One of the more intelligent surveys, *One Marriage, Two Faiths*, completed by James H. S. Bossard and Eleanor Stoker Boll in 1957, combined most of the common observations into the most elaborate and dispiriting portrait of all.

In their conclusion, Bossard and Boll wrote that ". . . it has been pointed out that people who make interfaith marriages apparently realize that children will cause problems or will have problems. The lower birth rate and higher rate of childlessness among such couples suggest this. A part of the difficulty is caused by a primary function of the family —to pass down the cultural heritage. When the parents are of different religions, the family is a cultural mixture and the child is torn, in choosing his religion and philosophy of life, between two sides of the family. This results not only in 'taking sides' within the family, but in inner conflict for the child. The divisiveness extends to brothers and sisters as well as to parents and tends to separate them even when they grow up, marry, and have their own children who are reared in various faiths."

As my research progressed, I found more up-to-date material written in the late '70s and early '80s, but it communicated the same feeling of danger and alarm, as if interfaith families were inevitably connected to something sad or destructive and little could be said to recommend them. Because rabbis and the representatives of most Jewish organizations were deeply concerned that interfaith marriages were dangerously eroding the Jewish community, their writings usually had an anxious and sad tone that also bore no relationship to my own positive delight and curiosity about being part of an interfaith household.

There were a few enlightened observers who noted that interfaith marriages and family relationships weren't as terrible as myth and propaganda would have them. But for couples like Jordan and me, who had made their decision to marry and raise children and who wanted advice and encouragement on how to live interfaith lives in a full and wonderful way, the material was as incomplete as it was disheartening. In a bookstore I picked up a new book called *The Real Anti-Semitism in America* by Nathan Perlmutter and Ruth Ann Perlmutter. Thumbing through its pages, I discovered the extreme prediction made by a Jewish leader from Boston named Philip Perlmutter that, "If trends continue, America will become one big dull glob of people who won't even know they had a grandmother." And in the final conclusion of the significant American Jewish Committee study called *Intermarriage and the Jewish Future* (1976), researchers Egon Mayer and Carl Sheingold wrote that, "The findings summarized above tend to reinforce the fear that intermarriage represents a threat to Jewish continuity."

The few Catholic writings didn't associate interfaith marriage with "fear" and "threat," because, understandably, extinction wasn't a concern for an American Catholic population of 52 million that didn't have to recover from a Nazi holocaust fewer than fifty years earlier. The ecumenism from Pope John XXIII's 1965 Vatican II also softened the church's official position on Catholic/Jewish marriages and the raising of the children. Though rare, there were some compassionate treatments of the needs of the interfaith family that mentioned divorce and the children's emotional tensions only in passing, and never as certainties. A 1973 book called *When a Christian and a Jew Marry*, written by a priest named Ronald Luka, was one of those welcomed works.

The Protestant literature was no help at all. I couldn't find a contemporary word on the subject. The best that well-intentioned advisers could offer me was the classic book written in 1954 by the late Episcopal Bishop James A. Pike. Called *If You Marry Outside Your Faith*, it was preoccupied with the crises of Protestants marrying Catholics—a hot topic years ago. In his final summary, Bishop Pike included Jewish/Christian marriages, however, and arrived at an all too familiar conclusion: "Sufficient has been said to suggest the idea that a mixed marriage is not a good thing."

Against that background of anxious voices who knew only the problems, I tried to reconcile my own sense of celebration and responsibility and come to know the successes *and* the penalties of others first hand. It was time to move to a second set of experts—the grown children who were the products of Jewish/Christian marriages like my own. That search wasn't any less complicated, however.

The myths about their problems and confused identities were all too clear to me when I started interviewing large numbers of adult Jewish/Christian children twenty-one and over. Once again the accepted "truth" about this forgotten population stood in stark contrast to what I kept discovering—that far from being wounded and downtrodden, these individuals were dynamic, intelligent, and very successful human beings who were proud of their mixed birth and the advantages that it gave them. Humor, adaptability, and openmindedness were among their many achievements.

Partly out of my hunger to reach out for a spirit that was compatible with my own and partly out of my determination to counter the lopsided and incomplete news about the children, I felt compelled to assemble a long list of dynamic achievers with Jewish/Christian parents. The names were easy to find through press clippings, leads from friends, and the various Jewish reference books that list individuals with a Jewish background. The detective work was simple and fun, and it was a pleasure to be doing something far more tangible than working my way through the abstract and complicated issues that surround the subject of this book. Besides, these personages, living and dead, were the most dramatic proof I could muster to show how effective Jewish/Christian lives could be.

The list was a colorful one, beginning with Jewish/Christian politicians like Fiorello LaGuardia and San Francisco mayor Dianne Feinstein, continuing with movie stars like Paul Newman, Goldie Hawn, John Houseman, Melvyn Douglas, Dyan Cannon, Kevin Kline, Michael Landon, Michael Douglas, Claire Bloom, Ally Sheedy, Carrie Fisher, Peggy Lipton, and Stefanie Powers. There were the musicians André Watts, Arlo Guthrie, Chico Hamilton, and Carly Simon and her sisters Lucy and Joanna. The writers included Mary Gordon, Eugene Ionesco, Marcel Proust, Romain Gary, and Dorothy Parker, and there were the brilliant researchers Dr. Erik H. Erikson and the Nobel Prize winners Hans Bethe and Wassily Leontief. To top it off, I discovered the comedians Peter Sellers and Freddie Prinze, photographer Margaret Bourke-White, the British financier Sir James Goldsmith, "Sesame Street" 's Joan Ganz Cooney, and professional football players Lyle Alzado and Larry Brodsky, plus dozens of others.

The list of famous people was varied and persuasive,

but I was also drawn to the adult sons and daughters who weren't famous and public persons. I interviewed over seventy-five of them for about two-and-a-half hours each in several major cities around the country. They were also easy to find. In addition to the names friends gave me, there was always someone "half and half" at every event I attended. They'd hear about my book and volunteer information, or most commonly, they'd exhibit some telling, mismatched characteristic, and I'd instinctively ask them about their roots. For instance, their names might be Maureen Cohen or Saul Birmingham. A six-footer named Max Shapiro would have freckles and blond hair, while Holly Brown would be dark and Semitic-looking. Sometimes a person with a name like Sidney Feldman had a cousin named James Allen Drexel III, or another's parents were named Morty and Marie. In many cases, the ethnic recognitions were more subtle because the Irish looks didn't match the Jewish intensity, or the adult daughter's mother was a judge while her father was an Italian tenor. If I count my useful but shorter talks with a wide assortment of other Jewish/Christian adults that I've run into over the last three years at the beach, in the line at the supermarket, at parties, PTA meetings, conventions, and religious services, I readily add another 150 alert and communicative people to my resources.

What struck me about most of the Jewish/Christian offspring I interviewed was their talkativeness, vitality, and humor. Because very few had ever been asked about this dimension of their lives before, they had a lot to say that was fresh and exploratory, and the discoveries came slowly and steadily throughout the hours needed to explain and consider a lifetime of experience. Although I learned from all of them, I found those adults who were struggling with a passage in the life cycle to be the most illuminating. Their periods of emotional change—during marriage, divorce, childrearing, separation from home, death of a parent, illness, and crisis, as well as the preparation for each of these transitions—often compelled them to reevaluate their identities, gather their emotional and spiritual resources, test their beliefs and commitments, and confront religious issues and institutions that hadn't been part of their lives for long periods of time. They tended to examine their ethnic and religious roots in a way that wasn't necessary when their lives were more stable. The complicated and highly individualized process of weighing and making choices about how to integrate the best of a Jewish-and-Christian background came into clearer focus, as did the conflicts that needed resolution.

Since it was not a process that had ever been explained or even valued by those around them, I sensed their deep curiosity about how it affected them. They didn't seem to realize that there were many other Jewish/Christian adults struggling with the same questions and experiences. They were sure that they were the only ones to feel that way or grow up in such an odd household, and they were surprised when they learned about patterns they shared with others.

Much of the time, I congratulated myself on having Jewish/Christian children of my own who could stand in such good company. They were smart and sensitive people, socially adept and loved by their families. They were infinitely more diverse and human than the one-dimensional, far from complimentary case histories had made them out to be. I realized that the great increase of Jewish/Christian marriages and children over the last fifteen years would begin to call attention to this complex group. Odds were good that the truth—rich and varied—would gradually be told about them.

There were ways in which the adult offspring didn't fulfill my hopes, however. In the early days, when I first wrote the proposal for this book, I'd anticipated that the grown half-and-half children were going to be the perfect guides to lead me knowledgeably through the Jewish and Christian worlds that I didn't understand. They'd point out the strengths and weaknesses of each culture and religion. They'd be fair and insightful as they did justice to each while nodding tolerantly as I aired my grievances and prejudices, which they, of course, would interpret in such a way as to make my distortions disappear. They would be better teachers than any rabbi, minister, priest, parent, or grandparent because they'd be informed and unbiased and, even though affiliated with one religion in some cases, they'd be knowledgeable about and loyal to both worlds because, after all, both worlds were internalized within them.

Unfortunately, it didn't take long to realize that few had that ecumenical depth and breadth of experience as a result of the way they had been raised. Until recently, the popular strategy had been to raise children within one or another faith exclusively or within no faith whatsoever. There were three basic options for religious instruction and exposure—all Jewish, all Christian, or nothing at all. More often than not, the children ended up as well-adjusted human beings with strong, clear identities. But on the subject of religion (and sometimes the culture and people associated with each religion), they were as limited as the rest of the population and unable to supply the wise and comprehensive information I needed.

Moreover, their experiences weren't models for what I wanted to offer my own children. I talked to people who'd grown up in homes where one parent's religion, often Judaism, was completely hidden from the children who'd never even known that they were part Jewish (or part Christian) until they became adults. I spoke to others who knew they had a mixed heritage, but one faith so totally dominated their religious education, school, environment, and family life that the other was minimized to the point of their knowing next to nothing about that part of their family's history. Also common were the offspring who felt torn between both worlds or so poisoned by parents and clergy against their Jewish or Christian alternatives that they reached out for a safe and often inadequate third spiritual choice, which could range from theosophy to martial arts.

The most disturbing experiences were those told by the survivors of World War II who were among 750,000 *mischlinge* (hybrids) in Nazi Germany when Hitler first severely limited their rights in the Nuremberg Laws (1935) and determined that anyone with at least one Jewish grandparent was a Jew. By the war's end, the consequences of their forced labor, their hiding, or their banishment to the concentration camps had shattered that population and left emotional scars and memories that took lifetimes to comprehend. These crises were the material for many of my longest and most intense interviews.

The research that hit closest to home, however, was the provocative study, "Children of Intermarriage," released in 1983 by the American Jewish Committee, under Egon Mayer's direction. It was a small, limited study primarily concerned with understanding how Jewish the adult children tended to become. Its major finding was that the children from intermarried families in which the non-Jewish parent converted to Judaism tended to know more and do more about their Judaism than the children of mixed marriages where there'd been no conversion. The differences were startling. In response to the statement that "Being Jewish is very important to me," for instance, 70 percent of the adults from conversionary families agreed, but only 18 percent from mixed-marriage families agreed. This meant to me that my children, growing up with a mother who hadn't converted to Judaism, could possibly grow up with the same intolerable lack of Jewish identification and knowledge.

Despite the fact that the AJC study was primarily measuring adults who were raised in a far less open and pluralistic society than Georgia and Rachel will know, I still couldn't discount those great disparities and assume that day-to-day contemporary life would naturally give my children significantly more information and connectedness to their Jewish roots. I knew that whatever faith or faiths Rachel and Georgia would ultimately embrace, it was imperative that our daughters be knowledgeable, accepting, and proud of both rich origins. Jordan and I wanted more for our children than what had been exhibited by the AJC subjects. As parents, we wanted to do a better job of honoring our children's Jewish and Christian roots than many families that preceded us. But how?

It was time to turn to the third group of experts—the clergy, and hear what advice they were conditioned to give interfaith couples who approached them for help in raising their own children. Their commands were gently but confidently offered, and once again I had to struggle to find my own way of adapting their convictions to fit my own. The heart of their message was that parents must choose a religious identity for their children. Their options were classic: Jewish, Christian, or Confused.

In a magazine article about interfaith marriages called "Mixed Marriage and the Rabbi: A Rational Alternative to Company Policy," the Chaplain and Hillel Director of Brandeis University, Rabbi Albert S. Axelrad, argued forcefully for the first choice and the advisability of "raising children actively, conscientiously, and *exclusively* as Jewish human beings." In doing so, he supported the standard dictum about avoiding anything more blended.

"By 'exclusively' I mean to exclude the syncretistic approach, i.e. practicing and/or merging both Judaism and some other tradition," he elaborated in the December 1983–January 1984 issue of *Reconstructionist*. "My experience is that such an approach often confuses the children, leaves them rootless, and fragmentizes the home, as well as failing to enhance the continuity of Judaism. I also mean to exclude the adoption of what some consider to be a neutral compromise, e.g., ethical culture, Unitarianism, the society of humanists, etc., or the absence of religion altogether, on the assumption that eventually the children will choose for themselves. This solution too jeopardizes Jewish continuity at home and deprives the children of our rich heritage."

Jewish authorities weren't the only ones to argue on behalf of one dominant faith. When I traveled to Montclair, New Jersey, to meet with a Catholic educator who had been married for twenty-five years to a Jewish book publisher, she handed me "Guidelines for Jewish-Catholic Marriages," which had been prepared by the Archdiocese of Newark. In it was the recommendation: "The only fair and unifying solution is to educate your children in such a way that they are committed to one tradition with knowledge of and respect for the other."

Even Reverend Daniel Heischman, an Episcopal chaplain at my older daughter's school where a large percentage of the students are children of interfaith marriages, started off what was to become a long series of evolving discussions with the statement, "It's more healthy to be raised in one direction or the other. Confusions are inadvertently fed by parents who don't want to tackle a child's question about what he is, so they remain silent or answer 'both.' "

Rabbi Helene Ferris, a leader of one of New York's largest Reform congregations, the Stephen Wise Free Synagogue on Manhattan's West Side, intended to be helpful when she allowed that such decisions don't have to be hasty ones. "Start talking, compromising, and taking risks," this thoughtful woman advised. "You don't sit down one night and list the pros and cons and come up with a neat decision. You have to honestly deal with it with open arms and hearts, and somewhere down deep in your gut you know what's right."

But unfortunately, my sense of what was right for Jordan and me, as well as our daughters, wasn't a sound alternative according to the clergy who still viewed "both" as a weak, even destructive choice. Down deep in my gut, I thought it was advisable to delay any decision, but the authorities didn't approve of that option either. "You have to decide," said Rabbi Ferris firmly, "and it's very bad if you don't."

The best I could do at the time, however, was to be aware of the challenge and move on to acknowledge another guiding voice that persistently echoed in my ear. It was that of my mother, who reminded me of my next responsibility when we were sitting in the den in my parents' house on Cape Cod, sipping tea and discussing the book. "Lee, what matters to your father and me," she said, passing me a ginger cookie, "is that you share all the good things about what your family stands for with Rachel and Georgia, and that you're fair to your heritage because there's a lot to be proud of."

Who could argue with such a request? Every major religion would approve of her words since it's considered im-

perative for Jewish, Catholic, and Protestant parents to pass
on their faith and traditions to their children. Certainly, the
essence of the advice was compatible with my sense of self-
affirmation and equal rights in my marriage. And basically,
there was so much good health to be gained by my children
who needed to be proud of what *both* parents represented.
My marriage thrived on balance and free exchange. And my
own emotional life needed the nurturance and self-awareness
that come from understanding one's own beliefs and background.

The problem wasn't agreement but ignorance. What was
my heritage? I hadn't thought about it in years, and only
when I sat down to write the book proposal and found myself
trying to explain what "the best of both worlds" could mean
to my Jewish/Christian children did I start thinking about it
once again, with great difficulty. At first, the only associations that came to mind about "the best" of my Christian
origins were reminders of a Scottish and Scandinavian ancestry generations ago. My grandmother's Norwegian
Christmas cookies and a print of a Scotsman named Fergus-
son wearing a blue-plaid kilt on my great aunt's wall on Cape
Cod kept reappearing, but their meaning eluded me.

The confusion increased when Georgia's Montessori
nursery school sent home a notice asking parents to come
into class and talk about "an aspect of their culture (ethnic
dishes, traditional clothing, instruments, art, etc.)" that would
give three-year-olds a sense of their friends' diversity. But
the word "ethnic" didn't seem to fit me, and the only thing
I could think to offer was a Shetland sweater, my native
costume from adolescent days in the suburbs of Boston. Obviously that wouldn't do. Wasn't there anything distinctive
about the culture of a white Protestant in America? Or to
borrow a term from a good friend, "What's to say about the
plain vanilla WASP?"

The books about Jewish/Christian marriages were no
help, because they always talked about "Jews" and "Non-
Jews," as if my identity, shared with almost the entire human
race, of course, was more a matter of what I wasn't—a

Jew—than what I was. The one encouraging article I discovered about children like my own, written by a Jewish/Christian writer from Boston, was inadequately titled "Half Jewish, Half Something Else." The day I found myself chatting away thoughtlessly about how "Jordan's Jewish, and I'm not much of anything," I realized it was time to take my mother's request to heart and think seriously about the family and religious environment that played such a big role in my life. I had to understand what it was that I valued and wanted to offer my children.

I was certain that if I had been Italian, Jewish, Latin American, or even a first- or second-generation American, I'd feel the intensity of my ethnic identity much more keenly. Jews were bound by their shared history and destiny, their peoplehood, and their responsibility to each other. Italians had their intense family loyalties to define them. And recent immigrants to America had their differentness from the dominant culture to heighten their specialness.

But the paradox was that my husband, the Jewish son of first- and second-generation Americans, was also self-conscious and disoriented when asked to articulate what his heritage meant to him. Like me, he hadn't been asked that question in a long while, if ever, and it was not a subject that had troubled him enough to examine it. Indeed, the experiences that came to mind when we first started talking about his Jewish background in relation to our children were solidly positive and comfortably tucked away in his memory. Since he was fifteen, he'd been traveling to Israel to study or work. As an architect he'd designed many buildings for Jewish institutions, including a new synagogue for the rabbi and congregation that he'd known since he was ten years old. His family was large and close with a long history of gathering together and participating in Jewish causes. Like his son, Alex, from an earlier Jewish marriage, Jordan had also celebrated a bar mitzvah that had been meaningful to him. "My identity as a Jew is a confident and comfortable part of me," he explained after he'd thought about some of these formative experiences. "But the truth is that I've devoted less and less time over the years to developing that religious and ethnic part of me. Being a Jew just doesn't play a major role in my daily life, not like it did with my father."

After years of not thinking about this matter, what struck my husband was how differently his father had expressed his Jewishness and how the contrast raised questions about the nature of Jordan's own commitments and his message to our daughters. When he and I talked about our children, his basic goals for them weren't hard to express. "I want them to develop enough pride in identifying as Jews, or at least knowing that they're half-Jewish, so that they will never deny that identity or turn away from it or find it threatening because of the pressures of society," he explained easily. "Once they've accepted the fact that being a Jew is OK, then they might go beyond and see that it's also challenging and stimulating and very meaningful to them."

The question for him was how active a Jew he should be in order to offer his children something that approximated his own parents' dedication and commitment in the years when he was growing up. For Jordan, the decades after World War II and the Holocaust were tremendously vital and creative as Jews around him were consumed with reestablishing Israel and building Jewish institutions in America. His parents were part of that mobilized community that was countering Hitler's threat of annihilation with a tremendous surge of participation and togetherness. For Jordan, the feelings were pride, excitement, and security as a Jew, and until our conversations, those background assurances had been important and enough. Only now as he looked for new ways to translate his loyalties to Rachel and Georgia was he questioning his own comfort and complacency. "If Jews fought so hard and were willing to dedicate and even give up their lives for their beliefs," Jordan asked, "then how can I be casual about Judaism?

"But the truth of the matter is," he added candidly, "I have been casual about it, and I don't think it's enough."

It was easy for me to join Jordan in helping our daughters feel connected to their Jewish roots. Too many Jews had been important in my life for me to feel anything other than love and respect for the Jewish community and what I expected it to offer Rachel and Georgia.

In addition, I'd begun to realize the power of the Jewish call for continuity and how that command and promise, as old as Abraham and the Book of Genesis, generated a responsibility so innate and understood, so strengthened by persecution that it was as if it were part of the genetic code of all Jews. In my mind, it was like a steady, rhythmic bass line that underlay and challenged all Jordan's and my choices about raising our children. I was relieved, in fact, to know that I accepted that urgent voice. To fight it would have been futile.

Nonetheless, I often felt that my broadmindedness ended with that plain and simple loyalty. There were a host of ragged feelings that kept pressing their way into my mind as a consequence of thinking about these complicated issues. It was clear from the beginning of my research that I needed as much help understanding each of them as I needed with all the intellectual and practical discussions about child psychology, religion, theology, and family dynamics. The litany of responsibilities for interfaith parents had ultimately become a long and depressing one, because there wasn't one category that I could either agree with or manage successfully. I had been told to: Prepare for a tough road in my marriage and childrearing; fight the likelihood of my children being damaged and deprived; choose one faith or else; do justice to my Christian roots; perpetuate Judaism and the Jewish people without conflict and ambivalence.

Now even the last of the requirements was complicated by a collection of uneasy hostilities and self-doubts that surfaced unpredictably as I tested out my responsiveness to Jordan's and my different options for our children. It galled me at first that our choices were tipped toward the Jewish side, as if Judaism had a moral superiority that inevitably created an imbalance. I remember expressing my resentment one evening to Ira Silverman, a friend who was then the Director of the American Reconstructionist College in Philadelphia which trains rabbis for Reconstructionism, the fourth, most liberal, and smallest arm of Judaism. In his Princeton, New Jersey, living room, the father of three nodded calmly, shrugged, and said, "You're right. It just doesn't matter to Christendom whether they lose a few followers. In the United States alone there are 142 million Christians. But there are only five-and-a-half million Jews here, and fewer than fifty years ago, Hitler did away with six million others around the world. Those facts add a weight to the equation that's undeniable." How deeply the element of ethnic survival has always run through the history of the Jewish people was even further expressed by those stark, contemporary numbers. With a new context, I found that my hostilities subsided.

But other feelings readily took their place—prejudice, jealousy, defensiveness, stupidity, rivalry, and even more resentment. Then, too, there was curiosity and pride, inspiration and hilarity, confidence and courage. All of those feelings were part of the complex process of growth and a more honest and informed approach to shaping our lives. Without that range of emotions to celebrate and confront, our resolutions wouldn't have had the depth and meaning they did.

No one knows the varied and changing emotions better than interfaith parents themselves, and without their insights and encouragement I couldn't have found my way through the many competing voices that argued persuasively about "the right way" to raise my children. In cities and suburbs around the country, I talked to a hundred interfaith parents in depth, often alongside their spouses and sometimes with their children present. In addition, there were twenty-five young adults about to intermarry and raise Jewish/Christian children, and there were approximately fifty grandparents who shared their feelings about their Jewish/Christian grandchildren and their children who married someone of the other faith. Added to what I was able to learn from talking to seventy-five adult children of intermarriage and fifty young and adolescent children of intermarriage, I ultimately had the benefit of 300 people of all ages, vital and observant members of interfaith families who generously shared their experiences with me. I would have liked to have spoken with even more mixed-marriage couples from more diverse geographical and sociological backgrounds, but the feelings and experiences of the people with whom I talked have a universal quality to them that, I hope, speaks to people in many walks of life throughout this country.

From the parents, however, I learned about the day-to-day choices that each of us must make in our adjustment to the dilemma and the opportunity of being part of an interfaith family and world. There are no formulas or models to copy, at least not for now as the dynamics of Jewish/Christian relationships are shifting so rapidly. Rather, there are countless parents, like Jordan and me, sitting at kitchen tables across America, answering our children's questions about "resligen" and identity, traditions and beliefs in the best way we know how. Our friends, families, clergy, the media, and especially our own children will offer the guidance and challenges that help our answers become richer and more sure. But I've learned that ultimately the touchstone is within each of us, and it takes time and talking and experience to reveal what it is that we love and fear and envision for our children's lives, as well as our own and those around us. I've learned that we make and understand our choices step by step. Economist E. F. Schumacher, author of *Small is Beautiful*, reckoned wisely with our first step when he advised universally, "Begin with yourself."

CHAPTER
2

COMPLETING OURSELVES

The barriers that have separated Christians and Jews have been like walls that have risen and fallen over the centuries. Until recently, the obstacles have been formidable enough to be Great Walls that were almost impossible to climb over. Once over, there was no going back, and the new territory on the other side—whether Christian or Jewish—was always imagined as a dark and threatening unknown.

The Great Wall wasn't erected in America, however. Today, in fact, the wall is more like a low fence between two broad, sunlit fields, and interfaith couples can easily climb over that fence to reach the other side. They can move freely back and forth, maintain their ties to their families and faiths, and raise their children with knowledge of both worlds, as they wish. At last, the opportunities involved in exploring this new and abundant expanse can outweigh the heavy sacrifices. Times have changed, and the interfaith families enjoying and accepting the challenge of this new freedom have changed, too.

Paradoxically, what makes them so able to address their

differences is the stunning fact that they have so much in common, more than interfaith couples have ever had in history. In the fundamental areas of education, economic background, and occupational status, they are indeed more alike than different.

When it comes to education, Egon Mayer concluded in his book, *Love and Tradition*, that "both Jewish and Christian intermarriers achieved significantly higher levels of education than those typical of the population as a whole." According to Mayer, over 75 percent of the interfaith couples share a college education, often from America's finest schools, and 30 to 40 percent of them also share graduate degrees.

Interfaith couples also tend to be overachievers with many professional accomplishments in common, as well. In Mayer's most recent study for the American Jewish Committee, entitled "Intermarriage and Conversion, A Study of Identities in Transition" (1986), he examined 309 individuals from a non-Jewish background who were married to Jews. Among other things, Mayer observed that a majority of interfaith partners were more similar than dissimilar in the status associated with their work. The wide discrepancies that were common in the past, when the doctor was married to the housewife, or the entrepreneur—the husband, of course—was married to the social worker, no longer exist. Except in marriages where the wife has converted to her husband's faith, interestingly enough, the common interfaith pattern is one of equal partners involved in related careers.

That finding was reflected throughout my own interviews as I kept meeting interfaith couples who were both artists (a painter and a theater director); both business executives (a banker and a publisher); both educators (a college dean and a university administrator), and so forth through one occupational match after another. What I noticed repeatedly was not only the similarity in what they did and cared about, but how important work was, in general, to both of them. Whether they were running a country inn together, teaching in different schools, or balancing a husband's law practice with a wife's unpaid community service, the work ethic and the intensity with which they carried out their work was a powerful bond between them and one of the most important gifts they offered each other.

The way that interfaith couples met each other also reminded me of their newfound equality. The pattern is a far cry from the earlier days when the rich landlord's son discovered the poor, very young daughter on the front stoop of her family's humble home. According to Mayer's statistics, half the Jewish/Christian couples meet at college or work and the other half meet through friends and by chance. As a group, they're not young when they marry. They're older, in fact, than the 1984 national average when men married at twenty-five and women at twenty-three.

"As likely as not," wrote Mayer, "intermarriers are also men and women who have already been once divorced." I've noticed a preponderance of couples within my own sample who've been married before. Even the meeting places—a political-science classroom, the Museum of Modern Art, the Metroliner, a business convention, the hospital ward—indicate how much interfaith couples have become equal members of mainstream America and how savvy both Christian and Jew have become in their ability to maneuver within that pluralistic world.

Adding to their confidence and comfort is the fact that interfaith couples and their differences are accepted by contemporary society in a way that was never possible before. Numerous surveys of the American public's attitudes about interfaith marriages have confirmed a changing climate. In a 1983 poll of non-Jewish Americans, the Gallup Poll found that 77 percent approved of Jewish/non-Jewish marriages. In 1968, the results of that same poll had been a considerably lower 59 percent.

Similarly, in a 1975 survey of the Jewish community in Boston, a researcher from the University of Massachusetts, Floyd J. Fowler, Ph.D., found that 60 percent of the participants said they could be neutral or accepting if their children married non-Jews. Earlier, in 1965, only 25 percent had said they could.

Economic success may very well be another interesting measure of how well interfaith couples have become comfortably integrated into society. After evaluating his 1986 statistics, Mayer concluded that "it is quite possible that intermarrieds as a whole enjoy higher incomes than the typical cross-section of American Jewry."

One doesn't need to consult the statistics, however, to realize that interfaith families, in general, have a freedom that's unprecedented. Nowadays, most intermarried Jews and Christians can maintain their relationships with their respective religious identities, their families, even their churches and synagogues if they wish. With rare exceptions, they can live wherever they choose. It's also possible for them to raise their children however they wish.

A major contribution to that open and tolerant spirit was made by the Catholic Church during the ecumenical era of Vatican II in 1965 and more recently in 1978 and 1983 by the Reform branch of Judaism.

The ruling within the Catholic Church reversed the centuries-old requirement that the non-Catholic partner had to sign a promise to raise all future children as Catholics in order to obtain the proper dispensation allowing him or her to marry under Church auspices. According to the new Canon Law, the Catholic is asked to promise, verbally or in writing, to do all in his or her own power to baptize the child and pass on his or her faith. The phrase "all in his or her own power," however, allows for personal interpretation.

The Reform branch of Judaism showed its responsiveness to the expanding number of interfaith families in 1978 when Rabbi Alexander Schindler led the Union of American Hebrew Congregations in a formal resolution calling for Reform rabbis and congregations to make themselves available and sensitive to the needs of interfaith couples and converts to Judaism. Outreach programs were developed to instruct couples in the basics of Judaism and help them with any emotional and social stresses. But more important, the Reform community called for a uniformly welcoming attitude toward interfaith families.

During its rabbinic convention in 1983, the Reform branch of Judaism took another significant stand when it legitimized the concept of patrilineal descent. Reversing centuries of traditional Jewish law (*halacha*) that defined a Jew as someone who converted to Judaism or was born to a Jewish mother, the Reform-based Central Conference of American Rabbis (CCAR) resolved that "the child of one Jewish parent is under the presumption of Jewish descent," and the children of intermarriage are officially welcomed into the life of the synagogue where they are invited to study and participate in Jewish ceremonies. Even though that open spirit had been in practice throughout many Reform synagogues prior to the declaration, and even though the Reconstructionist arm of Judaism had broken ground with a similar resolution in 1968, the official announcement sent another provocative challenge throughout the Jewish community. Although it has not been officially adopted by the Conservative and certainly not by the Orthodox branches of Judaism, the resolution reinforced a spirit of openness and flexibility within the Reform, Reconstructionist, and liberal Conservative community.

What the Reform ruling also symbolized was the recognition that interfaith couples had become the largest growing constituency in Jewish life. The traditional Jewish approach to intermarriage as a cancer that had to be excised from the body in order to keep the disease from spreading could no longer be applauded as the best and only treatment. Since the 1960s, intermarriage had begun to affect such a majority of Jews that little would be left of the Jewish community if that drastic response were the only option.

To come up with a new diagnosis, in effect, the Jewish community conducted a number of studies of intermarriage, beginning with the Jewish Population Study in 1970. Gradually, the results of these surveys have made their way into the media and the public's awareness, validating Jewish/Christian families in a new way and offering useful insights into their basic profile and characteristics.

The most comprehensive of these studies, by the way,

is still the 1976 examination of 446 intermarried couples, conducted by Egon Mayer for the American Jewish Committee. It was followed by Mayer's 1983 study of the children of intermarriage and his most recent 1986 study of conversion, and these have also made major contributions to the growing body of research. In addition, there have also been demographic studies of the Jewish and interfaith community in Boston (1975), Kansas City (1977), Denver (1982), New York City (1983), and Philadelphia (1984). But for me, the 1976 survey has been a gold mine that I keep returning to, time and again, to support and help me understand my own observations. None of the later work refutes the 1976 conclusions; it elaborates on them and reinforces the depth and perceptiveness of those original findings and their applicability today. As a result of Mayer's ten years of work, an additional profile of interfaith couples has emerged, indicating that:

- Twice as many Jewish men intermarry as do Jewish women, or in other words, close to two-thirds of all Jewish/Christian marriages involve a Jewish husband and a Christian wife and one-third involve a Christian husband and a Jewish wife.

- One-third of all intermarriages involve a conversion to Judaism while fewer than one-tenth involve conversion to Christianity. The largest proportion of intermarriages remain religious and ethnically mixed marriages without conversion.

- The ratio of Protestants who marry Jews to Catholics who marry Jews is 2 to 1, which generally reflects the proportion of Protestants to Catholics in America.

- Ethnic origins of those Christians that intermarry also reflect the composition of America, which means that almost 60 percent are English, German, Irish, or early American by ancestry, while the remaining 40 percent are Italian, Polish, Scandinavian, black, oriental, or otherwise European.

• Jews who marry Christians reflect the population of the three major branches of Judaism, as well, which means that close to 30 percent come from the Reform, close to 30 percent from the Conservative, slightly over 10 percent from the Orthodox, and the rest, slightly over 30 percent, are unaffiliated.

Despite this data about Jews married to Christians and the increasingly hospitable and open society that makes their interfaith lives far smoother than what confronted their predecessors, there is still an astounding lack of intimate knowledge about how they conduct their lives and what makes them tick. It's not surprising, indeed, that old, misleading myths still persist and color most people's understanding of interfaith families and the role that their differences play.

I'm always reminded of the conventional notions about this subject when I talk about my book with individuals who aren't directly connected to an interfaith household. Either they look bewildered and wonder why I'd worry about anything as benign and inconsequential as Jewish/Christian differences today. Or they congratulate me for choosing such a hot topic because, obviously, the stresses and strains between people who come from such different backgrounds are inevitable and real. Some of that latter group even mention today's big spectre—divorce—as the greatest problem that interfaith couples will have to deal with. I have no doubt that the warnings will start focusing on the maladjustments and confusion among interfaith children once again, as that population keeps snowballing. But for now, the newspapers focus their articles on the theme of divorce, offering the public its updated version of the stiff penalties that are still exacted by Jewish/Christian differences.

I've yet to read a news article about interfaith marriage that doesn't have a title using the words "problems" or "risks" and that doesn't conclude with an implicit warning about divorce. Surely, the news angle makes for good copy. But it also reveals America's belief in the old myth that there's still something not quite right about Jewish/Christian alliances and that the truth about them lies more in the problems and disasters than in the successes.

The real facts about divorce indicate that there is a slight increase of its likelihood if the marriage is an interfaith one. But given the reality that one in every two marriages ends in divorce anyway, that added risk seems irrelevant. Some tell me that an interfaith situation could be the straw that breaks the camel's back, or that marriage is difficult enough these days without one more difference to cope with. They quote Philip Roth's Portnoy whose well-known grouse in *Portnoy's Complaint* was, "It's just as my parents have warned me—comes the first disagreement, no matter how small, and the only thing a *shikse* [a non-Jewish woman] knows to call you is a dirty Jew."

Even my daughter Rachel when she was five had heard the bad news. Coming home from playing with another little girl, she rushed to tell me what she'd learned that day. "Daddy's a lot Jewish, and you're a lot Christian," she told me proudly. "You're not supposed to marry each other."

Nevertheless, Jews and Christians are marrying in record numbers, and they defend their relationships and their differences in a number of ways. They point to their siblings' marriages, which are often religiously homogeneous, and wonder where the others find their passion and challenge amid such sameness. Or they point to their siblings' homogeneous marriages that ended in divorce. They also insist that their own mixed marriages are stronger and much less boring.

As for the interfaith partners who've divorced (someone of the same faith, in most cases) and remarried (someone of a different faith), they tend to congratulate themselves for having the courage and honesty to leave a faulty marriage. When I tell them about various studies linking interfaith marriage with divorce, including a 1986 survey from Brigham Young University in Utah that confirms the expectation that couples who follow the same faith have slightly better chances of sustaining a marriage than those with different religious backgrounds, they shrug and often remind me that those few extra couples in the survey who stayed married because they had a religion in common might not have had much else going for them. Having been married unhappily themselves, the intermarried Christians or Jews realize that divorce can often be a smaller price to pay than years of eroding confidence, health, and well-being, a few of the hidden consequences of a bad, but continuing marriage that are never measured by the marriage surveys.

Many therapists take another position and argue that interfaith couples never divorce because of religious differences. They divorce for a variety of deeper reasons that may play themselves out in religious arguments, although not necessarily. "Many people want to believe that there are all these problems in mixed marriages," explained Edwin Friedman, a rabbi and family therapist who's counselled interfaith couples in the Washington, D.C., area for the past twenty years. "The problems just aren't there, however. Look at the evidence in your own marriage and in the people you know," he told me emphatically. "The vast majority of couples talk to each other and work things out. Despite the propaganda, mixed marriage isn't bad."

Nothing is more of a fixture within interfaith marriage, however, than the fact of Jewish/Christian differences. They're more subtle than they were. And they're set against a background of increasing equality within marriage. But these carryovers from 2,000 years of Jewish and Christian experience not only exist but act as a dynamic presence that's become a creative and complicated source of strength and vitality in interfaith marriages today.

What differences do couples notice, celebrate, and grapple with? For most couples, a simple comparison of the places where they grew up brings home the stunning fact that it's a miracle that they ever met. If it hadn't been for college and/or a few years of independence and work away from home, at least for one of the partners, they'd never have found each other. On a chart of vital statistics, the Jew and Christian may have a lot in common, but from the point of view of their disparate childhoods and family backgrounds, it seems more accurate to think of them as aliens from different planets.

Who'd have guessed that a Jewish girl with a seven-and-a-half-room split-level in a Chicago suburb would eventually fall in love with a farmer's son from the Oklahoma prairie who travelled twice a week to the Disciples of Christ Church forty miles away and ultimately grew up to become a minister (and ex-minister)?

Would anyone have predicted that another young woman, a Protestant, would spend her first seventeen years with her siblings and mother, who was a doctor, moving in and out of twenty-six communities, including an Indian reservation, while her future husband was calmly growing up in Brookline, Massachusetts, in a family with five rabbis?

City mouse met country mouse. Suburbanite met country bumpkin. Or suburbanite met city slicker. Even when suburbanite met suburbanite (like Jordan and me) or city kid met city kid, there were still such profound differences in the backgrounds of the people I interviewed that their meetings were still momentous and unexpected.

What exaggerated their differences, usually, was the religious and cultural homogeneity that characterized where and with whom they grew up. In Quincy, Massachusetts, or Great Neck, New York, or Manhattan, Kansas, their lives were dominated by a clear and self-conscious religious identity. They knew what they were—Protestant, Catholic, or Jew—and everyone who wasn't "that" often became a blurred montage of sensual impressions that weren't examined very much until marriage and childbirth when individuals were forced to confront them. Despite the liberating experiences of college and adulthood, the parents I talked with were struck by how indelible their childhood impressions had been.

"Being Catholic was queer, but being Jewish was so way out that you didn't even think about it," commented a New York novelist who grew up in Tennessee. Like many Christian parents he grew up in an environment far more parochial than his wife's. She was raised in a multicultural city, like many Jewish children who eventually intermarried. Others who are Jewish grew up in suburban neighborhoods that were ethnically mixed or predominately Christian. Some attended predominately Christian private schools. Like any minority, they were inevitably thrown in contact with the majority culture, even if only through the magazines, television, or sports events. As a result, Jewish young adults were generally more savvy about the Christians than vice versa.

But neither group was genuinely knowledgeable about the other. For both Jews and Christians, their early formative experiences with people different from themselves amounted to a collage of random impressions and myths based on a date here or there, a few friendships, or a neighborly exchange. Their solid learning began later in college, and the real learning began when they fell in love and decided to marry.

The hodgepodge of associations that they brought to their marriage are as hilarious and tender as they are embarassing. Everyone had some vital inaccuracy or distortion that was part of his or her legacy from childhood. One Jewish man expected his wife to ask him about his horns, a reference to an anti-Semitic image from the Dark Ages. Another Jewish man thought his wife's father probably drank a lot of beer and beat her mother because he'd heard somewhere that Christians behave that way. Another Jew told his Swedish fiancée that Jews, of course, love their families much more than Christians do, and that they even mourn a family death with more heart and sincerity. A Jewish friend of mine whose wife is Irish admitted that he still registers surprise when he discovers a Christian with a sense of humor. Yet another Jewish friend spent a night arguing with his Lutheran wife about whether Christians or Jews were more devoted to their dogs.

The Christians, of course, have just as many ill-founded notions floating around in their heads. As with the Jews, their sophistication and intelligence always belie at least one appalling area of ignorance (and usually more). The wildest admission I heard came from a sensible, very beautiful New York woman in her thirties whose mother had always told her, when she had been a child, to feel sorry for Jews because they had to spend their vacations in trailers. "No one would admit them to the best hotels, of course," she'd been told.

Along with that inheritance of misinformation, there's also a collection of appealing images that attract and impress interfaith partners and become more meaningful to them over the years. It's absurd to think that anyone could make a neat, thorough list of all the reasons why a man and woman fall in love and stay in love, let alone analyze those reasons from an ethnic point of view. As Edwin Friedman, the Bethesda, Maryland, rabbi and family therapist said wisely, "The decision to marry is like an iceberg; seven-eighths of it lies under the surface." Nevertheless, in my discussions with parents, certain themes were emphasized over and over because they were important symbols of their pleasure in their interfaith relationship and their belief that it had expanded their lives and helped them grow. The most popular and potent charm of all, one that could have been the subject for an entire book? Food.

"The lamb chops hooked me! Big, thick, juicy ones," drooled a Houston woman with her fingers separated by a two-inch gap. In her Irish Catholic home in Boston, she'd known about "thin, green, skimpy ones, rarely." It wasn't until she met and married her husband, a Jewish labor lawyer originally from New York, that she learned about a new set of life's treasures—fine meats, dark, rich chocolate, and bubbly champagne. "The generosity, the luxury, the attention to pleasure just knocked me out," said the tall, lush, redheaded wife with an infant son.

For a New York writer and her husband, a stockbroker who grew up in New Jersey, the joy wasn't in the eating but in the reminder of how far they'd traveled in their escape from lifestyles they'd outgrown long ago. In her chaotic Methodist home in Arizona when she was growing up, the standard food had been a pot of black-eyed Susans, ham hocks, and health-food experiments simmering on the stove for the family to ladle into a bowl whenever the parents or children got hungry. In her husband's highly structured kosher home in New Jersey, however, meals were punctual and predictable. There was meat loaf on Monday, tuna fish on Tuesday, in relentless order from week to week and year to year. For the couple, it was a proud miracle that two individuals with such different backgrounds could adjust to each other, and the liberation and the new patterns in their lives felt sweet. The forty-two-year-old writer found herself with calm meals around a dining room table with her husband and young children around her. Her forty-one-year-old husband had something that was equally revolutionary —a surprise on the table every night when he came home.

The marital payoffs connected with food are numerous. Some interfaith spouses report the fun of "indoctrinating" their partners into the lore of smoked fish, Swedish meatballs, or Irish soda bread, noticing how nothing makes a Jew feel more Jewish or a Gentile feel more Gentile than flaunting one's special ethnic food before an appreciative audience, touching base with childhood at the same time. In many ways, foods are badges of identity that define a husband and wife not only as separate and distinct individuals but also as a couple sharing values and experiences and feeling unique and close because of them.

For Jordan and me, one of our closest bonds is built on nothing more than a small white cucumber sandwich that's served at Episcopal weddings. Every time we spot one on a waiter's silver tray, we always laugh like conspirators with a secret that touches us on countless levels simultaneously. That tea sandwich has a way of confirming our history together, our differentness, our sense of how much we've changed since we met, and, most important I think, how our marriage can be broad and flexible enough to include everything about us, whether it's the cucumber slivers at the wedding or the gigantic Reuben with relish and a side of potato salad that we ate earlier at lunch to prepare for the skimpy WASP menu we knew was coming. For us, the intoxicating message, bubbling away with the champagne, of course, is that it's possible to have it all—fun, diversity, trust, and affirmation, a heady dose of self-congratulation, and even, vicariously, dreams come true. I'd always wanted a wedding with cucumber sandwiches (after the candlelight ceremony with the choir and eight bridesmaids that I didn't have, either).

Another asset that interfaith partners discuss a great deal is their sense that their spouse has coping skills and mastery of an environment that complement his or her own areas of confidence and expertise. For instance, Julie Nickerson, a forty-five-year-old abstract painter who grew up in Omaha, Nebraska, explained to me about how she was drawn to Saul Sheingold, a writer, because of his "Jewish intensity." She'd discovered such "power" back in Omaha during high school when the valedictorian was a Jew who was "serious, informed, and a great speech-giver."

"I wanted the self-confidence, the chutzpah, the expressiveness I associated with being Jewish," said the wife and mother of an eighteen-year-old daughter.

In turn, she fit her husband's very different dreams. "She was a Westerner, an artist. She even looked the way I liked women to look—pretty and fresh, straightforward but soft," said Saul, a bearded fifty-two-year-old who was raised in a small industrial city in upstate New York. "Her relatives went back to prairie days. Her parents ran the arts organizations and traveled to Europe, and they had servants and class that was natural and without pretense. I was fascinated by a family that knew how to sail and had a sculpture by Calder." Chuckling, the writer added, "I liked being a kosher crumb in Nebraska's upper crust."

Marianne Devin had different needs to fill, however. She was a smart and fast-talking graduate of New York City's High School of Music and Art who knew the inside of most major museums and concert halls, but she was less sure and adept when it came to nature. Very simply, she fell in love with a country guy, an Adonis, a big, strong football player who could take care of her in the California woods where she runs a small general store. For the twenty-eight-year old, dark-eyed Jewish mother of a young infant, "Woody Allen wouldn't do."

Despite the fact that interfaith couples are not immigrants to the large extent that they were in previous generations, it's still striking how mobile they are. I can't think of
one couple among those I've interviewed that doesn't include
at least one partner who's been transplanted from another
place in America or further. Even if the distance traveled was
merely a trek from the suburbs to the city, the adjustments
were always significant, and power and allure was given to
those—spouse, in-law, friends, and colleagues—who could
help the Christian or Jew learn the ropes and find his or her
footing in an essentially alien environment. Especially in the
cities, therefore, a place where Jews have traditionally been
comfortable, there's a preponderance of intense Jews married
to Christians from out of town. The exception to that rule?
A preponderance of intense Jews married to Christians, both
from out of town.

Although many of their stereotypes about each other
have roots in ethnic experience, the couples I talked with
were less concerned with reality and accurate sociology than
with the way certain myths and preconceptions confirmed
the wisdom of their own choices. Some touted their interfaith
mate because he or she was different from the negative ster-
eotype they held about their own ethnic group. In other
words, an Italian man from Albany, New York, told me he
couldn't possibly have married an Italian woman because he
needed "an equal, not a passive baby maker." A Jewish
woman from Denver, in turn, explained how her "Jewish
allergy" kept her from marrying a Jew. "I can't stand crude
men who wear chains, manicure their fingernails, and want
to go shopping with you all the time."

Needless to say, the stereotypes just as readily reverse
themselves, and one's criticism turns into another's flattery.
I know a Jewish publisher who adores his Italian wife, an
executive in a large bank, because "she's tough and sexy and
a fabulous, loving mother." I also know an Italian cooking
teacher who adores her Jewish husband, in part, because he
has an eye for clothes and shops with her and isn't afraid of
"feminine-type things that an Italian man would never do

—like cry when he's moved or really care what's on a woman's mind."

The point is that stereotypes are often playthings that interfaith couples use to best advantage, picking and choosing those, and only those, that support their favored argument. When they're looking for proof that they're a match made in heaven, they look to these images for evidence to support their conclusions, and with a little self-selection they're always able to find the necessary encouragement. Their own parents may have been part of a successful business partnership called O'Brien and Shestack or Kelly and Gruzen. In other cases, there are heroic family myths in which the Christian parent was saved during World War II by a Jewish buddy in the Army, or a Jewish parent in Nazi Germany was sheltered by a Christian official that he'd befriended years before. These and other stories become privately held imperatives that a Christian and Jew were meant to be each other's helpmate with needs and strengths that complement each other.

On the subject of sex, of course, the myths and theories really proliferate. Almost all the couples that I met hazarded a guess or two about why the Christian and Jew are sexually attracted to each other. They talked about the lure of forbidden fruit or yin needing yang, the seductive appeal of the shiksa or Freud's classic Oedipal complex. A Protestant innkeeper on Long Island kept nudging his wife and insisting that he married a Jew because "Jewish girls are loose."

The most interesting theory of all, however, was forwarded by the writer Molly Haskell in a provocative article, entitled "We Don't Match the Way Couples Do on Wedding Cakes." In it, the Southern WASP analyzed her own emotionally adventurous marriage to a Greek immigrant's son, and suggested that differences—in age, race, religion, height, or background—may be a new way for couples to experience "the spark of opposition" that used to be generated by a clear-cut separation between the sexes. "Now, as the line between 'men's work' and 'women's work' blurs, in the home and in the office," she wrote, "we seek to create and nurture opposition on other fronts. The differences may not be the traditional ones between man and woman, but the differences themselves turn out to be very important—the spice of life and sexual attraction."

According to Haskell, odd couples have even more going for them than that, however. They share the pioneering excitement of exploring and conquering new uncharted terrain, "reenacting the pioneer journey of . . . [their] forefathers—not geographically but emotionally."

Moreover, they're part of another kind of electric interaction. "Within every healthy pairing of opposites there's an underlying impulse not just to experience the thrill of differences but to reconcile those differences," Haskell continued. "This urge to fuse your differences into one radiantly complete being can become all the more challenging when you and your mate are divided not just by your sex, but by background, size, age or even color." Given this powerful, vital tension, in other words, interfaith couples can feel that they have it all—self-realization, commonality, adventure, sex, and romance.

Along with the romance there are the aggravations and problems that are inevitably part of the interfaith experience, however. Contrary to myth, the differences aren't cause for divorce, but as in all marriages, they're reason for thoughtful discussion, argument, negotiation, and growth. Here are five recommendations that have emerged from my own research that, I hope, put the very human needs of interfaith families into a useful perspective. They can help parents cope with their differences and consider what to do when those differences seem overwhelming or troublesome.

1. *Accept the fact that differences are part of the Jewish/Christian experience.* Realize that it's futile to deny them, coerce them into oblivion, or let them smolder in secret resentment. They come and go, popping into view when they're least expected, and they're infinite—either like beautiful stars or the cursed, multiplying sticks from the broom in the nightmare scene in

Fantasia's "Sorcerer's Apprentice." They exist despite a religious conversion. They're often misinterpreted.

In his book, *Love and Tradition*, Egon Mayer noticed how often the couples he interviewed reported surprise and shock when their differences began appearing for the first time. During their courtships the lovers had reveled in their commonality and the great shared areas of their lives. But suddenly the smallest detail (often to do with food) took on enormous emotional significance, and a gulf appeared between them that had never existed before.

When Jordan and I were first married I remember arguing ferociously about such things as smoked salmon and whether it was better served on Jewish rye or Norwegian flatbread. I was sure I'd become a bigot, consumed with family loyalty and ethnic pride, ego and prejudice that were not only abnormal but also dangerous. It took a long time to become more comfortable with my rivalries and to realize that skirmishes like that one are par for the course in all early marriages. "Things that are regular for one partner may be strange at first to the other one," observed Erica Bard Riley, a counselor to many interfaith couples in Louisville, Kentucky.

Couples never become so accustomed to each other that the differences stop proliferating, however. Every life cycle reveals a new array of ethnic conditioning, and it's a life's work to understand what differences can mean and how to deal with them. Fortunately, the task becomes easier and less threatening with practice. There's lots of practice.

2. *Be patient.* It takes time and experience to learn about another culture and family, especially in view of the poor preparation that most interfaith couples bring to their marriages. The most commonplace aspects of another's life take getting used to. A new last name like MacDonald or Shapiro can feel alien to a bride who isn't sure how she feels about being identified with her husband's religious and ethnic group. Rachel Cowan, a writer and rabbinical student, notes how non-Jews sometimes feel overwhelmed by the presence of a Jewish community they never even knew existed. Suddenly it enters their life, like a huge, unannounced family that can't be ignored, and it takes time to know and appreciate it. The equivalent shock for Jews can be Christmas, which they thought they understood. Suddenly, however, they find themselves in a Christian family that throws heart and soul into the holiday, for weeks on end, and they may take years to accept and ultimately value that annual encroachment.

At the same time as they're familiarizing themselves with new areas of life, they're also learning about their own personal way of responding to differences. The behavior is really a dance that people do with differences, and it takes time to trust its cycles. They reach out for differences and they push them away. They embrace the new experience, and they return to the old, familiar one. Everything and anything, from a flock of cousins to the texture of hair and skin, can be strange and threatening until they become a valued part of one's own history and circle of loved ones. Intimacy seldom happens overnight.

3. *Work toward a fair marriage where mutual respect and self-respect can flourish.* Because of the traditional assumption that marriage demands total unity and that differences are threatening rather than enriching, there's an underlying scenario within most interfaith literature that calls for one partner to forfeit his or her (usually her) background in service to this false ideal of oneness and total agreement. As the adult children of intermarriage proved, time and again through their reminiscences, the yielding of one parent to another often leads to deep resentments. The self-denial becomes a bombshell that threatens a family more than any forthright acknowledgment of differences ever could.

I've encountered many examples of interfaith marriages where one partner hasn't learned how to make compromises and show such respect or sensitivity. That's true of all types of marriages, of course.

What hit home within my own marriage, however, was not my husband's disrespect for my background or me; that's not his way. What I was shocked to discover was my own reverse prejudice and disregard for my background, a presence even more undermining to a marriage and oneself than anything initiated by a spouse.

In the course of writing this book, I don't think any incident was more important to me, in fact, than the moment when I realized how tightly my own self-image was bound to an ethnic identity I hadn't confronted or accepted in too long a time. The turning point took place on an evening after I'd interviewed an interfaith couple in my neighborhood. She was an auburn-haired Jewish woman who ran a large urban college. He was a dark-eyed, thoughtful Englishman who'd been raised in the Anglican Church. I liked them tremendously, and as I was saying goodbye, I wanted to give them a generous compliment to emphasize my appreciation. What I said haunted me all the way home and crystallized the real problem I was having in knowing my own mind about raising my children.

"Do you know what's been especially great about tonight?" I asked, buttoning up my coat. "I *loved* not having to interview another blond WASP woman! I spent this whole week talking to wholesome Protestant wives—one from Ohio, one from New Jersey, and another from Detroit. I've had enough.

"I've been thinking about them, however," I added, opening the door and hesitating. "It's so clear to me why their husbands love them. They're so easy to be with, so uncomplicated and cheery. And they're very pretty. But oh," I said, scowling and wagging my head, "they're so dull and simple, not complex enough for me. They're not like you."

My new friends shot a glance at each other, but the words didn't register in me until I was five minutes out the door. Suddenly, it became so clear that I wasn't talking about the interviews I had conducted with the substantive business executive, the psychologist, and the funny, articulate housewife who, in fact, had all given me a great deal of help in their honest discussions about their Protestant heritage. I was talking about *myself*—a blond, Protestant woman who hadn't outgrown a twenty-year-old image of herself as a sunny, all-American adolescent, desperately wanting to be a dark, wise, and sophisticated woman—anything but the commonplace, inconsequential person she was afraid of becoming. At thirty-nine, I was operating with old information that no longer fit my life. My self-esteem and attitudes about women like myself were colored by that unexamined contempt and rejection. I realized that the only way to feel secure about my identity, marriage, and interfaith questions was to learn how to be proud and honest about the woman I'd become and the heritage that shaped me.

"We all have ambivalent feelings about our ethnic background, but it is what we do with those feelings that count," explained Joseph Giordano, director of the Center on Ethnicity, Behavior and Communication for the American Jewish Committee. "Only by acceptance of your ethnic identity can you feel better about yourself and enhance your self-esteem."

When his words are considered in the context of a Jewish/Christian home, they become basic requirements for coping successfully with the ethnic differences that are always challenging husband and wife. In order to feel confident and relaxed enough to deal easily and equitably with those differences—enjoying them, accepting them, and moving on to learn from new ones—it's necessary to respect one's own distinctiveness first. It's a way to maintain a healthy balance of power.

4. *Enjoy what's common and shared.* Repeatedly I've heard couples say, "We're *so* different, but paradoxically we're really *so* much alike." They share many values, of course, including their respect for family, education, and high standards for work. But the commonality is also found in the ordinary places where many people who are bothered by differences would never look. It's found in a couple's commitment to things like big breakfasts, life outside the suburbs, colorful environments, and carefully planned birthdays. Maybe it's revealed in a spirited response to each day, a readiness to take out the garbage, a love for quiet walks together, or a propensity to break into song midway through the dishes.

In the anxious discussions about interfaith marriages, the play of such simple events is often left out of the picture.

Commonality is also more complex. It involves a shared acceptance of conflicts that are inevitably part of any marriage. It means noticing the intricate and highly individualized ways that two different people complement each other. Sometimes it means agreeing that religious differences are useful ways to siphon off resentments that have nothing to do with ethnic origins. All in all, it means that a couple has enough trust in its love and likemindedness to absorb infinite differences and allow that diversity to improve and animate their lives. They agree to disagree, and in so doing, they're continually reminded how much they truly have in common.

5. *Enjoy the diversity.* When the diversity seems wonderful or just another nuisance in the course of an exhausting day, it's useful to remember that a couple's comfortable respect for their differences and the honest and fair way they resolve them is one of their greatest gifts to their Jewish/Christian children. The rewards are manifest on many important levels. Children benefit by growing up in the company of two individuals who are stronger and wiser because of their marriage and the experiences that it has brought them. Children see the family's regard for its own differences and understand that the same combination within themselves is a source of pride and creativity. The way that differences are handled in the home teaches them how to treat people throughout their lives, and the spirit of compromise, patience, and sensitivity to others goes a long way toward preparing them to approach the world with the same openness and trust. In turn, when children see differences denied or reconciled because of one parent's bullying and another's abandoning his or her identity, a sadder model for dealing with life presents itself with serious implications for the child's self-esteem, understanding of how decisions are made, and overall adaptability to change and complexity.

To understand what it means to children to have their family's differences handled smoothly and sincerely, interfaith parents don't have to look further than their own childhood experiences. Odds are that their own parents came from families that seemed dramatically different from each other. In the children's eyes, each side of the family was a gestalt of distinctive characteristics that planted in their memory two models for living. Their parents probably weren't of different faiths, but the families were Ashkenazi and Sephardic, Orthodox and Reform, Methodist and Episcopalian, as well as rich and poor, citified and countrified, big and small. There were infinite ways that the families sorted themselves out into definite alternatives for the children growing up amidst both of them. How generously and proudly those alternatives were offered and how calmly and equitably the families handled the inevitable tensions between them was a legacy to children that had an incalculable impact. Parents draw from those memories in making their child-rearing decisions today.

When I imagine the two fields divided by the country fence that symbolize for me the open, proximate worlds of Jews and Christians, I begin to color in the green emptiness with the experiences and images that I believe I'm offering my own children. As if I'm illustrating a storybook, the pictures get more abundant and animated as the synagogues and churches with their different shapes and textures are added. The houses appear, with different pots on the stove and smells drifting through the air. Windows face mountains, the sea, or a bustling city. And the sounds of birds and music mix in with the background sounds of grandparents telling stories and people arguing, laughing, and talking their way through each day. Cousins are dropped like polka dots over the total page.

It's actually the scene I've dreamed for my own life, and I see my children moving surely in and around it, loving some images more than others and adding their own from experiences with a wider and broader world that stretches far beyond those pages.

I've no doubt that the Jewish/Christian differences in their lives, experienced against a background of love, will help them become their best and richest selves.

3

TODAY'S CHILDREN

We wonder what our children will do with their Jewish/ Christian identity—how they'll fit together the pieces of the puzzle that comprise their inheritance. When I look around my daughters' room, I notice things like the Easter basket holding Georgia's jewelry right next to the plastic menorah with orange bulbs chosen by Rachel because she loves its soft light. I hear music from *Fiddler on the Roof* and notice *The Night Before Christmas* on the bookshelf, and find myself wondering how Jordan's and my daughters will process the complexities and make choices about who they are and how they see themselves in terms of the two major religions and cultures that play such an inevitably powerful role in their lives.

It's almost impossible for parents to predict what aspects of the family's experience will form larger pictures in the minds of children—what they'll notice about the religious ceremonies and ideas their parents convey to them, and exactly what will take on significance and meaning. Sometimes things that seem major to us are overshadowed by perceptions we could never have imagined ourselves.

This was brought home to me recently when my friend Joanna told me about this year's efforts to celebrate Rosh Hashanah with her interfaith daughters. Garry, her Christian husband, came home early enough to prepare the apples and honey for the simple ceremony as a symbol of the sweetness anticipated for the months ahead. Determined to conduct a meaningful and proper ceremony, Joanna said the prayers in Hebrew, lit the candles, and talked about the meaning of the New Year and the hope it embodied. At the end of the dinner, Joanna felt quite triumphant as she looked over at her third- and sixth-grade daughters in the candlelight. Her eight-year-old, usually squirming in her seat by now, was settled in and looking very comfortable. Just as Joanna began to say how nice their Rosh Hashanah dinner had been this year, her eight-year-old looked up from buttering her seventh slice of challah with a beatific smile on her face. "Gee, Mom," she said enthusiastically, "I'm going to celebrate Rosh Hashanah every year for the rest of my life if I can have bread like this every time!" Little had Joanna realized that one trip to a new Jewish bakery would make this particular Jewish holiday an indelible experience.

Although with time, our children will get to the larger questions and commitments, these small observations and connections our children make are an important part of their developing sense of exploration, wonder, and attachment to their religious traditions. The things they notice all become a part of the way they interpret and understand their experience.

From a very young age they'll observe what's happening around them. The smallest everyday experience will add to that knowledge, whether it's watching *The Ten Commandments* on television or noticing that a friend goes to Sunday school in a strange building. The questions fly:

- Why does Daddy wear a yarmulke on his head at the synagogue?
- Why does Mommy wear a hat at church?

- Why do Jews go to services on Saturday while Christians go on Sunday?

- Why does Grandma say she doesn't believe in Jesus?

Children have an eye for differences and a strong need to organize and explain them, which is why young interfaith children will sometimes move around a living room and poll the relatives about who's Jewish like Mommy and who's not Jewish like Daddy. It's not unusual for a second-grade child to write a story for class about how she ate brown meat (brisket) at Aunt Shirley's on Passover and ham for Easter at Gramma Morrison's.

In the same automatic way that children classify people around them in terms of sex, race, age, and even the cars they drive or the grades they earn in school, children sort through their religious impressions and assemble a wide range of associations with their two heritages—facts, feelings, and memories of everything from a beloved holiday smell at their grandfather's house to a special round loaf of bread at a Rosh Hashanah celebration. As these impressions and memories sort themselves out, they eventually fall into an individualized categorization of traits that, by the way, is not necessarily objective. In Princeton, New Jersey, for instance, I met Jason, a lively eleven-year-old who introduced me to his three cats who all had acquired religious distinctions based on Jason's accumulated wisdom on such matters. First, he said, I had to meet "the Christian cat" who was "free and easy-going, like Dad." Then he showed me the Calico whom Jason had deemed Jewish because it was "the one who's picky about her food like Mom." Finally I met "the Nothing cat."

"She's the fat one that waddles around and sleeps and eats and doesn't rejoice in anything," Jason said.

It's almost impossible for an interfaith child in America *not* to notice and deal with the religious distinctions that the outside world cares about so deeply. Even when a family is highly secularized and genuinely indifferent to religious affairs, a child is inevitably sensitized to America's religious terrain through the media, friends, and relatives. The introduction might not always be accurate, clear, or friendly, but it guarantees that the interfaith child is never as oblivious to the subject as many parents believe.

A reminder of how alert most Jewish/Christian children are to their double heritage is the way they always mention it when you ask them to describe themselves. They seldom say, "I'm Jewish" or "I'm Catholic" and stop there. It's more common for them to volunteer a far more elaborate answer, such as "I'm Jewish, but my mother used to be Christian before she married my father." Or they'll say something like, "I go to Catholic school, but I'm part Jewish because my Dad is Jewish, and my Gramma and Grampa who live in Buffalo are Jewish, too."

"When they're asked to identify themselves, children will always establish a connection to both parents," explained Westchester child psychiatrist Morton Hodas, when I asked him about this tendency for exactness. "Who you are is a very concrete thing to a child. He'll always tell you, 'I came from her, I came from him.' Children are very honest that way."

When I interviewed interfaith children, I loved the ingenious and unique mixture of images that they used when trying to describe their dual identity accurately. Teenagers with whom I talked were especially creative and playful when it came to defining their origins. There were those who called themselves the predictable, scrappy, and somewhat self-denigrating names like "mongrel," "half-breed," and "mutt" or "Jewlic" or "Ca-Jew" (i.e., Catholic/Jewish). Some were more romantic. They were "a patchwork quilt," a "mélange," or a "star-crossed lover" who thought up her name when she eagerly scratched the Star of David beside a cross in my notebook. Some offspring were even more self-congratulating like the "Oye-vey Maria" from the Bronx or the son of a black Baptist mother and white Jewish father who announced he was "Blewish."

Children love both giving and knowing the thorough

details of their parents' backgrounds, and they also love the simple, clear labels that help them know where they really stand in relation to the two ethnic and religious domains. Having a neat designation isn't essential, but it helps children organize and focus their identity in a larger context.

When Chorizo Sato's daughter was filling out a school application, she went to her mother for help. "Am I 'Other'?" she asked, turning up her nose. "I'm not Caucasian or black, but I hate being an 'Other'!" When her mother suggested that she write in the word "Eurasian," she was delighted. As the child of a Buddhist/Japanese mother and a Jewish/Eastern European father, she suddenly had a label that made her a wonderful, simple, legitimate "Something."

It's assuring and useful for most children, whether they're seven or seventeen, to have an identifiable way to describe themselves. As New York psychiatrist Dr. Teruko Neuwalder explained, "No one wants to be ambiguous. It's nice to have an affirmation of who you are. It gives you a sense of belonging and recognition."

Reverend Daniel Heischman, the Episcopal chaplain at Trinity School in New York City, helps many of the Jewish/Christian students at his school feel proud of identifying themselves as "both" when they're asked what religion they are. A story he's told on occasion to children in the lower grades involves a little girl who couldn't make up her mind whether she wanted chocolate ice cream or vanilla ice cream. When she finally made up her mind, she said confidently, "I'd like a little bit of both, please." Heischman talks to many of Trinity's interfaith children about the richness of being "a little bit of both" and how that identity can be as meaningful and important to them as their friends' Catholic, Protestant, or Jewish identity can be for them.

Even with a certain clarity, however, a child's religious identity is anything but a fixed condition. It's a dynamic process that involves continual experimentation as the child keeps individualizing, reexamining, and shaping his relationship to his family and his belief systems.

As I see it, children have a very basic need to establish

a sense of mastery and self-esteem. This is true for all children, I believe, but children with a mixed heritage are particularly eager to acquire knowledge about the life around them that gives them a feeling of security and freedom to find their way within their own religious realities. In the children I interviewed, I observed these four basic necessities:

1. They need to understand the world around them. How does it work?

2. They need to acquire the knowledge and the skills to deal appropriately and feel comfortable with different communities, religions, and people.

3. They need to accumulate their own sets of beliefs and values, and find those people and institutions who will reinforce those feelings and help them grow.

4. They need to like themselves and feel loved and respected by the people who matter in their lives.

The needs of young children, for the most part, are simple and concrete. They begin by trying to master the skills associated with each religion. Parents will realize this when they begin to hear all the questions children ask about how to pray, eat, believe, and feel Jewish or Christian. When Rachel was six, she asked us what she should eat on Chanukah to be Jewish. "What do Jews eat?" she asked while Jordan and she spun the dreidel on the kitchen table.

Later in the year she asked us how Jews pray and how Christians pray. Very specifically she wanted to know if Jews flatten their palms together and whether Christians knit their fingers together. Rachel was demonstrating her curiosity and need to master the skills of both systems so she could be in tune with the customs of each.

Rachel's friend, Zachary, was busy the year earlier collecting information on the belief systems of people he classified as "Christmas" or "Jewish." At five, he was sitting cross-legged on the living-room floor with his mother preparing thank-you notes for the friends and relatives who'd given him presents for his December birthday. Midway through the process of dictating his messages to his mother, Zachary decided to decorate the outside of the envelopes. Suddenly he rushed excitedly from the room only to return minutes later, waving a page of colorful Christmas stamps that had arrived unsolicited in the mail from a fund-raising Bible organization. He tore off a picture of the Virgin Mary holding the baby Jesus in her arms and stuck it onto the envelope addressed to his observant Jewish grandmother.

"Oops, wait a minute, Zachary," said his mother, explaining that since his grandma didn't believe in Jesus and didn't celebrate Christmas, she might not like getting that particular stamp on her letter. She suggested that his other grandmother would probably like it just fine.

"What about Steven?" Zachary asked, holding up his letter to his good friend from school. "Does he believe in Jesus?"

"He doesn't believe in Jesus either," his mother answered, "because he's also Jewish."

Zachary thought for a moment. He stuck the Virgin Mary stamp on his letter to his Protestant grandmother and then popped up and disappeared into his bedroom closet where his treasures were stored. When he returned a moment later, he was waving a page of stamps from a wildlife society. "Alligators!" he exclaimed with a big smile. "Mom, I've got it! We can send these to anybody. It doesn't matter if they're Christmas or Jewish! Everybody believes in alligators!"

Through events like these, Jewish/Christian children like Zachary prepare the way for the inevitable choices they will make about their emerging religious identities. Gathering information and self-knowledge is an essential part of the process. Their intellect and curiosity compel them to scan, classify, and ultimately figure out how the religious dimension of life operates.

One of the best ways that parents—and grandparents —can help their children make sense out of the complexities of their dual heritage is to share their own ideas and listen to their children talk about their own feelings and beliefs. This doesn't mean handing children too much information too soon. It certainly doesn't mean ridiculing or ignoring any of their questions. It means responding to what they ask while remaining open to exploring religious territory together with them.

Grandparents have particularly good instincts about how to present information at a child's level. One grandfather who had survived the concentration camp at Dachau talked gently to me about his interfaith grandsons and how he wanted, above all, for them to grow up happy, to love him, and always to remember their Jewish side fondly, no matter what religion they might ultimately adopt. When he spends time with the six- and eight-year-old boys, they play games and talk, and often religion enters into their discussions.

"The other day, for instance," he recalled warmly, "I took the older boy to Greenwich Village to see some jugglers and fire eaters performing in the park. And on the way home, we discovered the old Jewish cemetery tucked in between the buildings on Eleventh Street. So we talked about who was buried there, and we got onto the subject of why there weren't any crosses on the markers.

"A little bit later, the older boy asked me about my parents and how they had died," he continued. "I didn't want to say too much. I told him they died in Europe during the Holocaust, which he'd heard of. I didn't say much more than that. When we got back, however, the younger boy was waiting for us, and I overheard him asking his brother what we did and talked about. 'Papa told me about his parents,' the older one said. This was an eight-year-old talking to a six-year-old, mind you. 'Even if I tell you a little bit,' the big boy said, 'it's so sad you'll cry.' "

Not only did this grandfather feel a responsibility to present his views to his grandsons in a low-key way when an opportunity naturally arose in the middle of their lovely times together, but he also realized how important it was for the boys to be respectful and knowledgeable about both sides of their heritage. Grandparents and parents who care about their offspring's wholeness take great care not to impart anti-Christian or anti-Semitic views to them. The rare grandparent who undermines a son-in-law, daughter-in-law, or that parent's traditions never finds forgiveness in the eyes of a grand-child.

The chance to participate in dialogues about their religious inheritance often seems to help children feel more compatible with it. I thoroughly enjoyed discussions with interfaith couples that took place in the presence of the small children hugging their teddy bears, or larger sons and daughters sitting around in their Levis and soccer shirts petting the family's cat in their laps. No matter their ages, these children listened acutely to their parents as they talked about their religious differences and choices they had made. When parents talked openly and comfortably, I was struck by how secure and free their children seemed to be with our discussions. I had the impression that they felt reassured by the fact that their parents were expressing their differences without creating schisms in their family unit. As a measure of the children's confidence, they usually drifted off to a basketball game or a good TV show after they'd reached their saturation level with the topic.

One of the biggest challenges to parents and grandparents is listening patiently and nonjudgmentally to interfaith children as they test out their theories and beliefs. Sometimes it's very hard for well-meaning parents not to overreact when their sons and daughters come up with outrageous pronouncements and judgments. In the face of declarations given to a Christian mother such as "I'm *all* Jewish, I'm not *any* Christian!" it's difficult to remember that this experiment is all part of a child's search for a religious identity. The search is essentially a process of trial and error, and when our children are small, it often seems as if it's their error and the parent's trial. For starters, children get their religious facts all wrong. Expect it. It takes time for them to get those facts straight. It takes time to sort out the calendar of holidays and the list of which belief belongs to which faith.

One time when Rachel was about seven years old, she matter-of-factly stated to Jordan that "Jews don't believe in God." Since she'd announced the week before that she was Christian, Jordan found himself having to take a deep breath before he could ask her in a calm and easy way where she'd gotten that idea. After his gentle inquiry, he was greatly relieved to learn she'd merely confused Christ and God. Just recently, Jordan was further relieved when he heard Rachel answer a friend's inquiry about her religion with a statement that she was "half Jewish and half Christian." His and my consistent reinforcement of that dual identity had paid off. In fact, when I asked her about her old answer, she didn't remember having ever declared herself totally Christian, nor did she remember her reasons for having done so.

I seem to remember that one of Rachel's main inspirations for previously declaring herself Christian was that "it was the girlish thing to do." At the time, she was identifying strongly with me and enjoying whispering confidences in my ear.

Now Jordan and I are experiencing a new test, one that reflects the various and unpredictable ways in which children assemble the elements and put them together. That test is being conducted by five-year-old Georgia who says that she likes being Christian because when she goes to church, "you get things." Georgia remembers all the very tangible rewards of Easter Sunday. There are the flowers, the Easter eggs, the jelly beans, and the tulip bulb that she planted in the back yard.

The testing and trying on of different behavior has many levels of meaning for a child. While it often involves the identity issues, it sometimes involves playing one parent off against another, using the vocabulary of religion to do it. Five-year-old Ilana, for instance, used religion as an effective tool when she said to her mother, "Daddy knows what the *megillah* is, but *you* don't 'cause you're not Jewish!" She said it in the same tone of voice she used the other day when she said to her father, "I love Mummy like the whole world, and I love you like my little pinky."

Sometimes parents find it very difficult to listen to their children exploring their beliefs and adopting different points of view. It's normal, however, for children initially to totally embrace the ideas they're learning about and only later to examine them with a more dispassionate mind. One first-grader told her Christian father that she would *always* be Jewish and *never* Christian, for instance, "because Jews are the smartest people in the world, and even God said they were the best!" Within a few months this same child was questioning the validity of the idea that any one group of people could "always" be the best. As her absorption with ideas of equality and fairness grew, her identification with the religions of both of her parents increased.

Sometimes it's difficult to listen as a child expounds on a theory that the parent can't accept. There's a fine line for thoughtful parents between respecting the search and affirming the belief itself. Knowing that the child's current belief is often held by one set of the children's grandparents, and possibly by the other parent as well, makes it very important, however, to respond without putting down what the child is feeling or articulating. It's equally important not to undermine the faith that's being exhibited. Sometimes that isn't an easy task.

One evening when Zachary was six years old he began telling his Dad, who's Jewish, all about how Jesus had brought a dead man back to life. At the time, Zachary was a first-grade student in an Episcopal day school partly staffed by nuns. Although the student body was unusually diverse both religiously and racially, the children had chapel every morning and heard Bible stories. Like most children his age, Zachary loved the dramatic stories and was able to believe without question the veracity of the events recounted. He also loved his teacher, Sister Mary Christine, and was identifying himself as a Christian.

"The man was really dead, Dad," he said. "He was so dead that he stunk. His relatives had wrapped him up in clothes and put him in a cave. But Jesus made the man get up and walk! He had healing power and he made the dead man alive again!''

"Zachary, do you really believe in those fairy tales?" asked his father, who had heard one parable too many that week.

"Yes, of course," said Zachary, "because it really happened. It's the *truth*."

"You can believe it's true," his father said, "and your mother can believe it's true. A lot of people can believe it's true. But I've never seen it, and I just don't believe it."

"Well, Dad," Zachary persisted. "I believe it because I *know* it's true."

When Zachary told his Jewish grandmother the same story about Jesus raising the man from the dead, she said, "Zachary, give me a break! Please tell me stories about Moses. Save the stories about Jesus for your other grandmother." To Zachary's mother, she said, "Is that school raising him to be a missionary?"

Not all children stand their ground so firmly, but Zachary's drive to know his own mind and find comfort in his own beliefs is a basic need that he shares with other children. It takes courage and self-awareness to stand up and express one's convictions, let alone dive into issues that have divided Western civilization for 2,000 years.

Sometimes, in the process of this kind of exploration, it's difficult for parents to remember that it's important for children to experience and understand their capacity for sureness and intensity and to trust the cycles of questioning, doubt, and self-examination that will naturally follow. Zachary's mother, who was raised a fundamentalist Protestant, was happy that her son was wrestling with these thorny issues at such a young age. She welcomed his exploration of the Jewish faith as well as the Christian faith. "At least if he's examining these ideas now, testing them, believing them and then reacting against them," she said, "he's not so apt to become a Moonie when he's eighteen years old and someone else comes along with a certainty about the way things are. I would be much more concerned if he didn't believe anything. I think a lot of the kids who get drawn into cults in their teen years are the ones who didn't grapple with these issues at a younger age. At some point in time we all have to explore spiritual issues. We know there's some larger meaning out there somewhere and, as far as I'm concerned, the sooner anyone's search begins, the better."

For her, another important result of her son's questioning is that he learns at an early age that the people he loves can disagree on important issues. Children become aware that people have different realities and values, and they learn not to take it personally when someone doesn't agree with them. Reverend Richard Spalding, a Presbyterian minister who teaches many interfaith students at Trinity School, has complimented his Jewish/Christian group, in fact, on their awareness that people support many different traditions and religious beliefs. "Those students who belong to one tradition uniformly are often far less aware that any other religion exists besides their own," he observed.

Although the process by which our children sort out their values, beliefs, and identity may seem chaotic to us, there's an essential consistency that they experience from their very real and unique reality. We're not "burdening" them with their inheritance. It's merely their reality they live with and learn from. Whether parents raise them as Jews, Christians, "Both," or secular human beings outside of any religious structure, the children will go through a natural process in which values, as well as the messages that have real meaning for them, will merge within them. Just as they'll see differences between the two religions, they'll also see the points of agreement between them, and they'll feel the compatibility between their parents' traditions and personal ethics.

It's less chaotic than it appears. "I don't see why children can't be bilingual on religion in the way they are with languages," said James W. Fowler, the Atlanta-based theologian and author of *Stages of Faith*. "Kids are attracted to the differences between their parents because they're pieces to build an identity out of. They're clues from their parents about what's meaningful to them, and they have no difficulty sorting them out. The crucial factor is seriousness, a deep understanding that life is more than individualism, that there are communities of faith. Children are not uncomfortable if parents' commitments are made visible and tangible and explanations are freely given."

What matters for parents is knowing that their children's search is valuable. What matters for children is feeling encouraged and loved through their search. It's how they'll come to know what it is they believe in—not just theological concepts but matters of faith, love, morals, and human values.

By the time the first-grader becomes a teenager, many of his views will no longer be so clear-cut. Like others entering adolescence, he'll find himself struggling to form a new, larger identity for himself in the context of his family and the world. The teenager is like a bird building a nest out of bits and pieces of information gathered from the world around him. He tests every shred for strength and suitability, and carefully fits it into his whole, intricate sense of himself. The process isn't always a conscious one, but it's all too evident to parents who suddenly find themselves—their behavior, attitudes, affiliations, and especially their faults—being mercilessly scrutinized by a teenager who's sifting through the clues for "final" determinations on who or what he or she wants (or doesn't want) to become.

Religion inevitably gets drawn into the adolescent's endeavor because it's a prominent part of each parent's legacy. When teens are weighing and measuring themselves and figuring out who they can model themselves after and what they can count on for strength within themselves, their attention is often focused on their Jewish and Christian parents and grandparents and the cultural and religious characteristics they represent.

To the consternation of most interfaith teens, their backgrounds are seldom as perfect and inspirational as the observing and romantic child would like them to be. Both sides of the family are often flawed. For nineteen-year-old Michael Leon, the fact that his father's Russian Orthodox background was marred by the Russian people's tradition of anti-Semitism and alcoholism became a very disturbing issue for him. He argued, in fact, with his friends, who were Jewish or half-Jewish like him, that these historical predispositions were not "a litmus test that disqualified a people from being worthwhile." Michael didn't want to be Russian Orthodox. Worried about his own feelings of prejudice, as well as his own emotional fallibilty during this passage to adulthood, Michael merely wanted to feel proud of his heritage on both his Russian and his Jewish sides, and he didn't want to feel that any of his father's, his ancestors', or his own weaknesses would disqualify him from "being worthwhile."

Teenagers seem to have a way of coming to terms with what's the best, and sometimes the worst, in their parents and grandparents. But the process of weighing and measuring each side of the family's values before they can comfortably blend them within themselves is often a back-and-forth experimentation.

Thinking about this, I'm reminded of John Rosenbaum, a tall, lanky high-school senior who stretched out on the grass in New York City's Central Park while he candidly talked about himself in terms of his perception of his grandparents' Jewish and Christian values. "The Jewish side of my background pushes me to achieve and be successful," said John, stretching his long arms behind his shaggy blond head. "I was really feeling that incredibly intense pressure when I was making out my college applications. I felt I had to make some kind of unique impression on the college admission boards. Unfortunately I think the colleges are just going to think of my application as another form from another Jewish kid from a predominately Jewish high school in Manhattan.

"Do you know what's really good about my Jewish side, though?" he asked eagerly. "My grandfather plays great chess.

He's also such an interesting guy. He and his pals are all in their seventies, and they ask me to sit with them while they argue passionately about politics for hours.

"My mother's Christian family is a lot different. They don't see life as success or failure," John explained earnestly. "Life isn't something to achieve, it's something to live. Like getting a good education isn't the ultimate goal in life, it's just part of experiencing your life fully.

"But on the other hand, my mom's family just doesn't know all that much," he added. "They're always quoting *Time* magazine. They're not very intellectual, to say the least."

He sat up on his elbows and thought for a moment. "I think my nonintellectual side is winning out at the moment. I've even thought about changing my name to my mom's, which is Anglund. John Anglund," he said, testing it out in his mind. "I had that name when I was a kid and did some commercials, actually. I probably should have used *that* name on my college applications. It might have given me more freedom!"

Odds are good that John's feelings and sense of himself will continue to shift, especially after he's completed four years at Harvard University where he was accepted on early admission shortly after our interview. His views will mature, and the differences that the seventeen-year-old sees so clearly will blend together and become integrated within himself as he becomes stronger and more secure within himself.

In high school and early college, teenagers usually feel a new imperative to declare their identity and come to terms with where they stand in relationship to their newly found status in the adult world. As they're evaluating their parents' strengths and weaknesses, they're also assessing their own selves and how *they* will measure up against the backdrop of their peers. Will their Jewish/Christian inheritance be a handicap? Will they make their way in the world as well, if not better, than their parents did? On a deeper level, they question their values, their courage, and their integrity. Would they have hidden during the Holocaust? Would they have denied their Jewish side and camouflaged themselves with their Christian family? Would they have handled themselves with honor? They grapple with these and other complex moral questions.

Adolescents are especially sensitive to the standards their peers set for "the right way" or "the only way" to look, feel, and live one's life. They want to belong to the chosen group and feel defined, secure, confirmed by that membership. Within that group they want to be enough like everyone else to feel comfortable. For the interfaith child, however, it's not always such a smooth fit. Because of their mixed backgrounds, they often stick out from the pack, especially in a religious school or homogeneous community where their name is different, a parent is different, a body type, hair color, or facial feature is different. Even their awareness of divided loyalties is slightly different from the norm, and to the teenager already suffering from awkwardness and self-consciousness, such distinctions can be painful.

There's some reassurance in the fact that the population of interfaith children is growing rapidly, so that Jewish/Christian children are no longer the rare commodity in the classroom, basketball team, family circle, or even religious school. If they look around them, they have company for sharing and confirming their complicated feelings.

The sensitivity of any teenager, however, is always complicated by prejudice by Jews against Christians, Christians against Jews, or Jews and Christians against children of mixed marriages. Adolescents often report feeling those stings of prejudice for the first time when they begin to socialize and, most particularly, when they begin to date.

Henry Bethe was fifteen when he woke up to a new set of confusing risks associated with his Jewish/Christian status. The son of Nobel Prize–winner Hans Bethe (who is also the product of a Jewish/Christian marriage), Henry was an attractive, energetic teenager. "I was dating this girl when I was in high school," said Henry. "One night her father pulled me aside and asked me to stop seeing his daughter because I was Jewish. When I was twenty-one, I was dating another girl from the University of Chicago. One night her father pulled me aside and asked me to stop seeing his daughter because he didn't think the relationship would work out since I *wasn't* Jewish."

Most Jewish/Christian teenagers have at least one slur or insult to report. There was the youngster who was called a "kike" for the first time at a WASPy summer camp in Maine, and a debutante whose first application to the dance committee was rejected because she was part Jewish. Some adolescents report having to speak up and tell their friends to lay off the offensive jokes about the *goyim* or the "hebes." Others ask their religious-school instructor to stop all snide comments about people who intermarry. Many ask their peers to allow them the right to think of themselves as committed Christians or Jews and not be told their dedication is suspect because of their mixed parentage. One of the greatest gifts parents can give their children is to prepare them to confront prejudice in all its forms and to stand by them for emotional support whenever they're hurt by it.

One adolescent whose mother is Japanese told me proudly that when she was a young teen sitting alongside her father at the synagogue, a member of the congregation leaned over and whispered to her father, "She's such a lovely child. She's adopted, isn't she?" Her father's answer was fast and sweet. "No, we didn't adopt her," he said. "We made her at home."

Interfaith adolescents have the greatest difficulty when they encounter prejudice or divisiveness *within* their own family. Whether it's a parent who hasn't come to terms with his or her own background or it's a grandparent who maintains bitterness over an interfaith marriage and never accepts the daughter-in-law or son-in-law, the result is arduous and painful for the teenager. Some misguided parents withhold essential information about their own experiences growing up. They may have severed ties with one or both sides of the family over religious issues, or they may just refuse to talk about them. Some parents deny or misrepresent their ties to a religion so profoundly that their children receive confused messages not only about the essence of either religion but also about their parents' strength of character and the honesty of their commitments. Adolescence has a way of revealing those disturbed relationships, and they place an unfair burden on the teenager who's left to grapple with larger issues on his own.

I've been told about some circumstances where a bitter divorce has separated a teenager from one of his or her parents. Sometimes, the child is the object in the parents' tug of war. In this situation, the parents put their own animosity above the welfare of the child. In a divorce situation where pressure is maintained to stay away from the other parent, or where one parent continuously puts the other down, the child has been offered a narrow and distorted understanding of that important part of his life at a time he most needs the nourishment and information about what he's made of and can draw from. Because this time of life is so formative and so important, undermining behavior sometimes wreaks long-term damage in the child's life.

Even under normal circumstances, however, there's somewhat of a contest underway. "When someone is struggling between the values of one parent or the other, there may be a focus on religion," explained Dr. Teruko Neuwalder in her New York City office. "Religion is a convenient organizer of conflict." Just as if they're evaluating a business deal, adolescents weigh their options and tally up the pros and cons. Obviously, identities aren't constructed in such a conscious and effective way. But for the average adolescent child of an interfaith marriage, such routines are part of the process of knowing their own minds and feelings.

"Mixed marriage really, really is an overblown issue," said Morton Hodas, the child psychiatrist from Scarsdale, New York. Dr. Hodas, who has seen many Jewish/Christian adolescents in his practice, was adamant that these children don't have any more troubles with their identity than children from a home with a uniform religious background. "There are a thousand issues that are infinitely more important and confusing to a child than the parents' religious backgrounds," he said. "When both parents suddenly go to work and aren't around or when parents make plans to move from the suburbs to the city without telling the child. Divorce is much worse. Lots of things are much worse.

"The truth is that two religiously homogeneous parents can screw up children in ten thousand ways. If religion is an issue at all for mixed-marriage children, it's *never* the only issue causing the problem."

For the most part, children of interfaith marriage learn to love the strengths they've inherited as a result of the differences between their parents. Time and again during my interviews, interfaith offspring told me that what counted for them was the worldliness and broadmindedness that their family's different backgrounds fostered in them as they were growing up. By the time they reached adulthood, many had learned to celebrate the differences. Teenagers and adults alike radiated a sense of adventure and pleasure when they told me about one set of their cousins who played contract bridge and argued about the purpose of life, while another souped up old cars and cruised around the 7-Eleven store. One set of grandparents introduced a teenager I interviewed to the glitz of the Florida shoreline, while her other grandparents made her comfortable in their cabin in the Minnesota woods. There was the one parent who knew the inner workings of ethnic politics in a big city, but the other who knew about yacht-club protocol. The contrasts in the cultures they belong to are infinite, and interfaith children are proud of how well they learn to navigate comfortably between those worlds. It often gives them a feeling of competence as world citizens, as people who can skillfully adapt to life's adventures and differences. They also learn that because of their love of such disparate people, they're not likely to succumb to parochialism and prejudice that limit the lives of many people they see around them.

New parents who are searching for their own ways to nurture and support their children may want to act on these tips that other interfaith children have given me. They've been clear and adamant about the ways they think others like them should be raised. Their rules have as much to do with enjoyment as with sound preparation. I think that parents who follow these guidelines will feel a new confidence about the way they involve themselves in this essential aspect of their lives.

- Be clear and honest from the start about the religious heritage of your children.

- Don't worry about them; let them enjoy their lives.

- Let them be themselves; recognize them for who they are.

- Laugh a lot.

- Make them proud of themselves.

- Prepare them for some prejudice and help them learn to stand up for themselves. (But don't make them *worry* about it!)

- Answer their questions as best you can.

- Fill the home with people of both faiths.

- Tell them about your disagreements about religious issues, but tell them about compatibility where it exists.

- Create an environment where a family can talk together about important things. Don't leave them to grapple on their own.

- Talk about religion—talk about what you believe.

- Tell them about your experiences growing up. What was life like for you? How did you feel when you were a kid?

- Listen to them when they tell you what they believe. Don't be hurt by their choices or their thoughts. Remember, they're learning.

- Don't close the door on any discussions about religion or life.

- No matter how they are raised, make sure they at least know their way around the synagogue and church.

- Point out who's half-and-half so they can have some models.

- Help them to get to know their grandparents. Encourage grandparents to share with them and to discuss themselves and their lives.

- Introduce them to the possibilities and diversities of life.

- Realize that they can be anything they choose. They may want to be a rabbi or a priest, a folk singer or a diplomat.

- Be sensitive to their differences and their unique personalities. They may not go about their religious exploration in the same way as their brothers or sisters did it. Each of them puts the combination together in a different way, and that's as it should be.

Parents should also remember to congratulate themselves on what they've offered their children. Reverend Heischman reports that one of the strengths he sees in interfaith children is that "they have so much less to unlearn than we do." Interfaith children themselves say that, more important than anything else, we should accept and enjoy their duality as well as the duality within the family. Teach them about it, and allow them to invest in it and build lives that do justice to their Jewish and Christian roots. Prepare them well so their self-knowledge, skills, pride, and interconnectedness with larger communities and subtler truths will continue to inform and enrich their choices throughout life.

4

YESTERDAY'S
CHILDREN—
NEGOTIATING
DIFFERENCES

The cultural differences at work and at play within every Jewish/Christian marriage can ultimately become some of the richest gifts that parents offer their interfaith children. Along with the love and guidance offered by the immediate and extended family and its religious traditions, these differences complete the inventory of resources that parents call upon to nurture their children and build their own lives and marriages. Although these differences sometimes challenge and test couples in ways that aren't easy, their combination within a family becomes an invaluable source of strength, vitality, and enrichment.

What are these cultural differences? They're the myriad ways of living and thinking that characterize a group of people who've been connected by centuries of history and experience to a particular religion and set of beliefs. "The differences between religious groups are fundamental and pervasive. They include differences in religious convictions, and these are not unimportant," observed James H. S. Bossard and Eleanor Stoker Boll in their study, *One Marriage, Two Faiths.*

Yet there is more to differences, the writers emphasized. "Behind the beliefs are differences in behavior, in observances in the daily life, in attitudes, in values, and in moral judgments. Reinforcing these often are the cultural survivals of different national origin groups, going back to the lives of their forebears in the country of their origin. In still other cases, there are differences in social prestige."

For interfaith parents, it's usually the tangible differences that are easiest to understand. Their childhoods were filled with those differences as a look around their own parents' homes today is usually quick to reveal. The food on the table is different, especially for parties and special events. The art on the living-room walls, its colors and favorite scenes, is never the same. The photo albums feature different holidays and rites of passage, and even the people in the pictures don't look alike. "Our faces are amazing cultural artifacts, aren't they?" Dr. Morton Hodas once commented.

The intangible differences aren't as easy to identify, but their impact on interfaith lives is usually far more profound. These chaotic, sometimes elusive and subtle differences are important to understand. As Bossard and Boll noted when they talked about values, beliefs, attitudes, and a moral code, a person's inner sense of what's important and necessary in life is expressed in his or her common behavior and, like Jewish and Christian names and faces, these expressions have deep, attenuated roots in separate religions and the experiences that Judaism and Christianity generated over time. Different ways of celebrating, surviving, and coping day to day have developed and created the cultures that surrounded and shaped Jews and Christians as they grew up.

As a result, wrote Joel Crohn, Ph.D., a California psychologist specializing in the study of interfaith marriages and ethnicity, "Ways of dealing with affection, conflict, child-rearing, kin, food, health, achievement, and male and female roles differ significantly between Jewish and various non-Jewish subcultures." In his study, "Ethnic Identity and Marital Conflict: Jews, Italians and WASPS," Crohn went on to observe that, "The ways in which couples deal with attachments to their respective cultural and religious traditions affect both the quality of those marriages and the future identification of their children."

What makes any study of these cultural differences so complicated, however, is that obviously no single, perfect model of a Jew or Christian ever existed in real life. A host of other forces, both ancient and up to date—nationalities, religious denomination, class, economics, family, neighborhood, life experience, and personality—all combined into countless permutations that, in turn, generated many categories of Jews and Christians, as well as an infinite number of unique individuals. When I started to classify these differences as a first step toward understanding their role in Jewish/Christian marriages, the job was mind-boggling. What generalizations could I make that could possibly apply to most intermarrying Jews who were a mixture of Eastern Europeans, Germans, Sephardim, and Reform, Conservative, and Orthodox varieties of Americans? Also, what could I say about most intermarrying Christians who included Catholics, thirty-two denominations of Protestants, some Greek and Russian Orthodox believers, as well as individuals with backgrounds as diverse as Italian, Irish, Scandinavian, Latin American, and many others?

The more I interviewed and the more I read about ethnic differences in a fascinating work called *Ethnicity and Family Therapy*, edited by Monica McGoldrick, John K. Pearce, and Joseph Giordano, the more the differences proliferated, like stars in the universe. As this thorough book indicated, the differences affected every aspect of interfaith lives from a marital argument to the number of telephone calls to Mom, from a menu to the contents of the medicine cabinet. Because of that profusion of differences, however, their patterns and relationships seemed even more impossible to chart. Moreover, on a practical level, it seemed miraculous that Jews and Christians ever fell in love and found something in common.

In fact, when I read the lengthy chapters on Jewish families and Norwegian families that specifically related to

Jordan and me, I found myself getting more hostile with every paragraph. When every typical ethnic characteristic was spelled out, from Jewish materialism to Norwegian depression, from a Jewish mother's intrusiveness to a Norwegian's chilly reticence, I couldn't believe that I'd married "that" or that I was "that." As a type, Jordan was too much to deal with, and I was as bad. If either of us had used that ethnic paradigm as our sole source of information about each other, we'd never have built our relationship and married.

Closing the book on ethnicity and returning to real life was a pleasure. I realized that in marriage, thank goodness, these differences seldom appear all at once. Like stars, they pop into sight and just as quickly fade from view. They can hover surely in the background, explode into prominence, fade with the sunshine, or disappear forever. Not only is the universe in flux so that stars are never the same from one night to the next, but the stargazers change, too, bringing their own feelings and experience to each moment, interpreting, selecting, and accelerating even more the mutability of the whole, flickering array.

I've learned that if there's any pattern, in fact, to the way that Jewish/Christian couples relate to the cultural differences within their marriage, it's best described as no pattern at all but rather a complex and dynamic process of interaction that's anything but fixed and predictable. Contrary to the tradition that maintains that interfaith differences only lead to trouble and alienation, I've found that they're a compelling, vital presence that is continually filtered through the evolving knowledge and emotions of every parent. They can challenge a person's identity on the deepest, most mysterious levels. But they can also flatter and entertain, inspire and guide, and illuminate one's own power and beauty. And on the same deep level, they can draw people out of themselves and help them reach out to become their richer and wiser selves.

Until this century, however, the differences within a Jewish/Christian marriage were not a rich cause for celebration. For 2,000 years, the divisions and boundaries between

Jews and Christians were such profound ones that crossing them socially, religiously, and certainly through intermarriage was a risky and difficult task with sobering consequences. For the Jew, intermarriage was a violation of ancient rabbinic law, called *halacha*, and the penalty for doing so was banishment from the family and the Jewish community. Parents sat *shiva* for the child who married a non-Jew, carrying out the rites of mourning as if he or she were dead.

"Intermarriage was considered to be a cancer in the Jewish community," explained sociologist Egon Mayer, "and the only thing to do was to cut it out, like removing a disease." In the hit play *Fiddler on the Roof*, probably the most widely known contemporary example of a Jewish parent's reaction to a child's marrying out of the faith, the passionate Tevye bellowed a "No-no-no!" when his youngest daughter, Chavaleh, "everybody's fav'rite child," begged him to accept her marriage to a Gentile. No matter how torn, he ultimately couldn't turn his back on the essentials of his faith—the Law, tradition, and his shared fate with the Jewish people. Before singing a poignant song of loss and bewilderment ("Chavaleh"), Tevye turned to his wife and said solemnly, "Go home, Golde. We have other children at home . . . Chava is dead to us! We will forget her. Go home."

The penalties confronting most Christians marrying Jews weren't any less onerous. They were often forced to leave their homes and families because of rejection or prejudice. The young Gentile groom in *Fiddler* couldn't live with his people's violent anti-Semitism that, in reality, destroyed many villages like Tevye's during the late nineteenth and early twentieth centuries in Russia and Poland; he and his Jewish wife packed for a new, presumably safer city. "As the Good Book says," warned Tevye, " 'Each shall seek his own kind.' Which, translated, means, 'A bird may love a fish, but where would they build a home together?' "

It's likely that a proportion of interfaith couples have always found a means, throughout history, to find safe havens for themselves. But still, there's no avoiding the reality that far greater risks than separation from their families threatened their well-being, even their lives and children's lives. By marrying a Jew, the Christian was inevitably caught up in whatever circumstances befell the Jews. Though the history of Jewish/Christian relations over the last twenty decades has had its "patches of light," as the renowned Jewish author and historian Yosef Yerushalmi emphasized in a powerful 1974 address to the International Symposium on the Holocaust, recorded in *Auschwitz: Beginning of a New Era? Reflections on the Holocaust*, edited by Eva Fleischner, the overall scene is much bleaker. "Much of the record is dark," Yerushalmi concluded.

"Our forefathers have been forced out of many, many places at a moment's notice," said one of Tevye's fellow Jews as the villagers packed and fled their home in a matter of three days. With rueful levity and words that fit the Jewish experience in Western Europe as well as in the East, Tevye shrugged and said, "Maybe that's why we always wear our hats."

No matter where Jews lived, their security was always in danger. As was powerfully illustrated in Abba Eban's book, *Civilization and the Jews*, as well as the public television series of the same name, Jews were banished during various eras from countries such as England, France, Germany, and Spain, sometimes for centuries. They were periodically forbidden from practicing their faith and marrying, even talking, with Christians. Although the barbarism and unfairness was by no means unique, the victimization that took place during the Crusades and especially during the Spanish Inquisition in the late fifteenth century was a particularly stirring statement that peace and comfort for Jews was never guaranteed, no matter how long they had settled peacefully into an apparently tolerant society. As Rabbi Joachim Prinz once wrote, "Never in their long history did . . . [Jews] leave a country voluntarily."

Day to day, however, there was a deeper, more pervasive presence that manifested itself as a roadblock to Jewish/Christian marriage. It was a prejudice toward Judaism and Jews that was woven into Christianity. "Consciously or subconsciously, anti-Semitism is profoundly rooted in Christianity," wrote the French-Jewish historian Jules Isaac in his widely accepted analysis, *The Teaching of Contempt*.

According to Isaac and many other scholars, the message passed down for millenia has been that Jews were simply too blind to recognize Jesus as the Messiah, and worse, they were evil enough to crucify Him. As a result of this and other Jewish violations throughout their history, God withdrew his love and offered it to the worthier Christians instead. In addition, God punished the Jews by destroying their Temple and exiling them forever, "their back bend thou down always" (Psalm 69) in their unending reprobation. In turn, Judaism was considered by Christians to be an inadequate religion, half-baked in a sense because it never developed and completed itself through acceptance of Christ.

Such a negative attitude didn't have to manifest itself in intense, violent anti-Semitism in order for marriagable Christians to stay clear of marriageable Jews. Throughout much of history, an inferior social, economic, and religious status of Jews was a deterrent, as was their physical separation because of where they lived and worked.

The image of the Jew wasn't an alluring one either. Commonly, Jews were cast in many ugly and frightening images. As the Christian theologian Rosemary Radford Ruether noted in another noteworthy presentation for the International Symposium on the Holocaust, one demonic myth after another circulated through society, spawning, by the late Middle Ages, a full-blown image of the Jew as a devil with horns, a tail, and a terrible smell.

Neither the Protestants or the Catholics were innocent of these distortions. Paris's Notre Dame Cathedral, which was completed in the fourteenth century, has statues depicting the Synagogue as a blindfolded woman alongside the Church who is crowned and triumphant. Calvin's Geneva wouldn't allow Jews to live inside its borders. And Martin Luther, the father of the Protestant Reformation, declared that synagogues should be destroyed and Jews exiled.

There were always individuals who transcended those

dictates, including many Popes who, according to Professor Yerushalmi, an authority on Jewish history, fought hard and effectively to preserve Jews and Judaism. Nevertheless, the prevailing social norms, buttressed by Jewish law and Christian theology, made Jewish/Christian intermarriage a rare and risky choice.

By the seventeenth, eighteenth, and especially the nineteenth centuries, however, there were big changes throughout America and Western Europe. With the Industrial Revolution and the French and American wars for independence, there was a tremor that sent waves of immigrants into America and many European cities. In Germany, for instance, the hold of Orthodoxy gave way to the creation of Reform Judaism, opening up revolutionary dialogues about intermarriage. Especially in cities, Jews and Christians met for the first time.

"Intermarriages between free-thinking Jews and Christians followed on the heels of emancipation in an inexorable sequence," wrote Egon Mayer in a detailed account of this turning point in history in his book, *Love and Tradition*. Shortly before 1800, the percentage of intermarriage among all marriages involving Jews had reached 29 percent in America. By 1900, it was close to 33 percent in Western European cities such as Strasbourg and Copenhagen. By 1933, in Germany, two years before Hitler prohibited intermarriage by passing the Nuremberg Laws, the rate reached a high of 44 percent.

As Mayer observed, the dramatic exception to this free, pluralistic matchmaking was Eastern Europe where Tevye and the other half of the world's 8 to 9 million Jews lived in small villages and communities set apart from the hostile Christian population. By the early years of the twentieth century, over half of these Jews fled their last pogrom and flooded to America where by 1925 they outnumbered the existent German Jewish population by more than ten to one. Ultimately they became the largest group of American Jews intermarrying today. Nevertheless, back in Latvia and Lithuania in 1933 the rate of Jewish intermarriage was a minuscule 2.64 and 0.2 percent respectively, and free spirits like Chavalah continued to be a rarity.

In America at the turn of the century, intermarriage wasn't very popular either. Such massive immigration brought a return to group consciousness and traditional religious separatism. By 1920, in America, Catholics weren't even marrying Protestants (and vice versa), let alone marrying Jews, and the Jewish statistics at the time confirm the conservatism; only two out of every hundred Jews getting married were marrying non-Jews. By 1960, when interfaith marriages began gradually increasing again, the numbers were still low; fewer than six out of every hundred Jews getting married were marrying non-Jews, a far cry from the 1980s statistics indicating that, on the average, thirty to forty out of every hundred Jews are intermarrying. Until recently, however, only the unconventional couples had the intensity to leap over the barriers that divided Christian and Jew, marry, raise children, and try to integrate a formidable set of differences into their complicated, often dramatic lives.

The parents who produced many of the grown sons and daughters whom I interviewed for this book could never be considered average citizens in mainstream America, no matter whose point of view one accepts. "Who out-marries?" asked two sociologists named J. S. Slotkin and Reuben B. Resnik in the 1950s. According to a summary of their findings that appeared in Bossard and Boll's *One Marriage, Two Faiths*, interfaith couples were best described as "unorganized or demoralized," "promiscuous," "adventurous," "detached," "rebellious," "marginal," "acculturated," or "emancipated."

"One gets the picture of a kind of person who is not deeply rooted in his own cultural setting," interpreted Bossard and Boll.

One also gets the picture of a maverick on the fringes —sometimes the lunatic fringes—of society. Many religious officials firmly opposed to intermarriage must have viewed these observations as further proof of their warnings about the negative aspects of "marrying out." With the exception of the "adventurous" and the "emancipated," interfaith partners sounded like the worst possible mates and parents.

When asked about their parents, the adult children of

these couples from the 1950s seldom see them in the same harsh light, however. Their emphasis is a different one, and more often than not, it's a warmer and more flattering look at the marriages and the miracle that those marriages even happened at all. Repeatedly throughout my interviews, adult children of interfaith parents talked about how proud, amazed, intrigued they were by the fact that their parents could be so different from each other yet stay together and triumph over the substantial odds against them.

The romantic stories about their parents' courtships were abundant. "My father was the young Jewish landlord from the right side of the tracks who joined his father one day to collect the rent from the family on the wrong side of the tracks," said Angela Marcowitz, a sixty-four-year-old grandmother from Florida. "He saw this young and very beautiful girl sitting on the stoop in Hell's Kitchen in New York City. That was it! He never stopped loving her ever."

Father Gary Gelfenbien, a Catholic priest from Troy, New York, spun another story that was less like a Broadway musical than a children's fairy tale. "My olive-skinned Calabrian mother with her long chestnut hair, the beloved daughter in a family of nine children, fell in love with a platinum-haired young man from Kiev who was sheer energy. His Orthodox parents ordered him to leave her or they would, in effect, bury him. But he became the favorite of my Italian grandmother," said the exuberant forty-two-year-old chaplain at Rensselaer Polytechnic Institute. "My mother became a beloved daughter to my Jewish Bubbe."

Full-blooded romance also fit the personalities who intermarried. Oftentimes, they were tough and compelling characters with substantial accomplishments. A passionate young daughter in Poland, for instance, said good-bye to her father, a rabbi, and walked to Paris to fight for Socialism. According to her son, a graphic designer in New York, she met her future husband soon after he'd been expelled from his Yugoslav home because his father, as the story goes, was tired of bailing him out of jail for his fiery political activity.

Closer to home in Jersey City, New Jersey, my husband

Jordan's aunt Annetta Brof met John Quinn, a Catholic, and married and raised a daughter. What made her such a remarkable woman was that she had been a polio victim since she was three years old. Despite her paralysis, this beautiful woman with clear, blue eyes became a lawyer, politician, and activist on behalf of the disabled. She was also a wife, mother, and candidate for mayor—an accomplishment that was difficult enough for a woman who was Jewish in the 1950s, let alone a handicapped one confined to crutches and a wheelchair.

At first, I was surprised when I heard stories like the one related by Toni LoPopolo, a senior editor at St. Martin's Press in New York. Her Jewish mother was a fourteen-year-old olive vendor in the Farmers Market in Los Angeles when a twenty-two-year-old Italian youth, going west, stopped to say hello, fall in love, and wait six months to elope with the girl he came to call his "exotic queen from Montenegro" for close to sixty years.

After many interviews and discussions, however, dramatic patterns like this one became so commonplace that I was surprised when I found an all-American couple who had met and married in their twenties after the young man moved to New York from a tame place like Ohio.

From the adult children now in their thirties, I was less likely to hear immigrant tales about the Old World meeting the New World, but I did hear about all the other standard differences that tended to characterize interfaith marriages during this era between the 1920s and the 1960s. One partner went to college and the other didn't, one was old and the other was young, one was high-class and the other was low-class, one was strong and the other weak. Obviously, similar combinations could be found elsewhere in the general population, and granted, not all these differences were equally difficult to negotiate. What struck me about the interfaith sampling, however, was how rarely these "odd couples" dealt only with religious differences. Not only did these individuals dare to be different from the prevailing social norms around them, but they also confronted enormous differences within their marriages as well. There was a tendency for huge gaps between husband and wife in one or more fundamental ways—age, economics, class, education, nationality, and sometimes emotional maturity. As a consequence their unions were often difficult, and there were high costs paid for their attempts to transcend the differences and find the common ground between them, penalties that today's interfaith couples aren't predestined to repeat.

A number of these costs became themes throughout my discussions. Some partners waited until their parents died before they married out of their faith, delaying marriage until their forties and fifties. Others were estranged from their families because they had rebelled against them or violated religious laws, the most moving account of which appears in Leah Morton's haunting book, *I Am a Woman—and a Jew*, written in 1926 and recently rereleased. Some permanently hid a spouse's religious identity from their parents and didn't see or talk to them very often in order to keep the truth from emerging. Others were ashamed of their family's lower-class status, poor education, and maybe its bigotry, so they maintained distant and awkward relationships.

In addition, there were a large number of other individuals, usually Jewish, who severed all but the most private, unexpressed ties to their religion because of its association with disturbing childhood experiences of prejudice, economic disaster, loss of a home or a loved one. To protect themselves and their children from reliving those memories, they tried to bury their original religious identity forever. In many cases, however, their children discovered those roots when they patched together bits and pieces of information as adults or found evidence, such as a crucifix in a mother's jewelry box or a Jewish birth certificate at the bottom of a father's bureau drawer, that revealed a carefully concealed heritage.

Self-denial inadvertently played a role in many lives as well. Since the Catholic Church and Judaism maintained strict requirements for marriage and raising children, many individuals conformed to those rules by converting to their spouse's faith, minimizing their own beliefs, or forfeiting both religions completely. In addition, others felt pressure to conform to the place where they worked or lived—a Quaker town, a Navy base, a religiously homogeneous suburb, or an Orthodox neighborhood in Brooklyn—in order to make life smoother for their children and themselves. Sometimes they converted to the dominant religion, although in most cases they merely tucked away their own religious backgrounds and put their energy into raising their children in the other faith.

Despite the fact that many parents seemed, on the surface, to accept their adjustments as a fact of life, I think that more of them than is realized suffered the consequences of their separation from the religious foundations, traditions, and family networks that nurture and strengthen most people throughout their lives. Without these spiritual and emotional supports that usually become more important as life goes on, many interfaith parents were weakened, some more than others, in their ability to deal with problems and stress. I think that many of them made greater emotional sacrifices than what's been generally acknowledged.

I'm reminded of a Kansas City English professor who sat with me on the steps of a church on a sunny June morning and questioned the degree of stress affecting her own parents' lives, leading her to wonder whether it had anything to do with their early deaths in their late fifties and mid-sixties. "My parents were so determined to prove to their families that religion couldn't divide them that I've often wondered if they just exhausted themselves," said the thirty-seven-year-old red-headed woman, the oldest of three children. Her father had been estranged from his Jewish parents since his marriage, and her mother had maintained very loose ties to her own German-Lutheran family. "My brothers and I have often talked about the pressure we felt to be happy, very happy, very successful, to prove that love, damn it, triumphed over differences. Maybe the price our parents paid for going it alone and maintaining 'super family'—as if we, the family, were 'our own thing,' separate and special—was bigger than anyone imagined."

According to the experts who were writing about inter-faith families between the 1920s and the 1960s, the ultimate penalty was displayed in the children, of course. They were exhibited as the living proof that religious and ethnic differ-ences couldn't be merged successfully in a marriage, let alone within an extended family or a child's identity. In the words of Philip Rosten, a Harvard College student, who wrote a 1960 honors thesis on fellow children of intermarriage like himself, the Jewish/Christian child is, after all, "a living bat-tleground for the interplay between the two cultures."

While the authorities consistently told sad stories about interfaith families, as if to counter the negativity, many in-terfaith families told their love stories, sometimes in an ex-aggerated way, as if that, too, were the only truth.

But reality is more complex than either of those ap-proaches. More often than not, the adult children that I in-terviewed were able to take a far more balanced and accurate reading of their families' varied lives. In effect, they con-firmed studies like Dr. Slotkin's and Dr. Resnik's, because they accepted the fact that there were tough and romantic parents with the grand achievements as well as the fragile, troubled parents with their disappointments and struggles with suicide, alcoholism, failed businesses, and mental illness. Many adult children saw their parents with a compassion and understanding that gave these larger-than-life figures —and indeed they were bold in their successes *and* their failures—a human scale that begins to set the record straight on what life was really like for interfaith families up until recently.

The truth is that it was difficult for many interfaith cou-ples to balance and resolve their formidable differences. Some people handled those differences well, and others failed. Today's interfaith couples have a wider range of options and far more positive stories to tell.

5

FAITH AND RELIGION: TAKING STOCK

The rabbi stood before a group of middle-aged Jewish parents in the basement of a small community center in Alpine, New Jersey, to discuss the problems of interfaith marriage. I had come to hear him talk because he was a scholar, family counselor, and the husband of a woman who had converted to Judaism from Christianity. Since it was rare to find a religious leader who'd chosen to marry someone raised in another faith and culture, I looked forward to a special kind of wisdom and reassurance from him, as if he'd be a calm voice sharing his own personal and professional experience. I quickly found a seat in the third row, next to a couple with two daughters engaged to Christians, and readied my notebook and ballpoint pens for an hour of helpful information. Immediately after the rabbi started to talk, however, I couldn't believe his words.

"Ninety-nine percent of the people who intermarry don't marry *out* of a faith," he declared roundly. "They marry *into* a faith, because they never had a faith to begin with. And certainly they never had one after the age of ten or thirteen!"

Was he talking about his wife, I wondered, shaken by his incredible certainty. There are statistics, after all, from the American Jewish Committee's 1986 study on conversion, that indicate converts to Judaism feel slightly more dissatisfied with their childhood religious experiences than interfaith spouses who haven't converted.

Was he basing his "facts" on conversations with the young interfaith couples who asked him to perform their marriage ceremonies? Sometimes they express a disconnectedness from their religious heritage that is natural to their stage of life.

Giving him one more benefit of the doubt, I wondered if he could be making a larger statement about the overall erosion of religious values throughout society and how inadequate the majority of programs for youth education have become in all three mainstream religions in America.

But no, those reasonable observations weren't the case. The rabbi, a fountain of misinformation throughout his heated monologue, was merely talking off the top of his head and presenting as today's truth a myth that no longer—if ever —fit the majority of interfaith parents. Just as the authorities had done for centuries, the rabbi was dismissing the religious life of those who dared to intermarry. He assumed—wrongly —that interfaith partners were indifferent to their inherited religious identities because of meager religious experiences during childhood.

If I'd asked him, I suspect he would have agreed with the conventional assumption that an interfaith marriage was proof in itself of a weak religious background. For if intermarried Jews and Christians knew and loved their traditions, the argument goes, they'd have married within those traditions and established a home that was dedicated to them.

I resented the rabbi's glib—and hostile—disregard for the Jewish/Christian couples, like Jordan and me, that have very real and sincere religious commitments and questions. After hundreds of hours of discussion around the country, it had become overwhelmingly apparent to me then, as now, that interfaith parents have strong feelings about their religious roots, and these are deeply imbedded in their experiences during childhood and adolescence. Interfaith parents may not know how to express their feelings as adults. They may need time to unlock their memories and discover which ones are meaningful to them. And they may not feel confident about how to translate their love and commitments to their interfaith children. Nevertheless, the majority of parents have a rich storehouse of memories and emotion to build upon, and their faith is an open and evolving process that is a valued part of their lives. It's time to accept and understand its complex presence and the way it weaves through a lifetime and affects the decisions that parents make for their children and themselves.

It's absurd to think that interfaith parents were raised without religious teaching. Anyone who takes a few minutes to quiz the Jewish/Christian couples around him or her will realize how religiously focused most of them were during childhood. If, as children, they hadn't been part of organized religion, including Sunday school and other sectarian activities, they were surrounded by extended families that were steeped in a religious tradition that indelibly affected their lives. From one source or another—and usually both—they developed a religious identity that became an important foundation in their lives.

When the interfaith parents talked about their religious background, they revealed a solid list of credentials. They had a classic American religious education, which means they got it all—Hebrew school, Sunday school, Confraternity of Christian Doctrine, or the old-fashioned catechism classes. They sang in the choir, played in the Catholic Youth Organization band, spent Sunday mornings as an altar boy or acolyte. Some studied five days a week at a yeshiva. Others attended Catholic parochial school for seventeen years. By junior high, high school, or college, many had become active members of the Sodality of the Virgin Mary, youth fellowship, the Newman Society, or Hillel.

The American Jewish Committee's statistics confirm that solid involvement with the churches and synagogues. In its

1976 and 1986 surveys, it found that the great majority of intermarried Christians had attended Sunday school and been baptized and confirmed; 75 percent of their parents belonged to a church.

As for the intermarried Jews, the majority of men and slightly less than the majority of women had between one to more than six years of formal Jewish education; 70 percent of their parents belonged to a synagogue.

Based on my interviews, I also sense that the majority of interfaith parents took their religious identities very seriously when they were young. They did a lot more than just show up for an occasional class. Their memories are elaborate and proud ones. They gave the student sermon to the church congregation once a year. They gave a bar mitzvah performance that was so brilliant the rabbi relaxed and sat down, and afterwards the congregants lined up at the door to congratulate the proud parents. Many chose to attend religiously affiliated colleges like Brandeis or Georgetown, and they still actively support their schools. The number of individuals who dreamed about becoming rabbis, priests, ministers, cantors, and nuns—and then intermarried—is also strikingly high.

Their own parents have told me how their children were so religiously dedicated as teenagers that they fully expected a daughter to become the first woman rabbi or a son to go into the church. Many future interfaith spouses did, in fact, study in seminaries or divinity schools, and some of those became clergy or religious professionals. An intermarried neighbor of mine loves the role he had when, at twenty-four, he was the once-a-week Jewish chaplain on an aircraft carrier in the Pacific.

There were the exceptions to this group who decided at eight or thirteen or eighteen that they had *too much* religion. There were the children who wanted *more* religion than their assimilated, agnostic, or atheistic parents offered them. There were the children of Socialists schooled in the idea that classic religion was "the opium of the people," so their faith was Socialism. An Omaha, Nebraska, child grew up with a father who claimed his only affiliation was "Nature," so when he filled out forms that asked about religion, he always sketched a maple leaf in the appropriate box.

But despite these and other variations, most children were essentially members of what theorist Will Herberg, author of the well-known sociological study "Protestant-Catholic-Jew," called "the three great religious communities in which the American people are divided." With few exceptions, family histories were clearly aligned with one of those three groups, and the result was a centuries-old accumulation of beliefs, traditions, and attitudes that inevitably shaped the children growing up in that resonant surround.

I was reminded of how concentrated *and* different Jordan's and my religious legacies have been when I started to compare our family trees that my mother and Jordan's uncle had assembled for us.

Jordan's arrived first—a neat, densely typed packet of papers that carefully listed seven generations of Gruzen descendants beginning when Tischel (Tillie) married Zorich (George) Gruzen in Latvia around 1830. I read page after page of the names that followed theirs—from Max Solomon Gruzen to Ida Ella Chivian Friedmann, from Samuel Handen Shrago to Norman Sumner Zimbel, continuing through a sequence of names that were Jewish and only Jewish. When my own name—Lee Ferguson—appeared on page four, it was shocking at first, like a neon patch against that tightly woven background, announcing in a sudden way that the religious predictability was lost and the pattern had a new design that had to be incorporated within it.

But the new design proved to be a subtly altered one. The Jewish names resumed, immediately after mine, and they unified the next four pages of genealogy in the way they'd always done. The few Christian names and the many new Jewish ones were naturally woven into a fabric unquestionably strengthened by its strong Jewish fiber.

What interested me was that all those names from 1830 until now were living ones that surrounded Jordan and me today, as if no one had been lost or forgotten in the passage through more than 150 years. The names had been given to new generations of relatives, and I'd either met or been told about three-quarters of the people listed. This large family, some of whom were Orthodox, and some Conservative, had stayed close, survived the Holocaust, accepted the new faces, and still maintained a constancy that made that history such a complete and vital one. To discount its presence as a source of support and Jewish instruction for everyone in that family —whether Jewish, Christian, or interfaith—was absurd.

My own genealogy was interesting in a very different way. The message from the Scottish and Norwegian sides of my family wasn't revealed in a long, thorough list of ancestors. Their own accounting was spotty by choice, as if it were unnecessary, almost inappropriate to memorialize one's forebears. "Why recall the names of people who have been sleeping peacefully in mother earth for decades, who never put me or anyone else under obligation to write an obituary they, so far as I know, have neglected about their own ancestors?" wrote my apologetic great-grandfather Lawrence Sorby in a letter to his daughter, my grandmother, that humbly went on to recount the names of three generations of Norwegian farmers that preceded him.

I loved the poetic cadence of the names—Seren Hansen, Simen Anderssen, Jens Rasmussen Forisdal, and Barbro Arnesen from Kalaaker Farm, among others. But since no one born after 1900 appeared on this or any other family list, I'd never met those people or heard their names before. It might seem that my lineage was nothing more than a romantic wash of Protestants, proving once again how disconnected I was from my religious and ethnic roots.

But that wasn't the case. What was meaningful to me was how much I recognized, with a sure knowledge that seemed uncanny to me, the spirituality and ethics that permeated those impressionistic histories. Even though Lawrence Sorby died when I was a baby, and my great-great-grandfather James Ferguson, featured in the Scottish family history, died in 1889, I knew these men very well.

Their reverence for God's "providence" coupled with

their moral pride in a "strong, inherited constitution, . . . indomitable perseverence, and . . . wonderful energy" were such familiar concepts to me. My grandparents, parents, brother, cousins, aunts, and uncles still interpreted the world in those terms, and I'd built those beliefs into my own faith, as well.

"What have we got that we did not receive?" concluded Grampa Sorby in his letter that was, in fact, a numerological query into the "strange" role that the "magical" number three played in his family's history. Even the way this father of nine children, a scientist and engineer concerned with practical and tangible pursuits all his life, had felt the wonder of life's hidden dimension was something that I had also known in my relatives. Congregationalists down the line, they'd all lived with the same private, dual trust in what's visible and invisible in the world ("all that is, seen and unseen," as the Bible says), especially as they got older. I hadn't realized how traceable and hardy my spiritual legacy was, however, until I saw those plain beliefs expressed so comfortably in my mother's yellowed documents.

For many interfaith parents, there were members of the clergy sprinkled throughout their family's past, articulating their religious continuity even more. Grandfathers were circuit preachers or officiants at their weddings. Their cousins were parish priests or the mother superior for an order of nuns. Some of their children were proudly named after famous rabbis in Jerusalem or clerics who founded churches in America.

Jordan and I can't find a single clergyman or famous religious leader in our own recorded blood lines (unless we believe a commercially prepared genealogy that tied my mother-in-law to King David or include my sweet uncle who should have been a minister). Nevertheless, there are plenty of interfaith couples with the best of family credentials (including the intermarried children of the three founders of the state of Israel—David Ben Gurion, Chaim Weitzman, and Theodor Herzl) to balance our own.

What counts, however, isn't the existence of heroic relatives (no matter "how tempting it may be to glorify ancestors because of the beneficial reflex it may throw over the progeny," wrote Lawrence Sorby). What's far more meaningful is the fact that most Jewish/Christian parents come from a long-standing and proud religious background that should be appreciated for the way it has seasoned and shaped their lives, loyalties, and identifications far more than they may realize. As the late rabbi Samuel Sandmel observed wisely in his useful book, *When a Jew and Christian Marry*, "The extent of escape from the past is often overestimated."

When my conversations with Jewish/Christian couples moved from their families' histories to their own individual passages, I learned even more about the formative experiences that molded the religious identities of parents like Jordan and me. Nothing was more personally meaningful, in fact, than listening to Jewish and Christian partners review the different periods in their lives and uncover the events, people, and emotions at the heart of their religious feelings today. Not only did their reminiscences unlock memories in me that I'd never weighed before but they illuminated the basic stages of development that gave me further insight into my own children's needs and capabilities.

While I was sifting through this enormous array of information, I discovered the remarkable book, *Stages of Faith: The Psychology of Human Development and the Quest for Meaning*, written by the religious psychologist, scholar, and United Methodist minister, James W. Fowler. No literature was more valuable to me, at any point in my research, than this classic analysis of how people develop in their ways of perceiving the world and finding meaning in their lives. Because *Stages of Faith* examined the entire span of life (and broke it into six definite stages), it helped me appreciate the special purpose and vitality within the important phases of life that parents had described to me. But most important, Fowler awakened me to the liberating idea that one's faith or religious identity isn't a fixed consciousness that never changes. To the contrary, it's a dynamic passage of awareness and commitment enriched by individuality, conflicts and upheaval, healthy revision, and a gradual deepening of beliefs and understanding. Ultimately, Fowler's spacious yet detailed perspective on the natural patterns in life helped me draw from my own experiences and those of others to arrive at reassuring guidelines that I could comfortably apply to my own Jewish/Christian children. I believe they will be useful for other such children as well.

I don't think parents, interfaith or those with a shared religion, can make thoughtful choices about raising their children without assessing the meaningful aspects of their own religious identities and identifying which experiences they wish to offer their children in an updated and appropriate form. To stimulate the memory, here are the religious experiences that other parents have loved and shared with me. It's my hope that these recollections, sorted into my own categories, will stir interfaith parents to address their strong and complex feelings about religion and express these feelings as they gradually unfold in the raising of their Jewish/Christian children.

CHILDHOOD

The writer (and interfaith parent) E. L. Doctorow summarized this key time of life well when he said during an interview for *The New York Times Magazine*, "A child is a perception machine. A child's job is to perceive, that's his business."

Children are, indeed, magnets for experience, much of it religious. This is their time to absorb an abundant amount of information and begin to classify it into useful concepts that explain the world and their feelings. Is it any wonder that interfaith spouses, raised in families so closely tied to their religious identities, absorbed such a classic array of data about what it meant to be Christian or Jewish? When I'm considering my own background in terms of what I'm offering my own children, I think about three advantages during childhood that conditioned my life and others. The first was a familiarity with the basics of a faith. The second was mastery of its rituals and ways of expressing its beliefs. The third was an emotional security associated with celebrations, religious services, and a belief system that seemed fair and orderly. This is how these simple introductions were manifest in many interfaith parents' childhoods, including mine.

Familiarity with religion was achieved in many ways, beginning with comfortable experiences in the churches and synagogues. Children knew these places well when they were growing up. They sat in the sanctuary for holidays, ceremonies, and many weekly services. They also spent time in the buildings after hours when they played basketball in the gym, joined their mothers for bingo or the annual church fair, studied Hebrew in the rabbi's study, or saw the priests' vestments drying over the basement washtubs as they walked the corridor to their catechism classes. They knew the reverent events, as well as the casual goings-on, and as a result, these buildings became their own friendly territory.

Children also built a relationship with the religious figures that represented each faith. There were the priests, ministers, rabbis, and nuns, of course, who populated their lives (like teachers, policemen, and firemen). But more significantly, there were the sacred heroes that were indelibly impressed on their minds. For the Christians, Jesus was a household name and friend of the family. Even my mother who always said she was more in touch with God than with Jesus would shake her head regretfully, on occasion, and tell me it was such a shame He had to die at thirty-three. "Just think of what He could have done if He'd lived," she said, sadly, as if she were talking about the son of a neighbor or a relative she knew well.

The Gospel stories, standard narratives in a Christian child's imagination, were also common property. By age eleven, most children had heard and seen, more times than they could count, the events that took place in and around Jerusalem during Jesus's life. Sites like the seashore of Galilee, the gates of the walled city, and the barren, stony hill of crosses were as real to many children as if they'd been there themselves. Naturally, the most evocative scene of all was the manger in Bethlehem with the newborn baby, a shining star overhead, and three kings with their exotic gifts; no drama settled so comfortably into a young child's imagination as the Nativity.

Since Judaism doesn't deify individuals in the same way as Christianity, the identifications were different for the Jewish children. Baby Moses tucked away in the bullrushes struck a chord in some youngsters. David who trounced Goliath became a superhero to others. Many Jewish children got a chance, at some point during their elementary school years, to dress up as Queen Esther or King Ahasueras and certainly to hiss when Hamen's name was mentioned on Purim.

But the deeper personal connections were extended to triumphant groups of Jews rather than to individual heroes or heroines. Holidays like Chanukah and Passover made the Maccabees and the Israelites an extension of each Jewish child's family, not by rendering them personalized members of the family unit like Jesus the Son, or Mary the Mother (who figured largely in many Catholic girls' lives), but by ennobling them as communities of ancestors, tied by blood and history to each Jewish child reliving their struggles and feats. As Jordan at age seven colored his pictures of the Exodus, ate matzoh, and heard stories about how the Red Sea parted as the Jews fled the Egyptians, the flow of his people's history, his own history, became real and personal to him.

Young children perceive the world concretely, and the first stage of their religious life is very much based on the many *images* that capture their experience and understanding of the world. According to Fowler, images are basic to a child's first stage of faith, beginning at age three. Not only are these images seeds for imagination but they give order to the child's world and condense emotions, values, the senses, and cognitive learning into units of meaning that, writes Fowler, "register the child's intuitive understandings and feelings toward the ultimate conditions of existence."

The images that interfaith parents know well aren't surprising ones, of course. They're the basic symbols of religion that speak to most Christians and Jews. The Cross, the Star of David, and the Torah begin the list. But sounds also resonate, like the Hebrew incantation "*Baruch Atoh Adinoi* (Praise be to God)," the Christian phrase "Father, Son, and Holy Ghost," or other beloved passages from Latin, Hebrew, and English liturgy.

Rituals at home generate meaningful imagery as well. A Jewish mother's lighting of the Sabbath candles is a classic memory. But Christian children may remember their mother as she painstakingly wrapped presents and stacked them under a luminous Christmas tree—a ceremony of another sort.

Since images express religious values, the *pushke*, a small box for collecting coins for charity, became an important symbol of giving in some Jewish households. Even a squeaky-clean polished hardwood floor in a Catholic school can embody principles of purity and scrupulous order that still stir Catholic daughters today, no matter how grown or intermarried.

A child's images can be classic or highly personal ones. No one absorbs the exact same array, no matter how many universal symbols are part of his or her basic collection. Among the standard memories of a *shofar* announcing the Jewish New Year or a choir singing "Adeste Fideles," there are always the more individual family memories—father with a stubbly beard on Yom Kippur, a long dining-room table packed with relatives for holidays, or a painting of a turbulent ocean with a shaft of light that Gramma said touched earth "like God." Images are serious in a magical way. But they can also be hilarious or full of fun, like the search for the *afikomen* during the seder or my own favorite memory of my brother's and my annual duel with the palms the church handed out on Palm Sunday. What matters is that children have the freedom to discover and create images that express their evolving feelings and comprehension of the world around them.

As children mature, they use stories as their more elaborate framework for organizing experience. The second stage of faith, observed Fowler, begins close to age seven, when children become deeply responsive to the narratives that explain their lives. As with images, the stories they hear and create for themselves are diverse and abundant, ranging from the biblical myth of Noah's Ark to a mother's graphic warnings about what will happen if her child strays from home or steals money from a friend. Whether these stories are universal literature or ad hoc scenarios, they are effective communicators because they're dramatic, concerned with themes of fairness and what's right, and clear in the way they transmit ethics, beliefs, traditions, and an understanding of cause and effect. Children's minds readily absorb information in that arresting and reassuring form.

During my interviews with interfaith parents, it was always amazing to them to discover how many stories—from the greatest books or family hearsay—bubbled to the surface with the same vitality and definition they had decades ago, hinting at the bottomless wellspring of narratives that continue to influence an individual's values and interpretation of life.

In addition to being struck by parents' familiarity with religion when they were growing up, I was also aware of how proud they were of having mastered the religious tasks that presented themselves. It had been a big deal to learn how to pray the Rosary beads or recite the list of Prophets. They liked having achieved First Communion, paraded the best costume for a Purim or Christmas pageant, or posed confidently in their beautiful new clothes for Rosh Hashanah or Easter. The churches and synagogues, even their homes during celebrations, were places of achievement where there was lots to do to feel grown-up and accepted.

In addition, religion gave many children a sense of security that was invaluable. The images that express that feeling stand out in their minds. Some adults emphasize their memories of sitting snugly between two parents in a pew or alongside an Orthodox grandmother in the synagogue's balcony. Others talked about feeling safe and sound as they said The Lord's Prayer at night in their beds, listened to their summer camp play taps at dusk, or watched their mothers light Friday night candles. Love and trust in the goodness and predictability of life were at the heart of these and many other intimate moments. Without such comfort and security, the other religious experiences would never have left such a positive mark.

ADOLESCENCE

"The texture of our religious pasts is shown in the memories of our high school years when we chose to become religious," said Joanna Shulman, an interfaith mother of two who expressed feelings about her husband's and her own teenage years that I heard more often than not from couples that I interviewed. For many interfaith parents, adolescence was an important time, if not the most important time, in the conscious development of their religious identities. The years between eleven and twenty offered them a variety of religious experiences that amplified their personal sense of power and independence while connecting them more intimately with a religion they felt they had chosen and made their own. Fowler characterizes those pivotal years as the third stage of faith.

For Joanna, who's Jewish, the passage from junior high school to the early years of college was a positive one. There were two years of Hebrew school, which she enjoyed because learning Hebrew was interesting. Best of all, the rabbi made her feel "special and different." Since the bat mitzvah ceremony wasn't a conventional ceremony for young women in the mid-fifties when Joanna celebrated hers, the thirteen-year-old satisfied her Conservative synagogue's requirements by creating a long, original sermon that integrated text with her own personal insights. Standing in front of the congregation that day thirty years ago, she'd felt smart and proud for having performed a tough, complicated task on her own.

But Joanna's sense of autonomy was only beginning. At

fourteen she started wrestling with the question of why she should be a Jew, an inquiry encouraged by the same supportive rabbi who challenged her to dig into Hillel's *Ethics of the Fathers* and probe many other existential questions. As her commitment gradually grew, she began attending weekly services at the synagogue, observing all the major Jewish holidays, and participating in a discussion group with a few other bright students gathered together by the rabbi. During her first year of college in New York City, 250 miles from her suburban Boston home, she kept kosher, took a course with the school's Jewish chaplain, and continued to feel "stirred by the primitive quality of the services" she attended regularly.

In parallel fashion, her husband, Garry Lloyd, was pursuing his own steady and serious religious course. His identification was with the Episcopal Church, however, and the aspects of religion that meant the most to him were more spiritual and less intellectual than Joanna's. Garry was particularly drawn to the liturgy and ritual that was part of every day's chapel in the boarding school he attended far from the small town where he grew up. By age thirteen, he was singing cantatas, attending morning prayer, finding solace from homesickness, and enjoying how clear and intense his feelings had become when he stepped inside the sanctuary and heard the exquisite music. Those feelings intensified through high school, especially during his junior and senior years. Nowadays, when he's asked to recall that period before college, he summarizes it as one "of enormous security, a profound love for ritual, and confidence in my own emotional and spiritual reserves."

Religion isn't a subject that most people normally associate with adolescence. Deafening rock music, pimples, packs of carousing kids, and bouts of moodiness are the references that are much more likely to come to mind. What's true, however, is that the emotional and physical upheavals at the heart of these very secular teenage expressions are the same internal explosions responsible for the religious intensity that Garry, Joanna, and many other interfaith parents experienced during adolescence. As teenagers, they grew so fast and riotously that they needed a variety of ways to understand themselves and feel stable and accepted; religion became one of their important vehicles for self-knowledge, strength, and self-expression.

Suggesting another image to explain this revolutionary time of life, Fowler wrote, "The adolescent needs mirrors—mirrors to keep tabs on this week's growth, to become accustomed to the new angularity of a face and to the new curves or reach of a body. But in a qualitatively new way the young person also looks for mirrors of another sort. He or she needs the eyes and ears of a few trusted others in which to see the image of *person*ality emerging and to get a hearing for the new feelings, insights, anxieties, and commitments that are forming and seeking expression."

There are many kinds of "mirrors." Peers naturally serve that purpose. For good reason, one of my husband's favorite memories and strongest associations with Judaism focuses on the rich array of Jewish students from around the world that he met when he was a fifteen-year-old working on a kibbutz in Israel.

Books by and about Jewish and Christian heroes, such as Anne Frank, Martin Luther King, Jr., Mahatma Gandhi, or Mother Teresa, are also useful. God, as well, reflects back to adolescents their deepest, most intense thoughts and feelings—a relationship that's important enough to discuss far more elaborately in Chapter 9.

But throughout my interviews, the "mirrors" that were most beloved were always grandparents and clergy. These were the teachers credited with having a lifelong influence on the adolescent's religious identity and his or her proud, clear sense of self.

My stepson Alex was twenty-four when he and I spent a long February weekend riding a series of New Hampshire ski lifts together and talking about the experiences that had given him such a strong sense of his Jewish heritage. Because of my book, we'd touched on this subject many times over the last few years, and he'd also begun to discuss it with the young Protestant woman he expected to marry. But gliding high above the tall pines, we had a peaceful, welcomed chance to look more closely at the people who'd reinforced his feelings about being a Jew and the experiences he'd have to build upon if, as planned, he becomes the father of interfaith children.

During Alex's adolescence, there had been an energetic and very sympathetic cantor who had spent nine focused months preparing the twelve-year-old for his bar mitzvah. A Protestant minister at high school had been another important confidant who'd taught him about ethics and the Bible. But the person who mattered the most was Alex's grandfather, Barney Gruzen, a gruff, charismatic architect who adored his grandson and spent a great deal of time with the growing child. Alex's last conversation with him made a powerful impression. Alone in the dying man's hospital room, the eleven-year-old had spent three hours listening to Barney talk about his love for being Jewish. The seventy-two-year-old talked about how hard Jews struggled for centuries to rebuild Israel and what pleasure he had received from his work with Technion (the Israeli equivalent to MIT). He also told Alex about Jewish persecutions and his own battles with prejudice. "But most of all," Alex recalled, "Grampa Barney emphasized how important it was that I feel proud to be a Jew. Whether I go to temple or not, he said, I should always remember what I am and that no one can take that away from me."

As a gift to his grandfather, Alex initiated his own bar mitzvah the following year. Later, at age seventeen, when his grandmother died during his first trip to Europe, Alex found comfort in a Paris synagogue. During his first year in college, he had his Jewishness further reinforced by a battery of relatives near school who made sure he was included in all Jewish holidays.

Alex's story isn't unusual. Many interfaith parents were deeply influenced as teenagers by authorities who cared about them, respected their autonomy, and lovingly shared their religious experiences with them. Because of the ages involved, it's not uncommon for grandparents or close relatives to have died during this sensitive decade in an adolescent's life, and many, like Alex, had their first experiences with a loved one's death during that period. Not only did many adolescents participate in the memorable religious rituals of a funeral and burial, but more important, the watchful teens saw how their grandparents and relatives found strength to deal with illness or death. "By their composure, parents and grandparents communicate to a child their sense of security in the universe," said Rabbi David Greenberg when we talked in his study in East Hampton, New York. "Their compassion, their lust for life, and the strength they find within themselves during such painful times are extremely important examples for a child. If parents and grandparents are afraid of death, a child will always pick that up."

For the adolescent, the conquest of these and other painful dislocations led to a heady feeling of confidence and self-congratulation very much remembered by intermarried adults today. As Fowler wrote, the adolescent "gathers and falls in love with a forming personal myth of the self." It's no wonder that the sentence most commonly used to describe these years was simply, "I did it myself!"

ADULTHOOD

For many individuals who ultimately intermarried, another dramatic awakening took place midway through college when, as Fowler noted, they began to feel "the freedom (and burden) to explore who . . . [they] could be away from home." Adulthood loomed, and with it came an expanded intellectual ability, combined with a host of demanding responsibilities that set them very much on an increasingly secular and independent path. According to Fowler, the decades between college and the middle of one's lifetime often mark the fourth stage of faith.

Garry Lloyd offered an observation that's helped me understand the passages through adulthood. "My theory is that you take a long trip out into the wilderness in your twenties and thirties," he said, "and then with parenthood and aging you're brought back home to your childhood memories."

In other words, during college and early adulthood when individuals are "out in the wilderness," they become rational and intolerant of all the unbelievability and fantasy associated with religion. Their favorite revolutionary phrase becomes "Why?" They feel strong, bold, and independent of symbolism, authority, the framework of organized religion, and the identities they got from their families. The people they want to be with and learn from are elsewhere, in politics, the arts, or business; the professional passions that are more central to their identities become their true dedications, and the laws, miracles, and wise people of that world, not the worlds they grew up in, become invested with an almost sacred power over them. It's not that religion disappears from their lives; many people still attend religious services once a year, arrange for clergy at their weddings, or express other aspects of their faith that continue to feel comfortable. But religion, now perceived rationally and with cool objectivity (even bitterness and cynicism in some cases) tends to fade into the background. The solid, mundane tasks of consolidating a career, lifestyle, marriage, and the basic patterns and commitments of adult life become all-consuming replacements.

But change occurs once again, as Garry Lloyd observed. The miraculous birth of children, a growing awareness of one's own mortality and profound need for continuity, and the illness and death of parents begin to sensitize adults to the deeper questions and feelings about life's meaning and purpose. What occurs is "a new reclaiming and reworking of one's past . . . an opening to the voices of one's 'deeper self,' " wrote Fowler, describing this period of adulthood that rarely begins before midlife. According to him, this "second naivete" or new capacity to know and integrate the conscious with the unconscious, the critical mind with the feeling heart, marks the fifth stage of faith, and the last plateau that most individuals ever achieve. (Only the rare visionaries—Mother

Teresa of Calcutta, Dag Hammarksjöld, Dietrich Bonhoefer, Abraham Joshua Heschel, Thomas Merton, Mahatma Gandhi, or Martin Luther King, Jr.—experience the universal love, leadership, and often the martyrdom, required of the sixth stage.)

Interfaith parents are often bewildered by their strange stirrings. Suddenly they find themselves reading Bible stories to their children, attending two seders for Passover rather than none, carefully scheduling Abba Eban's public television series *Civilization and the Jews* into their datebooks, or sitting glued to the TV set with their children through an Easter-week movie about Christ. They even find themselves praying, something they often haven't done, or expected to be doing, in the past fifteen or more years.

These adults are like bears coming out of hibernation— unsteady on their feet, blinded by the light, and confused by the changes that took place outside and within them during the time they were away. Interfaith parents often feel that awkwardness as they edge their way toward a new relationship with their old religious histories. It's not as if they can step back in time and pick up where they left off as teenagers, resuming old religious habits and proceeding on blind faith. They bring their reservations, ignorance, and maturity to bear on each of their new religious experiences with the rituals, symbols, and myths that begin to attract and move them once again.

As a result, even the simple act of praying can need time and experimentation to feel comfortable once again. Some adults haven't prayed since they were teenagers on their knees in the Catholic or Episcopal churches, and now that they've converted to Judaism or found themselves attending synagogues or churches where there is no kneeling, they're not sure how to sit or focus their minds in order to find the spiritual intimacy they knew years ago. In many other instances, the adults' concept of God as a presence within them conflicts with their old childhood image of God as "Our Father, who Art in Heaven." That common evolution can be a confusing one to understand and reconcile.

For the interfaith parent who's growing into his or her

own beliefs while struggling to share them appropriately with Jewish/Christian children, the process is, by necessity, a gradual and highly personal one. The search for institutions to enhance those beliefs in a genuinely ecumenical way often complicates the task further.

Although it's provocative and unsettling, this emotional and spiritual openness is what makes this time so rich for interfaith families. The parents' maturity inspires a new readiness to dig deeply into their own religious identities and heritage, while allowing them an expanded capacity to accept and learn from the other faith operating within their household. The mind has become complex and sophisticated enough to live with what's shared and complementary as well as what's ambiguous and contradictory in the dynamic relationship between the two religions. Some interfaith parents feel moved to convert to the other religion at this time. More, however, invest in their own faith while exploring their closeness with the other. They are able to respond to their different but equal traditions more powerfully, while trusting that the special Jewish/Christian synergy in their families gives strength and purpose to each of their lives.

In turn, interfaith parents satisfy another major goal for this stage of life—to nurture the next generation and help it find its own religious identity and meaning in life. Parents who take their own search and commitments seriously become their children's best model.

In Fowler's *Stages of Faith*, the word "religion" is broken down into its two origins: *re* meaning "back, again," and *ligio* meaning "to bind." In other words, religion means to bind again or as Fowler infers, to return to the powerful truths that one has been brought up to understand.

I believe that most Jewish/Christian parents have the seeds of a faith planted securely within them. Certainly everyone that I talked with had some distilled essence of religion, whether history or spirituality, culture or intellect, that was theirs to renew, build upon, and use as a guide for raising their children.

CHAPTER

6

THE REAL FAMILY LEGACY

As Woody Allen said in his movie *Hannah and Her Sisters*, "The heart is a resilient little muscle." It can heal itself and grow, give life and love and keep chugging along, day by day, regenerating and finding strength. With heart and soul, one might say, the interfaith family has that same vitality inspiring it to nurture its Jewish/Christian children and adapt to the changes that are part of its special experience.

The myth, of course, is that interfaith marriage shatters a family and alters its traditions and patterns of love and faith in destructive and irrevocable ways, with the children and grandparents supposedly suffering the greatest losses. I don't believe that's an inevitability in the course of interfaith lives, however. I've found too many parents, children, and their children—Jews, Christians, and Jewish/Christian offspring —who have built strong and loving bonds to each other, bridging generations, religions, and very different life experiences to grow and stay close. Their patience, humor, good sense, and, most of all, their love for their family and heritage, have been tested in ways they never anticipated.

So, too, the rewards have exceeded their expectations and offered them opportunities for continuity and pride that they never imagined. Interfaith families deserve praise, not sympathy, for how well they have adjusted to the changes in their lives while staying true to their deepest personal commitments. As a sixty-six-year-old New Jersey woman with three interfaith grandchildren proclaimed, "I've come such a long way. Who'd have guessed I'd grow so much?"

The accommodations, certainly the intimacies and harmony, don't happen overnight, of course. There are passages that families traverse in their years of building a relationship together. The interfaith couple's courtship, the wedding, the birth of children, and the years when the children are growing up are prominent benchmarks. Although each family has its own special profile of problems and triumphs, there's a reassuring pattern that's become apparent to me as I've heard about many families' evolutions over decades. Here are the feelings, issues, and experiences that have been shared with me.

COURTSHIP

The word that best describes it? Surprise! Indeed, the most surprised participants of all are the interfaith partners themselves. In my experience, the last thing that a man and woman were consciously searching for when they met and fell in love was someone of a different religion. Either the subject wasn't on their minds when they looked up from a book in the college library, struck up a conversation in a business meeting, or said hello to a friendly face on the beach and changed their lives forever. Or religion was very much on their minds, except they assumed they'd find someone of the same religion, not a different one. Whether carefully thought out or not—usually not—the matchmaking followed its own winding, unpredictable course.

Barbara Radin, for example, was thirty-four when she stormed into her Manhattan office one morning and called her best friend to complain about the foolish date she'd arranged to take place later that night. "Scanelli's his name," she said, groaning. "The last thing I need is a Scanelli in my life. A Goldberg, a Cohen, a nice Jewish boy, yes! But an Italian? No way!"

Only recently, the sensible, dark-eyed real estate broker had decided that it was time to fall in love and settle down "for real." She figured "for real" meant Jewish, of course, like her father and her fantasy husband from childhood and, actually, everyone else in her family as far back as she knew.

Everything favored marriage. Her work was going well. Her morale was the highest it had been in years. And her last two relationships, unsatisfactory ones that happened to involve a Catholic and a Protestant, were finally over, freeing her for what she described as "a mature and serious relationship that had a future." With amazement, Barbara had even begun entertaining her grandmother's suggestions about contacting eligible Jewish men she knew from her hometown, something she'd been loathe to do before.

The irony is that her grandmother's best friend's grandson, who was Jewish, of course, put Barbara in touch with his friend Peter Scanelli, a thirty-seven-year-old divorced lawyer who was raised as a Baptist.

"Peter Scanelli turned out to be the sweetest guy I'd ever met in my life," reported a radiant Barbara Radin Scanelli when we met for lunch two years after her dreaded date and weeks before the birth of their first child. "I met this very sweet man and fell in love."

According to Peter Scanelli, veteran of a first marriage to another Baptist, "Barbara was gorgeous and irreverent. I wasn't looking for a wife, let alone a Jewish wife, the night we met. I never knew what hit me."

Parents of the interfaith couples are often far less surprised by the turn of events than their children are. For some, it's the realization of their worst fears, so they may be shocked yet too forewarned to be surprised. In most cases, however, parents have had years to observe their son's or daughter's dating patterns and cosmopolitan adventures at school, work, or away from home. No matter how they feel about the relationship itself, parents usually admit that it's a logical one in keeping with their independent child's experiences in a pluralistic world.

What is far more disturbing and new to parents, however, are their own confused, intense feelings about the match, especially during the period before the wedding takes place. "There isn't a parent alive who doesn't want his child to marry within his own faith, to do as he did," said a Manhattan cab driver whose two Jewish daughters married a Protestant and a Catholic. As this dream fades, along with other long-held hopes and assumptions, it's not easy, at first, for parents to celebrate their child's newfound happiness with the wholeheartedness that everyone would love. According to Egon Mayer's 1976 statistics, only 20 percent of Christian and Jewish parents approve of their child's prospective intermarriage. Close to 50 percent of the Christian parents and slightly over 40 percent of the Jewish parents disapprove of it during that period leading up to the wedding.

I suspect a more recent survey would indicate greater acceptance among parents because of society's changing attitudes. Nevertheless, this introductory period continues to stir many unexpectedly sensitive nerves in both Jewish and Christian parents, and their emotional adjustments, whether subtle or more extreme, become an important part of the process of weaving a new family together.

Guilt is one of the first feelings to announce itself. "What did I do wrong?" many parents ask, as if their child's interfaith relationship were their responsibility and a dark sign of their inadequacy as Christian or Jewish parents. On religious grounds, they often feel they failed to instill enough love for Judaism or the Church to inspire their children to perpetuate its faith or loyalties. In turn, they often blame themselves for a host of child-rearing decisions that supposedly set their children on the wrong course. Maybe parents didn't go to the synagogue or church enough to set an example, or twenty-five years ago they took their youngster out of the yeshiva or Catholic parochial school and enrolled him in a secular school. A Massachusetts mother blamed her son's interfaith marriage at age twenty-six on a comparative religion course that he took at age eighteen.

These explanations can sound absurd. But for many parents, the sense of loss and guilt for having broken a long family chain of belief and tradition is very real and understandable. For Jews, in particular, there may be the added reproach of seeing themselves in the context of the Holocaust, unable, under the best of circumstances, "to preserve the link" that so many other Jews, under the worst of circumstances, gave their lives to continue. Learning to trust how their family is able to maintain its Christian and Jewish continuum, in spite of an interfaith marriage, is a task that takes time.

Other emotions also crowd parents' minds. For some, an interfaith marriage can feel like a slap in the face at first, as if the child were rejecting parents and their way of life by making different choices than theirs. Fear of losing a child is also persistent in parents, as if the marriage were going to separate the generations by a wide chasm and force them to wave goodbye from alien, religiously separate sides.

Then, too, there are the disappointments. Maybe the Jewish parents counted on acquiring a Jewish set of in-laws, so they'd have *mishpucha*, "family," to stick together for support and celebration. Or they wanted a prosperous doctor for a son-in-law and got a poor painter instead. Possibly, the Christian family wanted an understated, unassuming kind of guy who played golf or sailed, but they got a brash, young real estate whiz with manicured nails. Parents worry whether they'll ever be able to negotiate these differences comfortably. And more important, they wonder if their child will weather them or live out the classic myth about the extreme likelihood of interfaith marriages ending in divorce.

Most sons and daughters who intermarry are too full of joy and self-congratulation to identify with their parents' reactions, especially with the aspects of guilt and self-blame. Rather than assuming their interfaith relationship is the result of their parents doing something wrong, they usually feel quite the opposite, in fact—that their ecumenical romance came about because their parents did so much that was right. After all, the son and daughter were living out their parents' worthiest values by marrying for love, looking beyond labels to discover the human being within, and reaching out for broader experience that enriched their lives. In pursuit of education, stimulating work, and the rewards of the American dream, the Jew and Christian had met each other and fallen in love, and no one could fault parents for those sensible aspirations.

Couples who intermarry also know that interfaith relationships have become a sociological phenomenon with explanations that have little to do with their parents' actions, values, or religious upbringing. One of many theories suggests that the incidence of interfaith marriages naturally increases during periods of calm between Christians and Jews, as in America today. Another observation links interfaith marriage to the reduced Jewish birthrate following World War II and the need for Jews to reach beyond that limited group of eligible mates to find their partners. The fact that Jews have entered and found acceptance within the mainstream of American life suggests the third observation—that Christians and Jews work and live close enough to each other to discover the attractiveness of each culture and the personalities within it. In an increasingly secularized world where the impact of religion is less powerful and less important than it used to be, chance meetings that lead to romance are the consequences of freedom. My favorite version of that argument came from a student named Alisa.

"If your primary interest is Judaism, and most of the things you do are affected by the fact that you are Jewish," wrote Alisa in an excerpt from *The Jewish Family Book* by Sharon Strassfeld and Kathy Green, "it is likely that most of your friends, your circle, and the people you date will be, too. However, if your main interest is say, photography, and your life revolves around that, you are likely to run around with a lot of photographers, including nice photographers of the opposite sex, with whom you have a lot in common because of your photography. Unfortunately, *nice* photographers of the opposite sex are not always Jewish, and when you become interested in one it becomes very hard to become disinterested just because this photographer is not Jewish. You two have a lot in common, so why should it matter that there is one thing you don't have in common?''

The theory that means the most to me, however, was expressed by Edwin H. Friedman, rabbi and family therapist from Bethesda, Maryland. After counseling over 2,000 interfaith couples for the past twenty years, Friedman noticed the overwhelming number of first or only children among the intermarried Jews that came to him. As an expert on family dynamics, he knew that these children were often "focused" or "triangled" children, meaning that they tended to play a pivotal, stablizing role within their parents' marriage. They were the third party who siphoned off excess tension from the relationship and, like a leg on a tripod, added balance and stability to the family unit. When parents were newly married and separating from their own parents, the "focused" child became an especially useful support, but that child could continue, assume, or resume that position whenever circumstance or timing called for it.

According to Friedman, a child born five or more years after a sibling could have that same emotional interdependency. Any child, in addition, could inherit the role after an older sibling moved away or a grandparent important to the marriage died.

For those children, the process of growing up and extricating themselves from that snug and intense emotional network often became a difficult task. ''More powerful circuits need more powerful circuit breakers,'' explained Friedman in his provocative essay, ''The Myth of the Shiksa,'' which appeared in the useful book, *Ethnicity and Family Therapy*, edited by Monica McGoldrick, John K. Pearce, and Joseph Giordano. Interfaith marriage, in other words, became a welcome way to give a strong, liberating jolt to a family system that had become too close and intense to allow the child to grow and move freely.

Throughout my own research, I've found the same overwhelming incidence of "focused" children. But they're not just Jewish. Indeed, the Christian partner is almost always the first, only, or "triangled" child as well. Sometimes he or she was the beloved "baby" born late into a large family or the child raised by one parent and a close relative (which is also true in many Jewish cases). The common exceptions to that model, which I think will increase as interfaith marriage becomes more commonplace, include intermarried second and third children. Most of these children follow on the heels of firstborns who have already broken the ice if not by intermarriage then by another unconventional choice of a spouse.

What's struck me from comparing Friedman's theory with my own collected information is the sense that interfaith marriage, for many individuals, is a solution that gives them the best of both worlds. On the one hand, they establish just enough distance from parents to allow themselves the freedom to grow and establish independence ("My marriage gives me insulation from my parents' way of life!" announced one interfaith husband). On the other hand, interfaith couples stay close enough to their parents to maintain their relationship in an intimate, comfortable way that, in fact, might not be possible if they had felt their own self-realization were at stake.

Contrary to the old myths, contemporary interfaith couples, indeed, do stay close to their parents and in-laws. The 1976 American Jewish Committee survey confirmed the fact when it concluded: "All of the data make it clear . . . that the ties between the couples surveyed and their parents and other relatives were intact. Not only did most of the respondents say they got along well with their families, many even reported that their relationships with their parents were better than before the marriage. They saw their families as regularly as time and distance permitted, and in the vast majority of cases their spouses were accepted into the extended family. None of the respondents (446 intermarried couples were surveyed) reported a total break with their families as a result of their marriage."

I've observed that same success rate among the many individuals I've met. And I've also noticed that partners who intermarry the second time around after a first marriage within their faith, as in the case of Peter Scanelli, often report having the most warm and comfortable relationship they've had with their parents since childhood. Whether the success is due to maturity and experience or the presence of an interfaith spouse isn't the issue. What matters is that most Jewish/Christian families have the long-range assurance that their future children will be able to grow up with parents and grandparents who see, talk to, and care about each other—a future that was not the norm thirty years ago or more.

During the unpredictable craziness of the courtship, however, when parents and their children are stretching and learning to trust the flexible bands that tie families together, it's natural for the more peaceful, resolved times to seem very far away. For Dahlia Sklar, a New York psychotherapist who was born and raised in Israel, her prolonged courtship with Pudmani Kumar, a Pakistani businessman living in New York, raised many troubling questions and feelings that were beginning to become clearer and more comfortable as her wedding approached.

"I didn't leave home at twenty-six because of the classic reasons like rebellion or rejection," explained the thoughtful thirty-three-year-old when we met in a Greenwich Village coffee shop. "I feel extremely Jewish. I have a sense of shared history and fate with other Jews, and my mother was in Auschwitz. I grew up with a sense of identification and meaning from belonging to a group of people building a country, and I have a tremendous pride in being a Jew. I'm also the oldest of two daughters and very close to my parents," she said matter-of-factly.

"The question for me is why I needed differentness.

You can accept how your parents raised you and let them tie you in so you don't grow. But I couldn't do that," she said soberly.

"As a consequence, my choice has given me tremendous conflict. My parents were heartbroken. Many Israeli friends have never forgiven me. It's also taken six years to commit myself to a marriage. But," she added softly, wrapping her delicate fingers around an emptied tea cup, "I needed autonomy. It seems my husband and I needed to go out of the tribe, so to speak, to gather more strength."

"I had an incredibly close relationship with my mother. Imagine breaking apart!" said Susan Tolland, a graphics designer from Connecticut, who went through an equally turbulent passage before her marriage to Eli Mayer, a city planner from California. "My mother and I were one big amorphous entity," explained the twenty-eight-year-old Catholic woman when I met her in her colorful, busy house filled with two children, husband, and five artists on the staff of her growing design firm. When her German-born Catholic mother joined us later to pick up her grandchildren for a weekend visit, she was exactly as she'd been described by her daughter: "emotional, gorgeous, exuberant, and intuitive."

"All destruction broke loose when I told them I was in love with Eli," said Susan, the older of two children, as she remembered the early days of her relationship with the man who is not only a Jew and Zionist but also father of a grown child and seventeen years Susan's senior. "I moved in with Eli, and my father said the sanctity of the Tolland name was being desecrated. I was also trying to find my identity as an artist, and painting was my religion at the time. My parents said, 'How are you going to be a painter without an income? We wash our hands of supporting you!' I cried all the time."

Anything goes during this time of greatest adjustment between parents and children. Parents can behave with explosions, threats, hand-wringing, and urgent visits to the clergy—or the most warm and easy-going acceptance (and everything in between). There may be all-out warfare, cagey skirmishes, surprise truces, or happy pacifism all along. "All hell breaks loose" about a third of the time, said sociologist Egon Mayer, "but in most cases, the broken heart seems to mend quickly." Well before the Jewish/Christian children are born (and at least slightly before the wedding), the preliminary, often awkward introductions to the issues, feelings, and strange, new configuration of a Jewish/Christian family proceed along their course.

THE WEDDING

Attention shifts to family ties. When interfaith partners sit down to settle on the details of the guest list, site, menu, and the person who'll officiate at their marriage ceremony, spelling out their dreams and requirements for the wedding that will try to make everyone comfortable and happy, it's inevitable that their thoughts and feelings turn toward their families and the complicated bonds that play such a role in their lives. It's as if lovers suddenly wake up to the fact that their wedding ceremony and indeed their lives together will take place in the context of two families—two very different families, at that. Not only do they see how much their partner brings these loved ones and their shared history and values to the marriage, like a psychic trousseau, but they also feel the confusing tugs of their own loyalties to family and self, adding further to the blitz of new information and feelings to be absorbed and handled appropriately. For many interfaith couples, the mere job of gathering their two families together in the same room for a successful celebration seems touchy enough to need Solomon's wisdom.

Woody Allen knew what Jewish/Christian couples were dealing with when he created the movie *Annie Hall* and set Annie's Gentile family against Alvy's Jewish one in two of America's most memorable dinner-table scenes. In the first, the Hall family sat uprightly around the dining-room table and chatted delicately about the Easter ham, a swap meet, the boat basin, and the more alien matter of Alvy's fifteen years of psychiatry. Grammy Hall, spotted as "a classic Jew-hater" by Alvy, stared at him with total disaffection while he was transformed on the screen into an Orthodox Jew with a flowing beard and stiff black hat.

Suddenly, the film cut to Alvy's raucous Jewish family, the Singers, crowded around their kitchen table in a Brooklyn apartment. As they gobbled their food and loudly dissected the problems of an out-of-work fifty-year-old and his diabetic wife, they interrupted each other and piled one heated opinion on top of another; likewise, Alvy's aunt heaped food onto her husband's plate, as if it were her own. Whereas the Halls kept their distance by allowing each other space between words, bodies, and their carefully measured feelings, the Singers were intensely enmeshed in each other, physically and emotionally "like one big undifferentiated ego mass," to borrow an observation from California psychologist Joel Crohn. One was the all-American model of reserve and good health; the other was a hotbed of interactive characters attuned to disease and social distress. From the point of view of the potential interfaith son, Alvy, each family was ethnically worlds apart.

For interfaith couples all too aware of their families' own bizarre contrasts, especially during this time around the wedding when the differences assume such fresh prominence, Woody Allen's portrayals hit a nerve. The wonder is that so many couples, along with their parents, manage to accommodate their differences as well as they do during this first, emotionally loaded event together.

It's the small gestures that seem to count the most. When I've asked many parents who are close to their intermarried children what they remember about their son's or daughter's wedding, they often tell me about the touches of consideration and warmth that were deeply appreciated and viewed as an auspicious beginning for the years ahead. Before the plans were set, for instance, a future daughter-in-law took the trouble to ask her in-laws-to-be how they would feel about attending their Catholic son's wedding in her synagogue. Another couple decided to forego alcohol at the reception out of respect for a Southern Baptist mother who didn't approve of drinking. The minister, an octogenarian who was the groom's uncle, was humorously prepped to stay clear of his standard invocations to Jesus Christ and talk about God instead. In Jordan's and my case, we chose a beautiful and neutral site—Block Island, Rhode Island, which is midway between New York City and Cape Cod—to make our families feel at ease. Other couples put tremendous energy into shaping the wedding ceremony itself in order to connect that moment to their family's traditions. The choice of a warm, ecumenical clergyman has also gone a long way to make families feel at home.

Sometimes, the couple blunders disastrously in their handling of the event, out of rebellion, insensitivity, or too much spineless flexibility on the part of a young partner. I'm familiar with a recent wedding that went awry because it was so rudely lopsided. The bride's mother controlled every detail and, like a steamroller, assembled her 400 friends and relatives, her clergyman, and a token representation of the groom's unassuming family and pals. The twenty-three-year-old groom, who was cowed by the twenty-three-year-old bride's petulance and caught in the spell of her family's wealth, went along with the plans, despite a number of complaints and warnings by his friends. As a result, there wasn't a touch of his family's customs or traditions in the day's events— not in the ceremony itself, the toasts, or the spirit among the guests. The lack of respect for the groom's background was disheartening to those who noticed and, whether accurately or not, interpreted as a sign of problems to come in the marriage itself.

The classic troublemaker is a special kind of parent, however, who sustains his or her campaign to resist a child's intermarriage long after most parents have given it their blessing. The hysterical behavior and, indeed, the pain and resentment it causes are familiar to almost everyone who's heard about or seen these parents in action. They're the ones who've stood stiff-lipped and rigid at their child's wedding, like figures from a Grant Wood painting. Or they sulked in the back pew and left before the reception. Fathers refused to take their daughters down the aisle; mothers (especially widowed mothers with only sons) threatened to die an early death if the daughter- or son-in-law didn't convert.

In his practice, Edwin Friedman encountered "reacting parents" often enough to formulate a theory about them. He has suggested that the parent who overreacts is the one most troubled by the loss of the child from the balanced and interdependent family triangle Friedman associates with interfaith marriage. According to Friedman, "If the child occupying such a [triangled] position in the family does something that is perceived by the parents to be taking him or her out of that set of emotional dependencies, the parents' anxiety will immediately increase."

Many factors can further intensify that reaction, such as a strained relationship between the parents themselves. "Parents who are satisfied in their own marriage do not react with prolonged negative intensity to the marriage of one of their children," observed Friedman.

In addition, the parent may be too emotionally fused with a son or daughter to understand, as most parents are able to do, that ultimately it's not their own life and marriage at issue but someone else's to shape as he or she wishes.

According to Friedman, the overreactive parent may also have been a triangled or focused child who's caught in an unconscious web of obligations to his or her own parents, living or dead. Oftentimes this type of parent has unknowingly—and maybe unwillingly or guiltily—inherited the job of being the one to nurture and preserve the family, as if it's a sacred, homogeneous god requiring loyalty and obedience from its members. An intermarriage can be an enormous threat to that mission and the tightly controlled system the parent is determined to maintain.

What originally compelled Friedman to look at the special dynamics of reacting parents was his discovery that religious commitment was almost always offered as the reason for their fanatic response to an interfaith marriage when, in fact, there wasn't necessarily any evidence of that sincerity elsewhere in their lives. Because he found too many Ortho- dox Jews and Holocaust survivors who accepted their child's intermarriage and too many "reacting" Jewish parents who had never celebrated a holiday, attended a synagogue, or made any effort to express their Jewish identity other than through protesting the child's relationship, he concluded that, among Jews, "the degree of commitment to Jewish survival is almost irrelevant to the degree of reaction when a family member marries a non-Jew."

The child of overreacting parents could, of course, be Christian since the "neurotic usefulness of religious tradi- tion," as Friedman pointed out, is too universal an emotional phenomenon to be sectarian. Whatever the religious identity, the struggle to achieve a comfortable distance from parents may be especially painful and prolonged. With words that apply as equally to men as to women, the Bible said, "Hence, a man leaves his father and mother and clings to his wife, so that they become one flesh" (Genesis 2:24). In other words, a child "divorces" his or her parents in order to marry. But there are many parents, of course, who don't take those basic lessons about their child's right to emotional separation to heart, and it's difficult for their children to relate to them with the independence that's supposed to be an essential part of their growing up.

Even for those great many interfaith couples who are blessed with parents who try hard to make their weddings, marriages, and their overall emotional separation proceed smoothly, however, the process is still a deliberate, uncertain one that takes time to fall into place. At such a time of change, it's hard not to ruffle feathers. After all, this is a period when two generations, together and separately, are learning how to communicate with each other, make decisions, share and blend traditions, and establish the strong and joyful design of a newly configured but lasting relationship, one that will become more rich and meaningful when the third generation comes into the picture.

THE BABY ARRIVES

Does he have a Jewish nose? Isn't Bradley or Christopher too Gentile a name for Weinstein? How will he or she be baptized, circumcised, named, and fêted? How are a responsible parent and grandparent supposed to behave after all?

When the Jewish/Christian baby is born, the family clusters around the infant with a host of instinctive responses—not all sure, well-practiced, and diplomatic ones. The love and joy come easily, of course. That generous sense of wanting to do right by this tiny child springs up naturally. There are also spiritual feelings of wonder and connectedness to heritage and family history that intensify a family's commitment to honor its continuity. But which continuity? And which family history? And how can both coexist? When the two different generations from different backgrounds sift through their customs, traditions, and role models, as well as their storehouse of personal memories, to search for clues about how to celebrate and raise their new baby, they often find themselves faced with another round of confusion about how to handle the host of disparate assumptions and fantasies, dreams and fears that are stirred by this new stage of life.

For parents and grandparents, it's like learning a new job, after all, one that's even more exploratory and self-conscious because of the interfaith considerations that are now focused for the first time on a baby, not a marriage or a courtship. There's no tried-and-true rulebook, of course. Parents and grandparents learn as they go. They build on what they already know about each other. But inevitably they find themselves negotiating new emotional territory that can surprise even themselves with feelings they didn't know they had.

A New York grandmother, for instance, found herself holding her two-week-old twin grandsons and lecturing her shocked daughter-in-law, a Christian Scientist, about Josef

Mengele and his Nazi atrocities against Jewish twins. The words were meant as a warning to a Christian woman who might not know to protect her sons from anti-Semitism. But even the grandmother knew that hers was a poorly timed reference full of her own fear and overwhelming sense of duty, an association triggered by the touch and sight of her vulnerable, part-Jewish grandsons.

From memories of childhood to feelings of mortality and a need to secure one's legacy in the life of that growing child, deep emotions surface in a sensitive family, raising questions about its identity, values, and the role it will play in the new generation.

Naming the baby becomes the first nitty-gritty issue to handle with care. Or put it another way, it's the first symbolic, yet prominent opportunity for interfaith parents to establish their child's connectedness to both their families and backgrounds. The name becomes a collage of associations that draw from parents' fantasies and affections as well as their families' histories. Grandparents may not love the children's names as much as the interfaith parents do, but it's important that they're not offended by them.

Since the tradition among most American Jews of Eastern European background is for a child to be named after a deceased relative rather than a living one (the opposite being true among Sephardic Jews), it's customary for interfaith families to acknowledge that practice, at least with the first child. If the full name isn't used, which is often the case with loved ones unfashionably named Irving or Phyllis, parents incorporate the first initial of the relative's name into the first or middle name of the child. The middle name of my daughter Rachel Bara Gruzen, for example, was a tribute to Jordan's father Barnett Gruzen, who had died three years earlier.

But names are symbols that can resonate with other meanings as well, and for many interfaith parents, it's a source of pride that they're able to find names that pay tribute to their families and ethnic background in appropriate and original ways. Jordan's and my elaborate reasoning for our own children's names isn't unusual. The name Rachel, for instance, was chosen because it was a blend of her Hebrew and New England heritage, a name as comfortable in a Bible passage as on the stern of a New Bedford fishing trawler. Likewise, the name Georgia Bruce Gruzen sounded British, like half my ethnic background, as well as Russian, like half of Jordan's which is vaguely linked to the tough-minded province of Georgia where the Gruzen mountains are found (The name *Gruzen*, in fact, means "Georgian," we've since discovered. Our daughter is really Georgia from Georgia!).

For Georgia's middle name, however, it was important to me to give equal time to my family, so Bruce is culled from my mother's great-grandmother, a handsome Scotswoman named Mary Bruce. It was an added bonus that our names could allude to a few favorite aunts and uncles as well.

But names are easy in comparison to the diplomacy often needed to handle the matter of religious ceremonies and the pressures interfaith couples may feel to have a Christian baptism, Jewish *bris* (the ritual ceremony surrounding circumcision), or other traditional event in the church, synagogue, or home. For most families, these rituals have been standard operating procedure for generations. They're the assurance of Christian salvation and Jewish continuity, a sign of ancient covenants well kept and, traditionally, the first gesture that parents make to fulfill their obligation to pass on their faith to the child and prepare him or her properly for life. It's natural for well-meaning grandparents to associate "baby" with "bris" or "baptism" or whatever they gave their own children. Whether they press hard for a ceremony in their own image or quietly harbor their wishes for "something," they don't always communicate their feelings in the smoothest fashion.

Barbara Scanelli's Jewish mother Rose waited an hour after she heard the results of her daughter's amniocentesis to call to make plans for her future grandson's bris. "I couldn't believe my mother," she chuckled as she recalled her mother's excited conversation two years earlier. "Here she was putting together a guest list, pinning down a rabbi, and even figuring out which relatives would be in town in X months when Baby Edward would be born. 'Whoa, Mom!,' I said. 'That's Peter's and my job. Wait until I get finished with morning sickness, and I'll be happy to discuss it.' "

It's not always easy for interfaith couples to say "Whoa" and establish enough distance from their parents' demands and anxieties to find their own comfortable response to their child's birth, one that's a fitting and considered expression of their own particular values, style, and religious affiliation. Some heedlessly rush to placate an overbearing parent's demands, like a good friend of mine who arranged his son's bris without telling his wife, who had made him promise when they married that such a ritual would never take place.

A twenty-six-year-old Italian woman from the North End of Boston spent a difficult month mustering the courage to call a halt to her mother's ever-expanding plans for an opulent Catholic baptism that was making her Jewish husband and his family increasingly agitated. Her mother's and her tears, talk, and ultimate compromise led to a small private baptism after hours in the church, as well as to a family more in touch with each other's feelings and religious concerns. A sensitively planned ceremony that tries, as best it can, to take the needs and values of two families and faiths into consideration can open channels of communication and reveal feelings of concern, fear, and harmony that might otherwise have taken years to air.

For Jordan and me, as well as many other interfaith couples, however, discussions about ceremonies never progressed beyond a few sentences. Ceremonies were dismissed for want of interest, imagination, outside pressure, or maybe the birth of a boy. Some couples didn't dare tackle them. Other couples chose them, but the baby's service in the synagogue, church, or home routinely followed the tradition set at the wedding. For us, the magnificence and beauty of the birth itself gave us as profound and spiritual a ceremony as any we could have imagined, and we didn't feel a need for anything more.

Our problem, therefore, wasn't figuring out how to blend religious differences into a religious event. My discomfort stemmed from a more intangible and psychological confusion that had to do with how to blend our families into our lives and accept their differences, which had suddenly become prominent again. What Jordan and I had to get used to was, very simply, the different ways that our Jewish and Christian families expressed their love.

From having raised his own son, who was a mature teenager when our daughters were born, my husband was used to much more active participation from grandparents than my parents, living 250 miles away, were prepared to offer. With each birth, my mother and father had flown in from Boston to see me in the hospital for a brief, warm visit. And the following week my mother had stayed for two days to cuddle the infant, bring me breakfast in bed, and suggest a few ways I could handle my day more smoothly. Months would go by before we'd get together again, and our conversations on the phone averaged once every week or ten days. She didn't worry in the least about the babies who seemed fat and happy, like most babies, so nothing much upset our routine. And a routine it was, one that I'd grown up with and applauded for the personal space, the steady love, and the trust it offered.

But Jordan and many of my other Jewish friends knew about grandmothers who lived nearby and came to visit for weeks or months, who doted on babies, and helped young daughters (or daughters-in-law) choose furniture and clothing like a pal who was always ready with a cup of coffee, a hug, and plenty of advice. My mother-in-law was too old to fill that traditional role with me, although it was what she'd known with Jordan's first wife and the standard she'd set with her son who used to hate, but now missed, such intrusiveness. Even though Ethel Gruzen no longer came to visit to check out the refrigerator and rearrange the furniture, as she was wont to do when her son was married the first time, she was around me more than my own mother, and my feelings were a jumble as a consequence.

"If you could take a blender and mix your own mother with your mother-in-law," suggested the perceptive student of interfaith relations, Joel Crohn, Ph.D., "you'd have the perfect mother." But how guilty and defensive, ambivalent and confused I felt for even thinking such thoughts. What it said about me, of course, is that, as a new mother, I felt a powerful new connectedness to both maternal figures in my life, an unaccustomed closeness that revealed the strength and the limitations in both relationships. It took time for all three of us to trust our bonds to each other and allow them to coexist and evolve into a new configuration of closeness that had been accelerated by the birth of Rachel.

What added to the confusion is that these differences, reminiscent of Annie Hall's and Alvy's respective dinner tables, became silhouetted against ethnic backgrounds that not only exaggerated their opposition, like stereotypes, but judged them as good or bad. It was as if the Christian way of keeping one's distance and the Jewish way of moving in close were in competition with each other, applauded by each culture as the righteous way to show one's love and affection. My husband Jordan, like another Jewish spouse in an ethnic study conducted by Joel Crohn, couldn't believe that my father would come to New York on business for a day and not necessarily call or visit. I couldn't believe that his mother actually counted the number of times I telephoned her in a week. For all of us, this was a time for learning how to interpret the ways we showed our affection and for adapting to the different ways each of us liked to receive it.

What brought us closer together were the babies, of course. Rachel, and then Georgia, was the object of our love and a new opportunity for each of us to reveal the best part of ourselves, the caring center that made the differences fall away.

When the late writer Bernard Malamud talked about his family in an essay for *The New York Times Book Review*, he remembered how his father had sat in mourning when he had married a Gentile wife. Nevertheless, wrote Malamud, "After the birth of our son, my father came gently to greet my wife and touch his grandchild."

In our families we didn't have great obstacles to overcome. We had reached a delicate balance with each other long before the wedding, let alone the birth. Nevertheless, nothing softened our feelings about each other more than the small acts of tenderness we watched our parents bestow on their grandchildren. The images Jordan and I remember are such random ones: my mother-in-law, a former opera singer, singing a lush aria to six-month-old Rachel propped up on the dining-room table, waving her arms and hooting joyfully; or my father bundling up tiny Georgia in an over-sized orange life preserver for her first spin around the bay; or my mother at the Cape carefully preparing a special corner for the girls with my old dolls, cradle, doll house, and an oversized teddy with a freshly pressed bow.

These and many other memories are the ones that will remain with the grandchildren as they build very important relationships with their grandparents throughout their lives. These memories will also help the interfaith parents build stronger and more loving ties to their own parents and their spouses' parents.

When I've asked grandparents and their intermarried children for some words of wisdom about how to learn to live comfortably and enjoyably with each other, setting the stage for the harmony and openness that will nurture their children, they often echo three simple messages.

First of all: "Be patient," the grandparents tell me. "Let the priorities fall into place." What they notice is that the passing years remind them of what's really important in life and soften many of the anxieties they had way back when their child's intermarriage was first announced. They see that their children are happy and still married (or if they got a divorce, that the difference in religion had little to do with it). They applaud their son- or daughter-in-law for being sweet and steady with his or her own children. They're de-lighted that their children stayed in touch and kept channels of communication open. They praise the son- or daughter-in-law for making their child happy, even admitting at times that they've never seen two people better suited to each other.

What they also acknowledge is that relationships aren't necessarily any better with their children who married within the faith. They may have dreamed about the son-in-law who would join them at the Knights of Columbus meetings or their child's in-laws so compatible that they became "like family," but ultimately these and other fantasies may have turned out to be just as impossible with their children who married within the faith as outside it. The fact that two generations had a religion in common didn't mean they shared values, personality, lifestyle, interests, and family background. The favorite son- and or daughter-in-law is often the one with a different faith. Affection readily crosses religious lines, as grandparents will readily admit.

Interfaith couples would agree with that observation, of course. But when I solicit their advice, they talk more passionately about a second message: "Trying is what counts," they say. "We love it when our parents make an effort, step by step, to learn and accept the traditions we've brought into the family." The intermarried children applaud the smallest of gestures. They like it if a reticent mother starts talking to her friends who have intermarried children, in order to share feelings and experiences. Or they like receiving the positive, supportive newspaper clippings about intermarriage or interfaith relations from parents who've bothered to send on good news. It doesn't really matter what parents do for their intermarried children as long as it shows they're trying to grow beyond their negative predispositions and find ways to understand and feel a personal connection to their daughter- or son-in-law's family and background.

The interfaith couple's expectations aren't naive. They realize it can take years, maybe more years than their parents have available to them, to feel the closeness and comfort with the other faith and heritage that they, the intermarried couple, are beginning to feel themselves. Ugly regressions, such as a Jewish or Christian parent lashing out at his or her intermarried child with the old, unchanged litany of prejudices against Christians or Jews are deeply disturbing to the child who'd hoped that those roots, so solidly planted through history, had finally rotted away. What helps a child forgive his or her parents, however, is the knowledge that they're trying hard, for their children and grandchildren especially, to accept and adjust to a circumstance they probably would never have chosen on their own. Those gestures for harmony and understanding count a great deal.

Naturally, the grandparents have a keen and appreciative eye for the same engaging efforts on the part of a son- or daughter-in-law trying to learn and love their strange ways. Yet it was the third message that both generations most frequently agreed upon, often spoken with a shrug: "Sometimes all you can do is laugh," they all said.

The children laugh about the hard heads that Friedman calls "the overreacting parents" who'll die before they give their child's marriage their blessing. They laugh about the mother who still can't visit without pulling her Jewish daughter-in-law aside to ask about her soul or, after eighteen years, head for home without leaving a religious tract on the bureau in the guest room. They laugh about the circumstances that will probably never change—the parents who will always press too hard to win a convert, the parents who are stingy with their grandchildren, and most of all, the parents who don't know how to love without controlling and manipulating their children. The parents laugh, too, with resignation or affection, about the patterns and personalities they also can't change in daughters- or sons-in-law who refuse to adapt to needs other than their own.

More often than not, however, interfaith families improve with age. In their own gradual way, three generations build their strong and complex ties to each other, loving and nurturing each other, providing opportunities for growth and understanding, and surrounding the Jewish/Christian child with their greatest legacy of all—a family that can draw from its Jewish and Christian heritage to love and guide its children.

7

LESSONS
FROM THE PAST

When I began planning my book, which I called *Half and Half* during the early days of my research, I was often confused and disappointed by my discussions with Jewish/Christian adults who insisted that their mixed background was a relatively unimportant part of their lives. They felt their own religious identity was well established and comfortable. The structure of their lives, meaning their friends, jobs, relationship with parents, environment, spouses, and children, if they had them, had also settled into place. The subject of their identity, as it was shaped by their dual heritage, was closed and resolved for them. At a time when I was searching for help and insight into the way Jewish/Christian children integrate those influences into their identity, influences that were indeed very distinctive and provocative for me, I was frequently disheartened by their equanimity on the subject. It seemed too pat and unbelievable.

What I've learned is that many adult children of Jewish/ Christian marriages are indeed comfortable with that dimension of their lives. It may be an issue that's been placed on the back burner because other age-related concerns, from work to building a new house, are far more pressing. It may have been a problem resolved (or buried) long ago. It may never have been a problem because their families were comfortable and communicative about their Jewish/Christian partnership and the easy, appropriate ways they raised their children.

In many cases, however, it was a part of their lives they'd never been encouraged or allowed to think about. "Why would you want to interview me?" asked a bewildered Harvard University law student when I approached him for information about his Greek Orthodox/Jewish parentage. "Isn't it like having brown hair? I've always had it," he said with a puzzled look on his face. For him and many others, an interfaith background is an assumed, unexamined part of their history that is far more rich, textured, and essential to their identity than most have realized. I don't believe their lives are desperate tragedies, as the dated textbooks would imply. But I do believe this key dimension of their lives has been generally ignored, denied, and/or simply discounted—all of the above—up until now. Now that there is such a rapidly growing population of interfaith offspring who are no longer a minority in isolation from each other, it's important and timely to pay attention to the complex impact their Jewish/Christian lineage has had on their lives.

I wanted nothing more than to perceive and comprehend that complexity, but at first I could only identify the bold strokes, the gross interaction, the simplest and least subtle of feelings that operated within adult Jewish/Christian children. The individuals who gave me the most direction were those most aware of their Jewish/Christian struggles because they were usually in the middle of them, scrambling to sort out their discordant emotions and make peace with their Jewish and Christian roots.

For help in understanding my own children and what to do and not to do in raising them *and* for help in mapping out the most elementary of routes through the psyche of interfaith children, I found myself relying on the individuals who were very actively dealing with their religious identities at the time we talked. There were three groups of adults who led me through their conflicts and their exultant triumphs. There were those in transition struggling to find their emotional bearings at a time when they were getting married, losing parents, raising their own children, or coping with crisis and change. Others—a surprisingly large group—were struggling to uncover and understand a parent's heritage, usually the Jewish one, that had been hidden from them until they became adults. And finally, there were those who celebrated the wonderful moments when both sides blended and complemented each other so that the individuals felt whole and strong because of their double nurturance. What caused them to pay such careful attention to these special harmonies were usually stressful times that preceded and thus magnified the sweet times of adaptability and pleasure in their interfaith condition.

In other words, my early lessons came from sons and daughters going through experiences that triggered the troubled or changeable aspects of their heritage. I trust that the theme of my book expresses the opportunities and beauty of Jewish/Christian lives, and there are certainly examples of this happy variety within the adult lives I've discussed. However, essential lessons about what can go wrong in interfaith childhoods need to be drawn from many of these adult children's reported experiences. In addition, it must be remembered that the adult population of Jewish/Christian children has special needs that synagogues, churches, and families have yet to address.

One of my first interviews to highlight potential problems for children of interfaith marriages was with twenty-seven-year-old Donna Pitcairn, a Presbyterian graduate student who had met and fallen in love with Tom Rudolph, an architectural student from a closely knit, observant Jewish family in Savannah, Georgia. Donna had a Jewish mother who had rejected Judaism decades ago after a series of family quarrels many years before her intermarriage. While Donna was growing up, her mother occasionally accompanied her to church where the girl attended weekly Sunday school. Although Donna had a close relationship with a Jewish aunt and "felt more Jewish" than her conservative sister—and certainly more than her father, who was an uninterested Baptist—she accepted the Christian identity handed to her and valued the peace and beauty that she always found in church. Until she met Tom, who was an involved and well-schooled Jew, she didn't realize how ignorant and uncomfortable she was with a part of her life that had never received much attention. Donna's new relationship brought her into close contact with Judaism. When we spoke, she couldn't believe her surprising ambivalence about the new, demanding encounter.

At first, many of the standard questions that arise during a courtship took on religious implications. How would they raise their children if they married? What holidays would they celebrate? For Donna, it was essential that she'd continue to celebrate Christmas and Easter. But would Tom be able to participate comfortably in them? Who would marry them?

The practical questions weren't the big problem, however. What bothered Donna the most was her own defensive and critical response to the Jewish aspects of her fiancé and his family. When she accompanied him to the synagogue for Yom Kippur services, she argued about the high cost of the tickets and the shallow sermon. And despite her admitted attraction to the idea of belonging to a community because she'd never experienced that feeling with her own religiously rebellious parents, Donna criticized Tom's family for its "exclusive, small-minded" identification with a Jewish congregation where they lived. She repeatedly told Tom how much "[Jewish] elitism" disgusted her.

"I feel like I'm in *Body Snatchers*," she confessed nervously, referring to the horror movie about aliens stealing human souls. "Until a year and a half ago I went to the Presbyterian Church and didn't feel Jewish. Nowadays I'm afraid I'm going to wake up and be all Jewish."

The articulate and graceful young woman shook her head and blushed. "I can't believe I'm talking like this," she said. "In my liberal family, we were punished if we distinguished people ethnically, and it was very, very wrong to criticize someone on religious grounds. It's unbelievable to me that religious differences are suddenly an issue for me."

A round, blond twenty-three-year-old named Delia Michaels was "really nothing" religiously until she met and married an Israeli soldier named Sadja Cohen and rushed enthusiastically to embrace her Jewish heritage. She wasn't cautious or ambivalent like Donna. She was deliriously happy at the good luck that brought her to Israel where she met her quiet, bearded husband from the Jordan Valley and began a long series of Jewish discoveries that she could never have predicted at an earlier time.

Raised in New York City with a Protestant mother, Jewish father, her sister, and many relatives of both heritages around her, she had always thought of herself as "half and half." But except for a few years in a Jewish nursery school and an Episcopal elementary school, a celebration of Christmas at her home, and an occasional seder at her aunt's, there had been little religious observance in her household. She was so poorly educated about Jewish affairs that, when she visited her first kibbutz, she didn't even know that the letters PLO stood for Palestinian Liberation Organization. When the Israeli authorities asked her to state her religion upon entering Israel, she didn't realize that the fact of her having a Christian mother disqualified her from calling herself a Jew. Unaware of Orthodox tradition and its influence over Israeli citizenship requirements, she blithely wrote "Jewish" and sailed through another potential obstacle.

I met her shortly after her conversion to Judaism, when she was visiting her parents in New York. The exuberant young woman moved rapidly around the living room, bringing me tea and photographs and overflowing with enthusiasm for her serendipitous marriage and conversion. "See that beautiful skin and the detail on my grandmother's lace blouse," she marveled as she pointed to a tinted photograph of a clear-eyed, intelligent thirteen-year-old standing confidently in the middle of a garden in Germany. "My Jewish grandmother left Germany right after that picture was taken," she said softly. "She's eighty-one now, and she's still very beautiful. She still wears those rings that *her* grandmother gave her."

Since the conversion, many things about Delia's Jewish roots had suddenly come to light as her grandmother presented her with the old albums, her European linens, and stories about members of the family that had been lost in the Holocaust. For Delia, who knew very little about the Holocaust, the revelations and sense of continuity with a long, powerful history were her newest miracles, among many. "It's what I love about Jewishness," Delia said, turning another page and running her fingers tenderly over her grandmother's young face. "Judaism goes way back in a family. It has such history. I have such a good feeling about it."

Not every adult child of an interfaith marriage chooses a new religious path when he or she marries. Many mark out the known territory of their childhood faith and marry someone who confirms their beliefs, so the Catholic marries the Catholic, the Jew marries the Jew, or in some cases, the secular Jewish/Christian son marries the secular Jewish/Christian daughter. Maybe they marry individuals of the opposite faith and retain their own religion, so that their household has the duality that they knew as children. Whether the matches seem simple or not, there are infinite religious variables that can highlight differences within the couple and take getting used to.

For a short, pretty Chicago television producer named Anna Benenson, uncertainties about identity surfaced when her mother became seriously ill. Questions about her Christian mother's death, funeral, and burial crystallized her awareness of a shaky Jewish identity and her "misconnection" to her family and religious roots. Not since freshman year at college had she raised those stressful issues.

Twenty years earlier, she had chosen Swarthmore College, in part, because of its large percentage of Jewish students. After twelve years of private WASP schools where the Jewish part of herself had been submerged, Anna felt ready to explore her Jewish roots. The very first week of college, however, when Anna was standing in line to register for classes, a young woman, who was Jewish, stood beside her. When Anna mentioned to her that she, too, was Jewish, the other student cocked her head quizzically and said, "That's funny. You don't look Jewish."

The innocent remark was devastating to Anna. Whatever plans she had made to learn about Judaism evaporated immediately as her self-consciousness took over. She did very little to reinforce her fragile Jewish identity throughout her college years.

Now that she was gathering her strength for another difficult adjustment, she was painfully aware again of what her parents hadn't offered her.

Anna had been brought up without any religious instruction. Her Jewish father and Christian mother had divorced when she was six. Neither her mother nor her father had shown her very much of their own religious backgrounds, which were extensive. Her father came from a prominent Jewish family active in secular Jewish fund raising for Israel and Jewish institutions. Her mother was the offspring of an equally prominent Catholic family who'd had her educated in convents and parochial schools.

Her mother had let her own Catholicism lapse during much of her life, but it had been an important experience during adolescence. When Anna's mother became very sick, she resumed church attendance. "My mother took a bishop to lunch and became Catholic again," Anna said flatly, admitting that her mother's Catholicism gave the woman tremendous strength during her illness.

For Anna, however, religion meant resentment and confusion, not solace, and the specter of her mother's Catholic funeral only exaggerated the distance she felt from both of her parents and from a spiritual resource that could have given her needed comfort. She knew Catholic dignitaries would officiate at the funeral Mass. Burial would take place in a large family plot that had been maintained for generations by a special sect of nuns employed by her mother's family. "I used to think I had the best of all possible worlds and that I fit in everywhere," said Anna. "That connectedness was such an illusion, however. These days I feel so alienated, as if I'm looking and trying to fit in. I don't have a very strong sense of myself. I yearn to feel part of something organized and sure."

For adult children like Anna, there may not be a happy resolution. They may struggle to fit in, but never feel the freedom and confidence to make a solid commitment to one faith and its religious community.

Funerals are like a truth test, and in the same way that they reveal emotional conflicts they also express harmony, where it exists, and help heal a grieving son and daughter. Whether the parent and child share the same religion is not the issue. The quality of the relationship, as well as the spirit of the ceremony and the family's deeper understanding about life and death, are the factors that play a far more important role. For Joan Ganz Cooney, the founder of "Sesame Street" and Children's Television Workshop, the service for her seventy-one-year-old Jewish father felt complete and satisfying because it reflected the religious mixture within the family's experience.

Like her mother and siblings, Joan Cooney was raised as a "conscientious" Catholic; her father was a proud Jew throughout his life, though he rarely went to the synagogue and always insisted he was an atheist. "When my father died we got a young rabbi to do the service," the gracious, slim executive explained in her office across from Lincoln Center in New York City. "The rabbi had gone to Notre Dame. In fact, he was the Notre Dame fund raiser for the Southeast. He was perfect. He came and did a service at the funeral home, and then we went out to the cemetery, which was religiously mixed, and he said words in Hebrew over the grave. We all dropped to our knees, and most of the pall-bearers were Catholic. My mother crossed herself, and we prayed in silence."

New York architect Michael Braun drew strength from both his Jewish and Christian roots during the funeral for his son, a twenty-seven-year-old lawyer who died suddenly in an accident. Accepting and relying upon his double identity hadn't come easily to the fifty-six-year-old German-born architect, however.

He had grown up in Berlin during the Nazi era. His father had been half Jewish and his mother was Christian, and their house was always filled with friends and relatives who were mixtures of faiths and backgrounds. The child was baptized and confirmed as a Lutheran, but it was always made clear to him that his Jewishness was an important part of his life. "My mother said, 'Be proud of your Jewish ancestry, because it gives you the strongest elements of your character,' " he recalled. Even with these strong family foundations, however, he found it traumatic to be a fifteen-year-old Jewish/Christian child in Germany in 1938.

"In Nazi Germany it was perilous to choose," Michael explained during one of our many long interviews in Manhattan where he was, at the time, an associate partner in a large architectural office. "You were endangered and victimized if you were Jewish. And you felt such shame if you were German (i.e., Aryan). Especially after the war when the horrors came out in the open, the realization of what it meant to be German was devastating for me."

He believes that the story of the adult children of interfaith marriage who escaped the gas chambers "was not a hero's story. How could it be when the war was such a black-and-white situation?" he asked. "The bad and the good were clearly delineated, and we were the *mischlinge*, the hybrids, caught in between in a miserable gray zone. We were outcasts with very few rights who had to position ourselves to stay safe and unnoticed. I remember constant stomach cramps as a boy. The tension must have been terrific," he recalled.

At sixteen, Michael was drafted into the German Army because his father's records had been doctored to remove his half-Jewish status. Within weeks of service, however, the young teenager managed to be captured by the American forces and sent to the United States as a prisoner of war. After briefly returning to Germany in the late 1940s, he settled in the United States, married and raised four sons. For thirty years after the Holocaust, however, he was unable to resolve his internal conflict and establish a clear and committed religious identity for himself. It took a severe emotional crisis when the architect was fifty-four to force him to come to grips with his faith and find an answer that would allow him to live with both of his religious roots. "I had to make a commitment to be a Christian once again," he explained. "I needed the strength to survive."

When Michael's son died two years later, the architect felt very much at home in the local Episcopal church where he and his wife had become active members. Reminiscent of his German Lutheran childhood, the funeral service supported him in other meaningful ways, as well. The Psalms, which are, after all, from the Hebrew Bible (or Old Testament), were comforting. The friends who flocked to the church were an even mixture of Jews and Christians, and that duality also moved him. "I felt as if I were among family," Michael said, recalling that afternoon. "Even the minister was sensitive to the special spirit in the sanctuary that day. As we were leaving, he told me, 'How rare it is that the church feels like 'the real church' grounded in its Jewish origins'."

Not every adult I spoke with needed a crisis to bring them in close touch with their religious roots. Sometimes the midlife maturation that theologian James Fowler described was the circumstance that helped them deepen their faith and appreciate the good and strong aspects of their Jewish/Christian background. I've spoken to many adults who were proud and intrigued by the surprising turns their lives have taken. For example, a Catholic professor began an intense commitment in her forties to study the Holocaust and its rootedness in Christian theology. A Jewish woman, who had been raised in her stepmother's Methodist household, restored her Jewish ties when her children were half-grown and became a prominent leader within the international Jewish community.

No group experiences a greater, more disorienting surprise, however, than the surprisingly large number of sons and daughters who discover that they're half-Jewish—and to a less extent, those who discover that they're half-Christian—when they become adults. It's been astonishing to find out how common it was for parents to cut themselves off from their origins and allow their children to grow up without knowing and experiencing half of their family history. A friend of mine was riding a bus en route to her freshman year at Barnard College when her mother decided that it was time to tell her a few facts about her Jewish childhood. For my friend, those were the first words ever spoken about the matter, and very little has been said since.

For me, that was the first of many such stories related by other friends and people I interviewed. In many cases, the truth had only come to light because the children themselves had uncovered the facts. At seventeen or twenty-seven or older, they were suddenly asked to integrate an entirely new and confusing experience (a non-experience is more like it) into the fabric of their lives.

In *Present Tense*, the magazine published by the American Jewish Committee, Susan Jacoby, a New York writer, wrote an intense article about her own struggle to penetrate "the thicket of a mixed heritage." In it, she explained how she had been a twenty-year-old reporter for *The Washington Post* when she realized the obvious: that "naturally someone whose last name was Jacoby, whose paternal grandmother was named Sondheim, and whose ancestors in the export-import business had emigrated from Germany in 1848, was a half-Jew." Her Jewish father had converted to Catholicism when Susan was seven, but his Jewishness had never been discussed in their Catholic home.

Susan's complaint wasn't that she was religiously deprived; her Roman Catholic education had given her "a touchstone" that she valued. Her own fervid cry as an artist focused, instead, on the risk of hurting her parents, the emotional pain, and the hard work that would be necessary in order for her to understand and draw from "the particular moral and cultural tensions inherent in being a *Mischling*." Without sorting through the confusion and knowing her own "native ground," she worried that she could never write valuable literature or mine the deepest, most imaginative parts of herself. "All this can seem to be a high price for the satisfaction of elucidating the statement, 'I am a half-Jew, American-born,' " she concluded. "But I find the sentence so charged with untapped energy that no price seems too high to me."

An important national organization was formed in 1985 to deal with the complicated needs of adult children of interfaith parents. It's called Pareveh (paar-eh-va), or the Alliance for Adult Children of Jewish-Gentile Intermarriage. Pareveh, a Yiddish word, refers to the neutral foods, such as fruit and vegetables, that are neither dairy nor meat products. Because they can be eaten with either food group without violating the Laws of Kashruth (kosher foods), they are therefore acceptable according to Jewish dietary law. According to Pareveh's press release, "This concept . . . humorously summarizes the family status of the offspring of Jewish-Gentile intermarriage."

The thirty-six-year-old executive director, Robin Elizabeth Margolis, is herself a pareveh, the child of an Episcopalian WASP father and an Orthodox Jewish mother. Robin discovered her Jewish heritage in 1984 when she was sorting through her late mother's belongings and found yellowed documents featuring strangers with Jewish names. "My God, my mother's parents were Jews!" she realized in shock. "My mother was a Jew. I'm a Jew!" Robin had been raised as an Episcopalian with her father's last name of Smith. Neither she nor her father had known about her mother's real religious and ethnic identity. The discovery changed her life, and the very articulate, forceful journalist set out to piece together her buried heritage.

Her search led her to many Jewish relatives, a deeper compassion for her mother, and ultimately to the needs of parevehs, like herself, who are coping with many similar internal and external conflicts. Ironically, Robin had considered converting to Judaism four years before she uncovered her mother's Jewish identity. "My mother shielded me from Judaism to the best of her ability. I found it!" exclaimed the woman who has, since her discovery, made a commitment to Judaism and changed her last name from Smith to her mother's maiden name of Margolis.

"I look like my WASP father, and I have intense, very meaningful memories of my Episcopalian childhood. But I had been searching for a new religion for a long while," she explained when I asked her for a further explanation of why she became a Jew. "I feel that the half of me that's my mother has pulled me to her religion and peoplehood. I identify as a Jew. I feel extremely blood-tied to the Jews. But I can't think of my choice as 'conversion,' which implies snipping off half of my personality and family. I think of it as *living out my Jewish half*."

Although Robin welcomes her powerful new identity, the disadvantages of learning so much so late is obvious to anyone sensitive to the needs of a mixed-marriage offspring. Under normal circumstances, the pareveh takes a lifetime to sort through a potentially confusing array of Jewish and Christian experiences in order to understand the world and himself and where he stands within it. The experiences of childhood and adolescence are crucial to that process. But the late discoverers, as I think of them, are deprived of those experiences, and much of what they have learned has been inaccurate as well. It's as if they've been suddenly introduced to a complicated, very confusing game that they're not prepared to play. They don't know the rules or the players. They haven't developed the tricks to master it. And they're not sure where their old skills and knowledge fit into this new arena. For many individuals, the need to make sense of this new area of their lives is an all-consuming, urgent one that can radically alter their lives.

The advantage, however, is that they see the problem with fresh eyes that the adult children who have integrated their dual heritage don't have because the forces have become so blurred and assumed in their lives. Robin Margolis, for example, is able to separate and articulate the pressures acting on her with a clarity that many other adults lack because they have already gone through the integration process. She's proud of the fact that she had a solid Episcopal identity when "the lightning bolt hit," because it gave her the strength and understanding to accept and expand into her new identity as a Jew. She also knows what commitment involves. Her late-in-life identity crisis gives her a unique basis of comparison that's as perceptive as it is hilarious in the way it delineates the pressures tugging insistently on the interfaith child. For instance, Robin once said that "being a pareveh is like having two repertoires of behavior, two head sets, two world views.

"It's like running a hotel with two conventions going on simultaneously," she continued. "The Jewish side is in one wing, and they're very noisy and demanding. They're always flying into rages. They call room service a lot, because nothing is ever quite right. They have suitcases all over the place which they're always unpacking and tripping over. They tip very well, but they're emotionally exhausting.

"In the other wing are the WASPs. They're polite, controlled, restrained. They all have light hair, like I do. They *never* ring the bell," she said emphatically. "But when they do it's with a very well-placed suggestion, and you'd better listen carefully.

"Neither side, of course, can understand why you're paying attention to the other wing," she said, sighing. "Trying to keep both sides happy and comfortable is very tiring."

Robin's creative way of handling her dual heritage was to form Pareveh with the help of another Jewish/Christian offspring, Leslie Goodman-Malamuth.

Leslie, the daughter of a secular Jewish father and a secular Christian mother, was raised in California with "a reverence," as she puts it, "for beach real estate." Unlike Robin, the tall blond woman had always known she was part Jewish. As a child she had eagerly read books about Jewish children, and when she was nine years old she had been fascinated by a seder at a friend's house and resolved to learn more about Judaism when she grew up. While Pareveh was taking shape in 1985, Leslie married a Jewish man and, since then, she has formally converted to Judaism.

What Leslie shares with Robin, however, are many painful realizations of the difficulties that adult Jewish/Christian children often encounter as they search for knowledge and acceptance of their religious identity. Throughout her life, Leslie had been rebuffed by many individuals who were quick to tell her that she couldn't possibly understand what it was like to be a Jew because her mother was Christian, her looks were Gentile, or her religious training was meager. When she visited synagogues and studied Jewish materials as a college student, and later as an adult, she found that the children of intermarriage were seldom addressed at all. No helpful materials on the subject existed, in her experience.

Moreover, she remembered, "many people were mystified to see me there. Some were even horrified to see me. It was as if I'd climbed out of a lagoon. The children of intermarriage were supposed to be lost to the faith, never seen again, because of their parents' terrible sin of marrying each other. But here I was, and they didn't know what to do with me!

"I wanted to be treated as a thoughtful, seeking person looking for answers and involvement," she continued. "For years, however, I slipped in and out of services, avoiding any discussion about my background as much as possible. In a synagogue, it was always easier to 'pass' when you have a Jewish last name like mine."

Pareveh's phenomenal growth over the last year has proved that there are large numbers of other Jewish/Christian children with the same compelling needs. Since Pareveh's first press conference in September 1985, the organization has created two operating chapters in Washington, D.C. and New York City, published a quarterly newsletter, created a tape library, and assembled an extensive mailing list based on inquiries and offers of support from several hundred concerned individuals and organizations. In addition to lobbying for change within Jewish and Christian institutions in the treatment of interfaith families, Robin and Leslie have also begun writing a book, *Split at the Root: Children of Jewish-Gentile Intermarriage.*

Based on its experiences over the past year, Pareveh recently spelled out a series of principles that I find to be exceedingly clear and illuminating for interfaith parents with young children today. These are Pareveh's premises:

1. Throughout their lives, the children of intermarriage carry a Jewish "half" and a Christian "half" within themselves—all descendants of intermarriage are influenced by both heritages.

2. However parevehs choose to live—as Jews, Christians, or neither—they must learn to live comfortably with both heritages, or go through life with a divided sense of self.

3. Pareveh defines a "pareveh Jew" as an individual with some Christian blood who chooses to live as a religious or secular Jew—pareveh Jews do not acknowledge the divinity or spiritual leadership of Christ, or the key doctrines of any religion besides Judaism.

4. Pareveh defines a "pareveh Christian" as a religious or secular Christian who has some Jewish blood, but acknowledges Christ as God or as a spiritual teacher, or who lives by some version of Christian ethics.

5. Pareveh defines secular parevehs as those with some Jewish blood who have rejected both Christianity and Judaism to follow other religious or secular teachings.

6. Pareveh respects the integrity and value of each religious culture in its members' backgrounds—the Alliance has no interest in false religious syncretism, and firmly rejects all attempts to create a "Jewish-Christian" religion, considering such a move both anti-Semitic and anti-Christian.

7. Regardless of how parevehs choose to affiliate, it is the organization's goal to help them love and respect both "sides" of their personality and heritage.

The address for the organization is: Pareveh, Alliance for Adult Children of Jewish-Gentile Intermarriage, P.O. Box 2554, Washington, D.C., 20013-2554.

Pareveh is addressing these concerns on a national level, but every Jewish/Christian adult continues on a personal and daily basis to draw from the strengths of a dual background to create a satisfying life.

For example, Father Gary Gelfenbien from Troy, New York, is proud of having been able to take an anti-Semitic incident and translate it into a lifelong commitment to be a loving and ecumenical Catholic priest. During his early years in the seminary, his beloved Russian/Jewish grandmother had died, and after her Orthodox funeral he had returned to school and encountered a fellow student who reached out and touched him on the arm, saying, "I'm sorry."

Thinking the youth was offering sincere condolences over the loss, Gelfenbien nodded. But the fellow added, "I'm sorry she wasn't saved." The statement became a turning point for the young Gelfenbien who vowed that he would become "a different kind of priest, someone who gets through the sectarianism to the love God was meant for." To keep that promise he went on to become resident Catholic chaplain at Rensselaer Polytechnic Institute, complete a doctorate in art history, assist the pastor of a large local parish, perform interfaith marriages, choreograph a dance troupe, sing, cook, feel pride in his Jewish name, and "give humor back to God."

Not all the resolutions are religious in nature. One of

New York City's most famous mayors, Fiorello LaGuardia, turned his mixed parentage into a political asset when he gave campaign speeches in Yiddish and Italian.

In his 1970 biography, the father of the psychiatric study of identity, Dr. Erik H. Erikson, admitted to the author, Dr. Robert Coles that, "Yes, if ever an identity crisis was central and long drawn out in somebody's life, it was so in mine." According to the great psychiatrist who was part Jewish, part Christian, part German, part Danish, and raised by a Jewish stepfather, "I had to try to make a style out of marginality and a concept out of identity confusion." In turn, Erikson wrote over a half-dozen pivotal books elaborating on that personal theme.

In the literary world, there's Marcel Proust, Montaigne, Dorothy Parker, and Eugene Ionesco whose Jewish/Christian origins were part of their creative storehouse for their lasting works.

More playfully, there's a young Jewish/Christian comedian that I heard on the radio who mined his childhood experiences in a church confessional with a routine that begins, "Father, forgive me for I have sinned. . . . But first, let me introduce you to my lawyer, Mr. Cohen?"

For many Jewish/Christian adults, their choice of a neighborhood and workplace may be a meaningful way of expressing their Jewish and Christian ties. Some choose to live and work in mixed environments because such surroundings are familiar and stimulating. They talk about feeling "at home" in a place where the faces, body language, verbal expressions, styles of problem solving, and the lively array of ethnic diversity surround them. Oftentimes, they may also be the "bridge builders" in such settings, linking disparate groups in the way that Dianne Feinstein does as mayor of San Francisco, or Joan Ganz Cooney as the founder of "Sesame Street," or Joseph Murphy as chancellor of the City University of New York. Their skill in "carrying messages between sides" has become their useful way of employing skills often developed in interfaith households.

Whatever their creative solutions to the ongoing complexities of living in two worlds, adult Jewish/Christian off-spring need to draw from the best of both of them and feel that it has blended creatively and comfortably within them so that their lives are richer because of that presence. It's understandable that the moments when they feel that perfect harmony are especially important to interfaith children. A Roman Catholic bride from New York felt "the coming together of two sides in a way that wasn't all torn and confused" during her wedding when her husband's Greek Orthodox church resonated with the rich sound and imagery of both the Hebrew Scriptures and the Gospels. On a trip to Israel, another New Yorker squeezed a tightly rolled prayer into the crevice of the Wailing Wall and accompanied his Catholic mother to the Garden of Gethsemane. "All my roots were there in Jerusalem, and it felt like a total coming together of my entire life," he recalled. But for another young man in New Jersey, "a profound sense of well-being" came over him when he returned home for an opulent spread of kreplach, chopped liver, borscht, baklava, and hot cups of cappuccino in honor of his huge, multiethnic family that gathered around him at the dining-room table, "just like always."

Whether religious or secular, these feelings connect the children of interfaith marriages to their roots and remind them how intricately and uniquely they have woven them into the structure of their lives and their identities. These are the sweet achievements that parents and children deserve to celebrate and enjoy.

What lessons emerge from these rich and provocative experiences? How can parents today distill those joyous and disturbing stories and clarify their own goals for children growing up in a contemporary environment? Here are five recommendations that have a special application to today's interfaith parents raising Jewish/Christian children.

1. *Be clear and honest from the start.* This first rule seems so easy to follow, especially in this era of openness and truth telling where it's no longer fashionable—or necessary—to keep secrets tucked away in the closet. Nevertheless, many people are still uncomfortable with their own religious differences, and they don't know how to handle them except by denying that they exist at all, minimizing their importance, or exaggerating the primacy of one faith at the expense of another. The denials, evasions, and hypocrisy are still evident in my interviews with couples, and nothing is worse for the child.

There are interfaith parents who feign religious loyalty in order to get social acceptability. Other parents pretend indifference in order to adapt to a controlling spouse and in-law or a concept of what family life is supposed to be. Many interfaith couples are totally out of touch with their feelings, while others believe they can wipe out an uncomfortable past, as if dropping a curtain over an image of themselves they don't have the courage to face. If the testimonies from adult children prove anything, it's that truth ultimately wins out. "Kids are sharp little bunnies, and they're not easily fooled," said Robin Margolis. "Look at me! I was raised in a totally Christian home. Both parents were devoted Episcopalians. But I still received subliminal Jewish messages. At Christmas, for instance, I watched my mother set up an elaborate Christmas tree with a crèche, and then, suddenly, sink into a terrible depression as though she'd committed a crime."

The penalties exacted on many children who received those deceptive messages were stiff. The dishonesty interfered with their relationships with their extended families. It often gave them an erratic, shallow, and uneasy religious education. "Deceit and deception sometimes permeated into the rest of their lives," said Robin Margolis, who believes that many Jewish/Christian adults never learned how to deal squarely with religious differences. The parents who compressed a religious identity into a pitiful yellowed document at the bottom of a garment bag, a rosary in a jewelry box, or a prayer shawl carefully buried under layers of clothing in a drawer were often psychologically weakened because of that amputation of their identity and the energy that was necessary to maintain it. In turn, the children were left to build an identity out of confusing clues that distorted their knowledge of life and their family's character. It's a parent's responsibility to come to terms with his or her religious identity so that it's possible to express it, accept it, and discuss it with the children as a natural part of life.

2. *Offer children a fair, informed exposure to both faiths, no matter what religious choices the family has made.* The call for an easy, comfortable introduction to aspects of both religions was almost unanimously sounded in my interviews with adult children. When they were growing up, the norm was exclusivity, which meant that children were raised intensely within one faith, with almost no contact with the other. The children who were raised as Jews seldom saw the inside of a church, even with Christian grandparents. The children raised as Catholics and Protestants, especially if they grew up in places other than Eastern cities, usually didn't even know that Judaism was a religion, let alone what a rabbi and the sanctuary of a synagogue looked like. In turn, the children who were raised as "nothing" were doubly denied.

Another problem occurred when the children tended to be in much closer contact with one side of the family than another because the other family lived far away, and transportation and telephone communication were limited, so another potentially broad avenue of communication was narrowed. There were some children, like Gary Gelfenbien, who moved easily between the church and the synagogue, Nona's Italian kitchen and Bubbe's Jewish kitchen, but twenty-five years ago, his easy-going, ecumenical experiences weren't the interfaith norm.

Today is entirely different, however, and it's possible for parents to give their children experiences from both religious domains so that, at the very least, they know relatives, holidays, places of worship, clergy, and, above all, the different ways that people express their faith, whether it's through prayer, music, giving, working, or dozens of personal modes. Since that familiarity is so important and so available, I'm always incredulous when I find individuals who opt for the provincial approach that believes these contacts are somehow dangerous to a child's developing body of beliefs. I have a close friend in Chicago, for instance, who asked me if I thought it was all right for her school-age children to take a tour of the pretty white clapboard church in rural Minnesota where she grew up. My friend had converted to Judaism many years ago when she married, and her children were being raised as Jews; therefore her respectful parents, who were sincere and unassuming people, had asked permission before they took the children inside the doors.

I assured her that her son and daughter had everything to gain and very little to lose. They'd accumulate one more loving experience with their grandparents. They'd feel closer to their mother's and family's history, as well as to a basic fact of American history. They'd improve their chances of growing up to be individuals whose ultimate religious choices are based on knowledge and self-acceptance, rather than a defensive denial of a major dimension in their lives about which they're ignorant. They'd also develop a balanced respect for both parents' backgrounds, rather than a condescension and contempt for one of their two "halves" that I've found in a number of poorly adjusted Jewish/Christian adults.

It's crucial that parents never denigrate themselves or each other's faith, which means that divorced and widowed parents must make every effort to treat the other faith fairly, especially if the other parent isn't available to represent it. Above all, a parent mustn't poison children against either side of the family without being well aware of the permanent damage it does to the children. My interviews with the adult sons and daughters proved that coping with a legacy of cynicism, prejudice, bitterness, and contempt was a far more formidable and insidious proposition than the blank slate that Robin Margolis and Susan Jacoby were handed.

3. *Be prepared for the realities of organized religion.* Practice "preventive medicine" wherever possible. There are two heated conflicts that have been a source of pain to many interfaith adults, and the patterns don't have to repeat themselves.

The first issue focuses on the idea of "belonging" and the profound ambivalence that the children feel about something that's often been denied them. Every time the subject has come up in my interviews, as with Donna Pitcairn and Anna Benenson, the contradictory responses have been classic. On the one hand, the adults will long for a group identity and the security that it offers, while romanticizing their parents' guaranteed membership in a childhood religion that will unconditionally accept them. But on the other hand, they'll exaggerate the threatening aspects of organized religion, equating it with an organization of "body snatchers," and resent the fact that a parent can so easily and hypocritically return to a natal faith after years of non-interest. Simultaneously, the adult children also applaud their own intellectual independence and their freedom from causes and ideology. "They want an 'in' without being 'sucked in,' " observed Egon Mayer after completing his 1982 study. "They're fierce loners," summarized Robin Margolis. "And it's not too helpful for them. They need to share their experiences with each other, and they need to learn that good things can come from causes, ideologies and religions. 'Community' is not a dirty word."

It's possible for today's children to have a much healthier relationship with sectarian communities. After all, the community is the way that values are perpetuated and tasks are accomplished, and contact with "the Jewish community," "the Catholic community," or "the Protestant community" shouldn't be such a threatening proposition to today's interfaith child, as if she or he is little David face to face with a hostile monolith like Goliath. There are many groups of people within each faith who gather together around a shared goal, whether it's to pray in a sanctuary, build a hospital, shelter the homeless, organize a New Age festival, mount an art exhibition, or fight for nuclear controls. Young children and teenagers should be encouraged to participate in a variety of these services so they never dismiss them out of hand or feel excluded by them.

Obviously, the experiences should be positive ones, and it's wise for parents to research a religious institution, particularly the church and the synagogue, for its attitudes about interfaith families and the opposite faith. Press the rabbi, minister, and priest for their true personal feelings about interfaith marriages and appraise how much they genuinely value an interaction between Christians and Jews and how sensitive they'll be to the needs, present and future, of one's own child, the converted spouse, or the spouse of the other faith.

The sad adult stories also prove how important it is to know the religious rules that govern churches and synagogues, so that there aren't any devastating surprises when it comes time for important ceremonies, like a wedding or a bar/bat mitzvah. The churches demand a baptism before any of the sacraments can be performed. As described in Chapter 11, the synagogues demand that the participants in their pivotal ceremonies be Jews, and since the definition of who is a Jew varies within the Reconstructionist, Reform, Conservative, and Orthodox branches, it's essential to understand the differences and take them seriously. The debate over these issues is almost 6,000 years old and it's as passionate as ever. Bitter stories from the interfaith children of Christian mothers who suddenly discovered that their Jewish identity wasn't accepted by the religious authorities should remind parents how important it is to plan wisely and avoid the conflicts with tradition wherever possible.

"When I informed the parents of my wife-to-be that I had a Catholic mother, her father went berserk," recalled a Jewish film editor whose memory of the events leading up to his marriage fourteen years ago is still vivid and angry. "My father-in-law kept saying, 'A Gentile, a Gentile! There's never been a drop of Gentile blood in our veins!' So he asked his friends what I had to do to convert, and there was a ritual re-circumscision by a rabbi who pricked my finger and drew blood. He stuck it, it bled, I was hugged, and he said, 'Welcome to the tribe.' I remember my bloody finger and my stained shirt and a feeling that my integrity was being violated. If they line up Jews and shoot, they'll line me up. Isn't that enough?"

But the reality is that an offspring's self-definition as a Jew or a Christian is not enough to "legitimize" the person in the eyes of the particular faith community they wish to join. The synagogues and churches have their rules and traditions and the flexibility with which they'll amend those guidelines in order to meet the needs of interfaith families varies considerably. The smart interfaith child has to learn how to maneuver through all these realities, so they don't become an insurmountable obstacle that inhibits a youth's religious search and identification. My personal strategy is to offer my children many positive experiences with each religious community and its membership so they'll essentially trust and respect these resources. The search for the most welcoming, stimulating religious environment where our children will grow in self-esteem, adaptability, and good sense is key. Nevertheless, it's also necessary to prepare children for those communities and individuals who may, in the future, question their religious credentials and, worse, treat them with prejudice and scorn. Parents are always there to stand by for moral support when a child feels rejected or self-conscious because of his interfaith roots.

4. Last of all, *free them for their own choices.* Of course, it's important to offer children a variety of positive religious experiences so they have information to make a choice about their religious identity. But what matters even more is that parents don't poison the child's growth with the negative associations that curtail their curiosity and impede their exploration. No hidden agendas, in other words. No tugs of war with spouses or families. No hostile undermining of either one's own background or the other parent's.

"Children must be free to make a choice not only whether they'll be Christian or Jewish," said Rabbi David Greenberg from East Hampton, New York, "but which aspect of either faith—morality, ethics, social justice, or culture—they'll identify with. Parents want their children to have the experiences that spawned and enriched their life. But children will always modify and make their own adjustments to what's been offered them.''

As the lives of many interfaith adults prove, defining and accepting their identity and deciding on religious commitments are a life's work. Odds are good that their passage through their rich and increasingly accessible heritages will be smoother than those of children of interfaith marriage born in previous eras. Odds are also good that today's interfaith parents can do a better, more honest, and comfortable job of assisting their children's development than parents of interfaith children in centuries when interfaith marriage was socially and religiously unacceptable.

CHAPTER

8

WISE CHOICES

"Why in the world are you here?" asked Myrtle Spellman, my late mother-in-law's old friend and neighbor, as she rushed to greet me in the gray stone lobby of Stephen Wise Free Synagogue in Manhattan. Three years ago, I was waiting for an interview with Helene Ferris, the temple's assistant rabbi, when Myrtle, a short, ebullient sixty-eight-year-old, wrapped her arms around me, popped two hearty kisses on my cheeks, and took my hands. Before waiting for my explanation, she looked up and said, beaming, "How it would thrill dear Ethel to see you here! On that Saturday before she died when I was sitting beside her bed, do you know what she told me?"

I shook my head. "It was her deepest wish that little Rachel would be brought up Jewish," she said.

I wasn't surprised by the request. My mother-in-law, who died before Georgia was born, had been deeply involved in Jewish activities all her life, and it was natural that she'd want her grandchild to be part of a world she loved and knew well. But Ethel had never breathed a word of this wish during our seven years together, and she'd always seemed comfortable with our handling of the religious part of our lives. I pressed Myrtle for more details of their conversation.

The report began to change, however, once the bright-eyed woman began to tell me about her own reasons for seeking out a synagogue on a midweek afternoon. Her only son and Protestant daughter-in-law were having their first baby that week, and Myrtle, a widow, had stopped by to search for a reassuring pamphlet about the children of intermarriage. "I've been thinking about Ethel so much these days," she said, after telling me that she'd also undergone a recent cancer operation. "Maybe what Ethel really said was that she wanted Rachel to understand her Jewish roots."

I was relieved at first. That wish was such an easy and natural one to satisfy, and Jordan and I had always been clear about that basic goal for our children.

But minutes later, when I'd said good-bye and started to climb the stairs for my interview, I felt let down, disappointed, as if something momentous and transporting should have taken place—but didn't. What I'd wanted Myrtle to give me, I realized, was a pronouncement from my mother-in-law that would resonate in that sacred space and decide, once and for all, the issue of how Jordan and I would raise our children. My mother-in-law's supposed words on her deathbed would become my inspiration. Fired with love and altruism, I'd make a noble choice—Ethel's choice—to raise my daughters exclusively as Jews. But she hadn't issued such a clear imperative after all.

I'd have loved the easy deliverance of obeying her order, at least for that moment. Instead of a loosely held collection of inchoate feelings, instincts, and unresolved questions, I'd have an orderly, simple plan that would please at least one side of the family. I'd have a certainty that would supposedly take all my loose ends and formative thoughts and squeeze them into a neat, purposeful goal.

I knew such a solution wasn't an answer, however. It was too arbitrary, too premature. The truth was that I loved the slow and steady way that Jordan and I were making choices about how we blended our backgrounds into our lives and introduced them to our children. We were celebrating each other's holidays, joining each other's families for their important ceremonies, enjoying friends from both backgrounds, and learning about the religious experiences that mattered to each of us. This process was like our courtship, in fact, another gradual evolution full of discoveries, tests of our commitment, and the fun and promise of three years together before the certainty of a wedding on Block Island and the start of a new stage of life for ourselves. As with the issue of raising our children, there had been outside pressures to declare our intentions, and there had been aggravating times when I wondered if we'd ever take that extra step of commitment. But all along, there had been a trust that our relationship was unfolding in a strong and natural way. Any false acceleration or crowding would hinder a growth that felt so comfortable and vital to both of us.

I realize that interfaith couples have many approaches to the issue of raising their Jewish/Christian children. Slowly, rapidly, confidently, or warily, they construct their relationships with their religious traditions in the same way they build their relationship with each other. As a result, there aren't any hard and fast rules, timetables, or patterns for decision making that fit everyone's search for an answer to the classic question, "What to do about the children?" What has become increasingly clear to me over the years since my pivotal visit to the synagogue is that every family has its own special package of considerations and resources to honor and enjoy at its own pace. Although families need courage and patience to grow into their own solutions (as well as the wisdom to refine them), it's essential that they allow each other the freedom to shape and amend this important part of their lives.

To encourage interfaith parents to consider the choices available to them, however, here's a representative array of decisions that other families have made. These are the success stories, for the most part, meaning that they seem workable, comfortable, vital, and well-suited to each particular family. These options aren't flawless experiences, by any means. Each has its weak spots, unfinished business, penalties, and risks that are readily identified by one or another generation. These routes aren't certifiably ideal for the children either, primarily because the interfaith sons and daughters raised in today's freer environment are still too young to reflect on their parents' choices or to display the effects those choices have had on them.

But instinctively I've chosen these examples because they give life to one of the most useful pieces of advice I've received in the course of writing this book. A few years ago when I asked a New Jersey priest for guidelines about how to raise my own Jewish/Christian children, the gentleman, who asked not to be identified, paused to think about the question, then said simply, "Go with the strength. If one parent is more involved and committed to his or her faith, then offer that to the child. If the other religion is the more vital one within the home, then honor that one," he counselled. "What matters is that the child is nurtured in the richest way possible."

For the priest, the choices were simple ones—either Christianity or Judaism—and in his potential support for a faith other than his own, he was unusually generous and open. But his phrase, "Go with the strength," has acquired greater meaning for me in the course of observing how interfaith parents choose to raise their children and establish a religious philosophy for their homes. They find "the strength" in many arenas—in Christianity, Judaism, a blend of both religions, their extended families, their primary families, various communities, and/or patterns of celebrating and perpetuating life. Each family in its own way reaches out for the resources that are the most meaningful and available to it. As my friend from California would say, they go where there's "juice." Or as my Italian friend would say, gesticulating for emphasis, they go where there's "heart." Interfaith couples gravitate toward the people and ideas that generate in them the energy and power, love and search for wisdom that enhance their lives and children's lives. They have combined those possibilities as best they can.

In the simplest sense, their choices for raising their children are these: Christian, Jewish, Both, and Secular.

CHRISTIAN

For Howard and Mary Michaelson, the decisions about raising their children came early in their relationship. When they met thirty-four years ago at Yale University, the Catholic Church exacted a promise from the non-Catholic spouse to promise to raise his future children as Catholics. But for Mary, the product of sixteen years in parochial school, the requirement was merely an expression of something she would have asked anyway. "There was no question about my faith wavering or how to bring up my children," Mary recalled. "Howard had loose ethnic and religious ties. His bar mitzvah had been perfunctory. And his mother was always saying, 'It's better to be good than religious.' But I cared a lot about my ties to the church. I figured it was only a matter of time before Howard would go along with me."

When I met Mary Michaelson, she was the mother of five children in their late teens and twenties and, for the past twenty-nine years, married to Howard, a publishing executive in New York. The soft-spoken woman sat at her desk in the book-lined basement office where she worked full-time, directing the educational programs for a large Catholic parish in New Jersey. To reach her for my appointment, I'd had to jog right at the statue of the Virgin Mary just inside the entrance to the church's rectory, smile hello to two priests eating lunch in the kitchen, drop down a flight of stairs to a freshly painted hallway lined with classrooms and a washroom hung with white vestments drying over set-tubs, then turn right at the big room with the easy chair and the cheerful orange curtains covering small, high windows. "Welcome to my submarine!" Mary greeted me warmly, crossing her office to greet me.

Seeing her so immersed in Catholic activities, I could understand the value of Howard's and her agreement three decades earlier. Within that religious framework she'd been able to flourish and create a rich, spirited religious experience for her children and others. Once a week for many years she'd taught prayer and the Bible to all five of her sons and daughters gathered around the dining-room table. To supplement a Ph.D. in English, the former college professor had also begun studying for an advanced degree in religion and become particularly interested in Christianity's rootedness in Judaism. She had always cared that her children knew about their Jewish traditions, and when it came to their Passover seder, especially within the last few years, the family joked that she was more Jewish than anyone because of her enthusiasm for reading the Haggadah so thoroughly and saying all the prayers. But recently her own studies had made her realize how much richer her children's Jewish instruction could have been and how sincere but vague her efforts had been for most of the time when they were growing up. Her newest concern was developing an ecumenical curriculum for her Catholic students at the church and advising the local diocese on ways to help interfaith couples. "Parents must make an effort to know each other's traditions," she counseled.

In Washington, D.C., the Tannor household makes that effort in a sincere, effective way. Theirs is an unusual circumstance because three sets of traditions operate in the lives of their eight- and five-year-old son and daughter. Renata, the children's mother, is Catholic, and Sam, their father, was born Jewish. But twenty years ago, when Sam graduated from college, he converted to Christianity through a baptism in the Presbyterian church. Nowadays, the basic religious structure in their home is Protestant, and most Sundays the family goes to the Presbyterian church where the children are enrolled in Sunday school. Nevertheless, overlaid onto this clear-cut commitment is an abundance of other religious and cultural experiences that ground the children in a very mixed, rich heritage. Their Jewish and Italian grandparents live nearby, so they celebrate Christmas, Easter, and the evening of Yom Kippur with them. Every Passover, they join Sam's extended family for a seder. Their stepsister and brothers from Sam's first marriage to a Catholic woman have been raised with their mother's strict Catholicism, to add to the variety of religious choices that are exhibited around them.

It might seem that such an array of experiences would be chaotic and confusing, too distracting for young children building their own religious identities. But there's a consistency with which Sam and Renata approach this area of their lives. Their thoughtfulness and agreement become a deep and steadying guide for their children.

I'm reminded of a statement by Edwin Friedman, the therapist and Reconstructionist rabbi from Bethesda who became adamant when asked about the supposedly inevitable confusion that the children of mixed marriages undergo as a consequence of growing up in a family with different religious affiliations. "Contrary to popular opinion, the issue isn't how much of a mixture or how many differences the child of mixed marriage can absorb," he declared. "The issue is whether or not the parents have their heads straight.

"By that I mean, 'Are they well defined in knowing who they are, what they want out of life, where they're headed, where they stand, and what they believe?' The more straight the parents are about these essential questions," he continued, "the more differences the children can absorb."

For Sam, the serenity of weekly church services and the beauty of sacred choral music are the aspects of his spiritual life that have the most meaning. During college, he sang in a professional choir with compulsory chapel performances ("the best part of the college experience"), and he still plays a requiem from Beethoven, Mozart, or another of the masters every day. "I go to church regularly," he explained during our interview, "not for the intellectual exercise, but for the security I feel, the peacefulness and understanding I find in a place of worship. It's an important part of my life. It's where I feel in deepest touch with myself and my feelings."

The forty-six-year-old will be the first to admit that his decision to convert was "peculiar and odd." Indeed, it's taken years to understand why he took such a step. "On the surface I know I went to Hebrew school at the Reform synagogue for a year and a half, was disruptive, and quit at twelve without a bar mitzvah," he explained.

"But my conversion had much more to do with psychological factors than anything so simple. I certainly didn't choose it after weighing Christianity against Judaism," he said, shaking his head, then continuing slowly, thinking out his reasons one more time. "As a reaction to certain things in my background I converted. I wanted to be different from the model I knew—my father."

When I looked around Sam's ground-floor office in his home, where he balances an active career as financial planner, volunteer activist, and at-home daddy while Renata, an advertising executive, commutes to work in Georgetown, it struck me how successfully he's been able to forge his own private world. The bulletin boards are layered with as many children's notices and gifts of crayoned artwork as professional announcements. The walls are decorated with colorful photographic collages of all five of his children at play. And there always seems to be time during the steady flow of phone calls for a thoughtful word or two about what's going on in the caller's life. The values are clearly placed on family, gentleness, introspection, and service, without pretension.

Renata supports Sam in these choices. In addition, the exuberant former Peace Corps volunteer reinforces (more singlemindedly, in fact, than her husband) the Jewish aspect of their lives, making sure that it's a part of her children's upbringing and identity. "If you ask my son what he is," Sam explained, "he'll always say 'half Christian and half Jewish,' which is a reflection of Renata's thinking. My wife broke out of the narrow Italian community where she grew up and has flourished in the Jewish community. She's become unbelievably comfortable in it, especially since we got married. She loves the idea of a mixed background for our children."

Sam, however, hasn't fully resolved what he calls his own "two-channel life." When he joins his parents for High

Holy Day services or attends one of many ceremonies in a synagogue, he's of two minds in that he's at home in the familiar congregation yet coolly separate from it and aware that it's something he rejected many years ago. When his small daughter comes home on Fridays from the nursery school she attends in a nearby Reform temple, an enrollment that was Renata's idea, he also feels conflicted as she prances into his office, proud as punch that she's "a *shabbat* girl."

"I'm not reaching out for more of my Jewish heritage," he said calmly. "There are tensions within me, inconsistencies, feelings that are still in opposition, but I'm gradually understanding them more. My goal is to reconcile them."

The choice that Sam Tannor made is not a common one. It's estimated that only 3 to 10 percent of intermarried Jewish partners convert to Christianity (in contrast to over 30 percent of the non-Jewish partners who convert to Judaism).

For interfaith couples, the choice to raise their children as Christians is also a minority decision. Or so it seems from the only statistics available, which are those gathered by the American Jewish Committee in their 1983 poll of the adult children of intermarriage. In it, only 20 percent of their sample identified themselves as Protestant or Catholic, while slightly less than 50 percent considered themselves to be Jewish, and slightly over 30 percent said they were something else or nothing. These statistics were based on parental decisions made a decade or more ago, not recently. Also, since the sample was gathered by a Jewish organization working closely with synagogues, members of the Christian community were not thoroughly evaluated. Therefore, these numbers are not reliable indices of choices that interfaith parents are making today or will necessarily make tomorrow.

Nevertheless, I was also hard-pressed during my own research to find many interfaith families baptizing their young children and decisively agreeing, as Mary and Howard Michaelson did, to raise them within a Christian church. If I'd combed predominately Christian communities like those in which I'd grown up and also surveyed the churches more extensively, I've no doubt I could have uncovered many more examples. Nevertheless, the search takes detective work, a measure of how today's Christian-affiliated families are often camouflaged, distributed more randomly through the population and not at all clustered around a nationwide array of outreach programs to match what's increasingly available to interfaith couples within the Jewish community.

What interests me about the Christian-affiliated families is not the rarity and privacy of their choices, however, but the individualized process by which they arrived at them. In the Michaelsons' and Tannors' cases, their choices evolved out of deep spiritual and emotional needs within one of the partners, and the decisions were, in effect, made long before the children were even born.

There are others I've met, however, who rely on common sense and insist on making practical, if not conventional, choices once they're confronted with a tiny baby. "When we were first married, the children's religion didn't seem important," a Catholic nurse from Huntington, New York, explained matter-of-factly. "But once we started having children, I had a maternal instinct about giving them some religious training and having them all belong to something. All I knew was that when I was growing up there was a family where one child was Catholic, another was Protestant, and another was Jewish, and they were in and out of psychiatric institutions. I wanted unity in our family. I wanted our children to know who and what they were and where they belonged."

Joined by her husband, a Jewish doctor whose parents eventually attended all three children's baptisms, she found a small Catholic congregation near their home that had a welcoming priest, a few interfaith families among its members, and a Sunday school presently attended by their two oldest children. "Our main interest is that the kids be happy and not torn between either side," summarized the thirty-six-year-old woman, a product of a Catholic/Protestant marriage. "Our responsibility is to teach them something solid right now."

For many other interfaith couples, however, the commitments are much slower to evolve. It may take time to accept the reality that one parent cares much more about his or her religious attachments than the other parent does. It may also take time for parents to work through their negative or ambivalent feelings about a heritage before they can comfortably introduce its richness to their children. "How long it's taken me to accept my background. Not to advocate it. Not to want to return to it. Just to feel relaxed about it!" said a forty-three-year-old Kansas woman with an interfaith son. Getting older and somewhat wiser had helped her gradually see her family and the symbols of her childhood in a more forgiving, acceptable light.

Sometimes a crisis is necessary to force a choice and a reevaluation, however, as in the case of a New York City artist whose younger twenty-three-year-old brother died suddenly in a boating accident. In the face of that traumatic loss, the woman found herself relying upon her religious beliefs and her Protestant family for comfort and assurance. The factors that had dampened her religious commitment for years before the accident—her Jewish husband's lack of religious conviction and, in her eyes, the disappointing models her parents had become—no longer mattered or dictated her plans for her children. Indeed, her parents displayed incredible strength during their ordeal. Her husband, who will probably always cover his eyes and groan when his wife talks about prayer or heaven, found security as well in a loving family unit (something he'd never had as a child) bound together by a shared experience.

"It took time for me to have respect for my background and accept how much I cared about it. I'm finally taking initiative," the young mother told me, two years after her brother's death. She had recently enrolled her daughter in Sunday school at her parents' Methodist church.

"Among other things, I love the idea that my child will learn the hymns," she continued. "It's a way for them to feel close to her own history, her family and community around her. She'll know she's not alone."

Whatever the timetable or the particular synthesis of

considerations at work, all of these interfaith parents approach their child-raising decisions with openness and regard for each other. They've tested out their choices, supported each other's feelings, and dared to weigh the disadvantages of their plans.

Some of the Christian spouses wish they could share more about the inner workings of their faith with partners who aren't as immersed in religion as they are. Many also keep searching for a more perfect church where their special interests would be better met. Some parents question whether the Jewish component in their family shouldn't be handled with more intensity and effort; it's usually the Christian partner, in fact, who wonders whether the annual seders and visits to the Jewish relatives are enough to connect the children to the Jewish parent's heritage. Some of these Jewish parents, in turn, realize they have more to resolve in their emotional revolt against their parents and background, a search that can only help their children feel more assured about their Jewish inheritance. Nevertheless, all the children in these families benefit from the spirit of honesty and fairness in their parents' carefully considered choices.

JEWISH

When I think about the reasons why such a large percentage of the couples I've met have decided to raise their children within the Jewish faith, I keep finding three guidelines at work. They feel love and affection for Judaism. They feel a responsibility to contribute to it and do their part to guarantee Jewish survival. And in some cases, they feel pressure from family and community.

The love is easy to understand. It's what Aaron Burt Siegel, a Reform rabbi from New York, talks about when he explains his feelings about Judaism. "It's a gargantuan interest in my life. It always was. I sing Jewish songs in the shower; I dance Jewish dances. I feel that everything about me is Jewish—every feeling, every attitude, every value," he explained in his office at the American Jewish Committee. His wife, Karen, who grew up in a Lutheran family in Wisconsin, had begun studying to convert to Judaism shortly before they met at the University of Wisconsin. But given her future husband's religious commitment and professional plans, it was natural as well for her to become Jewish and guarantee a Jewish home and identity for the son they'd eventually have. Her husband's passion and full-time dedication spilled into all corners of their home and became an experience they could share.

Not everyone, of course, is as absorbed by Judaism as the warm, exuberant rabbi. Barbara Radin is not a cleric but a real estate broker who attends a synagogue three times a year at most. Nevertheless, her heritage is an important part of her life that she wants to offer her young son, Edward. "My childhood memories are positive ones," the thirty-seven-year-old New Yorker explained. "I've always loved the peacefulness in the synagogue. And to me, Hebrew school means learning that there's over 5,700 years of history to be proud of and lots of prayers and stories to learn and act out. Why wouldn't I want my son to have that continuity? What's religion for, after all, but having a link to the past that gives you perspective on how important and unimportant all your troubles are?"

Barbara's choices for her son are made somewhat easier by her husband's negative associations with his own religious instruction. Raised Baptist, a religion he angrily associates with "a thousand controls and laws about what not to do and feel," Peter Scanelli has no interest in offering his own child the regimen that's given him such trouble over the years. What the lawyer loves, instead, is his family, its rural values and deep connectedness to the land it has farmed for generations. Recently, he and Barbara built a weekend house in his family's back pasture so they could feel part of that heritage and community and expose their son to its special beauty.

Barbara, meanwhile, eases her husband into the Jewish aspect of their lives. Well aware of Peter's wariness about all organized religion, she's initiated a gentle and cautious progression of ceremonies and introductions that have, in fact, pleased her husband and made him feel at home. After she had suggested that a rabbi marry them, Peter found one through a friend, and two years later, when Barbara asked to have an informal religious ceremony to name their baby after her late father, Peter warmly invited the rabbi back. "I listened carefully to every word the guy said, and nothing was amiss," the lawyer recalled, a year after the naming ceremony and a year before they agreed to enroll their son in Jewish nursery school. "Actually, I liked the whole event we had for Edward, especially the part about the baby being part of such an ancient culture."

When she heard her husband talk so comfortably about his experiences with Judaism, Barbara laughed. "Peter and I have always agreed that a child doesn't need religion to be a human being. Our relationship is much more important than our little boy dressing up as King Ahasueras in the Purim play; that's always been clear. Whenever this subject starts to make Peter crazy, I'll drop it." Turning toward her husband with a broad, infectious grin, she added, "But so far, so good."

Paradoxically, it may be the Christian parent's affection for his or her background that also influences the choice of a Jewish education for the child. Many Christian mothers and some fathers take the initiative to teach Judaism out of fondness and regard for their own memories and dreams about what childhood should involve. "I'm the one who's pushing Judaism," said Aileen Jacobsen, a stockbroker who grew up in a churchgoing family in Minnesota. When her son turned six, he began a once-a-week class after school at the Reform synagogue in her Manhattan neighborhood. "Why doesn't it bother me that he's going to a synagogue rather than a church?" asked the accomplished executive. "A lot of my best friends are Jews. I trust them. They're nice people with good values. My own upbringing was very positive and not threatened by the religious instruction I received. I assume religion helps people learn to be better people."

Her husband Benjamin, a lawyer whose own religious

experiences as a child were "tepid, at best," is delighted by his wife's affection for Judaism. He'd never celebrated a Passover seder, in fact, until Aileen gathered his Jewish family together at their home the past spring. "Ben's parents found it 'absolutely charming,' " Aileen recalled. "We were scrambling through the book, learning as we went along."

Love and affection, as well as responsibility and a dose of pressure, shaped what can only be called the evolution of Bob and Nancy Lebenthal in their chain of decisions affecting the religious life of their large family in a suburb outside Boston. Their history is a shifting series of considerations, beginning with their own emotional preferences fostered by the similar ways they grew up.

Bob, a tall, blond, muscular man, was the oldest of five children raised in a Conservative Jewish home in a suburban town near where he lives today. His parents' synagogue was a vibrant community with a charismatic rabbi who inspired his parents to immerse themselves for decades in active support for Israel and other Jewish causes. "I learned that it was important to preserve Jewish people and never walk away from them. But I was torn," he added, "because I never learned anything that made religion very relevant to my life. After my bar mitzvah I was disgusted by all that rigamarole and how little I learned about real issues and human relationships that could help me live in this world. I drifted away."

Nancy, a lithe, outgoing woman who runs a complicated household as well as an extensive business she manages with her husband, is also the oldest of five children and the product of a childhood involved in the life of a suburban religious institution, in her case a Methodist church outside of Chicago. Her liberal-minded parents sang in the choir and contributed time and money to a host of Christian-sponsored social services. Whereas Bob's friends came from Hebrew school, Nancy's came from Youth Group. She went on uplifting retreats and loved the sacred music and teen discussions, important religious memories that remain with her as an adult.

But once the Lebenthals got married, had two small children, and moved to a new town with an array of religious choices, they scanned the possibilities and settled on the Unitarian Church. The minister had the warmth and charisma that Bob had seen in his parents' rabbi, and the community was as cosmopolitan, religiously mixed, and vibrant as any they'd ever experienced. Nancy heard the hymns and felt peaceful; Bob, as well as Nancy, loved the intellectual stimulation and the many friends they met during the wide-ranging discussions. "My head is in the Unitarian Church but my heart is in the Jewish Center," Bob once told the minister. What moved the Lebenthals to turn their attentions to the Jewish Center was not that contradiction, however.

"Our daughter was about nine when she started talking about a bat mitzvah. My parents who live nearby had been prepping her," Bob explained when he started to discuss the reasons why they eventually drifted away from the church and began attending services at the Conservative synagogue in town. "My son, who was seven then, zeroed in on the money he was going to make if he had a bar mitzvah; our daughter wanted to please her grandparents. I must say I felt some relief when we agreed to enroll our daughter in Hebrew school twice a week and show support by attending the services at the temple. I don't think I would have insisted on it without being nudged."

"It was pretty much the right choice," Nancy added, as she buttoned up the sweaters on their two youngest children, five and three, who were born around the time the family made a commitment to the older siblings' Jewish education. "Adolescence is difficult enough without one more uncertainty to have to cope with. Besides, Unitarianism isn't so great for kids," she said, looking up for a moment before tackling the children's untied shoelaces.

Bob continued her thought. "It's much easier to teach children about the specific beliefs and traditions of their ancestors than it is to introduce them to big, open questions that adults are prepared to explore," he said. "At the very least, our kids have an identity to work with, a secure place to begin. Otherwise, I think they're subject to a generalized anxiety."

For their suburban neighbors, Carol and Tom Weiss, the responsibility that decided their plans to raise their three children as Jews was more rational and practical than anything else. "Where else would they learn the basics of half their heritage if they weren't taught in a synagogue?" they asked themselves. Hebrew, Jewish history, the reasons for the founding of the State of Israel, the basic prayers in a Sabbath or holiday service were not such an integral part of American culture that their children would absorb them, as if by osmosis. "We made a decision at one point, based on the fact that there are only five-and-a-half million Jews out of a total population of 200 million people in the United States," Carol explained, while her husband, a surgeon who is Jewish, served us cups of tea in their large living room full of holiday poinsettias. "It's a Christian world, and if we didn't give our children Jewish training they'd get nothing," Carol continued. "The kids started Hebrew school, two to three times a week. I did the carpooling."

When their first child was born, Carol had converted to Judaism, something she thought was necessary to keep any mixed marriage intact. After five years, however, she realized her marriage was stable, and the choice wasn't working for her. "I was trying to be something I wasn't," she remembered. "I felt fakey, as if I were living a lie." When her Midwestern father became ill and moved in with them for five months of nursing before he died, Carol continued her family's Jewish observances as consistently as ever, but she also began attending the Presbyterian church, alone or with her husband and one or more of their three children.

The Lebenthal and Weiss families are similar in the honest way they've tried to integrate Christian experiences within their primary and resolved commitment to Judaism for their children. "We kick and scream, but we're willing to work on doing both in this household," said Tom Weiss. "Among other things, it makes our marriage work."

"I like it that our kids won't be ostriches with their heads stuck in the sand, locked into a phobia about Christians and Christianity," Bob Lebenthal suggested. "They see their mother comfortable in a synagogue. They see their father comfortable in a church. I think it's just as important, in fact, that they understand the majority religion as well as their own minority one. They live in a country where Christianity is dominant, after all. It's shaped everything from the art on the museum walls to the issues argued every day in Washington. My kids should understand where so much of American politics and culture comes from."

For Deborah Levin, however, that ecumenical and intellectual blend of religious experiences is not the dream guiding her choices for raising her children. "We're not one big merry band celebrating everyone's religious holidays," explained the mother of three who decided at thirty, before her first baby was born, to convert to Judaism. "Originally I converted for the kids," the dark-haired woman with a round, friendly face recalled. "I figured the burden of child rearing was mine, and though I've never been a particularly religious person, I took that aspect of their education seriously. I knew my husband couldn't see his children raised as Christians. If I was going to stay at home for a few years and be a 'MaMa,' which I was because I had two master's degrees and was studying for a doctorate, I figured I'd do my job right. I took the plunge and called my husband's old rabbi in Boston to talk about converting."

When we talked in her comfortable New York City apartment filled with pictures of the children, Jewish objects on the bookshelves, and a sweet-smelling bald toddler circling around her knees, Deborah reviewed the many ways her choice had been a joyous and liberating surprise for her. "It's my thing!" she said jubilantly. Not only did she discover a closely knit Reconstructionist congregation that stimulates and warmly accepts her husband, an insurance executive, and herself, but she found in Judaism an outlet for her intelligence and commitment to her family and community. "Judaism adds so much texture to our lives," said the mother who recently became president of the congregation. "At home we light the Shabbat candles, sometimes I bake challah and we always seem to be preparing for one holiday or another. At Hebrew school a few afternoons a week, our children study Jewish history and learn the songs and dances, the prayers, the language and rituals. I'm not looking for someone or something to direct our lives, but every day I find it comforting to hook up with a culture and belief system that are so old and complete.

"Conversion is like moving to another city," she philosophized when asked whether she missed Christmas or anything else about her former identity as a Methodist. "If you love the new city, you don't miss the old one," she said assuredly.

Indeed, for Deborah there wasn't a sense of abandoning much of her past when she converted, first with a *mikvah*, the ritual cleansing bath, and then with a ceremony in the synagogue during which she renounced her former beliefs, pledged to raise her children as Jews, and cast her lot with the Jewish people. As with most converts, according to a 1986 study by Egon Mayer, she remained close to her family. When she first announced her plans to convert, in fact, her Methodist mother smiled and confessed she'd always wanted to be a Catholic.

"My mom is proud that her grandchildren have a religious background," Deborah explained. "She brags to her church group all the time, and I tell her, 'Mom, don't you know you're supposed to be ashamed?' "

Deborah is like the majority of converts in other ways as well. She's a woman, as are 90 percent of them according to Mayer's findings. She converted before or close to marriage. And since converting, she's become far more religiously committed than she was as an adolescent.

She's also one of an increasing number of converts in leadership positions within the Jewish community. On the West Coast, for example, Lydia Kukoff directs a nationwide program for adult Jewish education. On the East Coast, Rachel Cowan is a rabbinical student who has spent the last five years counseling interfaith couples and administering educational programs for a revitalized Manhattan synagogue, Ansche Chesed. Both women have written books about their experiences.

The expansive, committed joy that Deborah, Lydia, and Rachel exhibit is not always the case, however. I've met other women who feel their choice to convert has cost them more than they've gained. "At twenty-three, I went along with my husband and mother-in-law, and it was easy. But the older I get the more I feel I made a big concession," said thirty-seven-year-old Karen Miller, a Milwaukee mother who drew up an agreement shortly before she and her husband Donald were married. In it, she promised to convert to Judaism, have a bar mitzvah for a son, and enroll all children in Hebrew school. He, in turn, promised not to press for a bris (a promise he violated) or any more religious observance from her than her conversion; they agreed to celebrate Christmas in a secular way (without church services, a crèche, or talk of Jesus).

Karen would be the first to agree with the clergy's common recommendation that interfaith parents reach a decision about the children's religious identity sometime before they're born. "We laid our cards on the table early," she said. "My parents have had plenty of time to reconcile themselves to our choice. If my husband and I hadn't agreed, we'd probably argue about this issue eternally."

No matter how clear-cut their decision or how much it appears that their potential conflicts have been put to rest, however, there are other issues, both marital and spiritual, for the Millers to address. Karen resents that she sustains the children's Jewish life without help from her husband or his mother. "Donald pays that godawful membership fee to the synagogue, saying, 'Whatever it costs, of course, of course.' But does he ever darken the doorway? Does he ever do the carpool? Does his mother ever do more for Chanukah than send a check to the children in January?" she asked heatedly. "I was willing to convert to fit into a family and a community. My husband never conceded anything."

Edwin Friedman, rabbi and therapist from Maryland,

feels strongly that the Millers' pattern is a classic one. "The woman who converts when she gets married (as opposed to those who choose conversion at a mature age after years of consideration) tends to be adaptive, and her husband is a rigid man under the thumb of his mother," he suggested. Conversion, he feels, is often a coercive tactic by families far more interested in emotional control over their children than religious or spiritual commitment to Judaism and its continuity.

Indeed, I've talked with many converts to Judaism who made their choice in response to pressure from in-laws. Diplomacy and accomodation dictated a religious commitment they wouldn't have made otherwise. In some cases, it resulted in a feeling of forfeiture and loss, as if they severed ties to an old way of belief and participation without replacing them with new bonds that nurture them emotionally. Karen Miller feels that disconnectedness, as if her religious identity has been on ice, suspended for too long.

I've found other cases, however, where the compliance was always an easy price to pay and one that ultimately led to a warm, resonant surround of family and faith for future children as well as the converted parent and spouse. "I really love God. I adore my husband. And I love my family who wasn't concerned about my becoming a Jew," said one of many women whose decision led to positive results.

"I never felt I was losing my identity, my family, or my ethics and morality. I felt I was joining a culture and becoming part of another mainstream of humanity," explained a documentary filmmaker who also chose Judaism to pacify an insistent in-law. One of the rare 10 percent of intermarried men who do convert, he was a thirty-five-year-old "open to new ideas and experiences . . . hardly wet behind the ears" when, ten years ago, he underwent a ceremonial circumcision in which a drop of blood was taken from his penis (a simpler Reform ritual than the hospitalization that would have been required if he had converted under Orthodox and some Conservative auspices). "Not bad at all," he said.

But moreover, the preparation, ceremony, and especially the decade he's had to develop a sense of tradition and closeness to a family and the Jewish community have been meaningful, "more so every day." His son, his marriage, and his own identity have been able to grow within that choice —the key, of course, to a wise and thoughtful plan for handling and enhancing the Jewish dimension of interfaith lives.

"BOTH"

No choice available to interfaith parents is as exploratory as this one. Without the imprimatur of organized religion or a history of successful implementation, this option to raise children within both traditions is the new, untested, yet compelling one for many families. Step by step, they're negotiating their way with each other, their children, and their faith communities. With hindsight, their choices seem logical and consistent in the way they've unfolded. But to the parents themselves, all of whom are still trying to make the most of this experimental course, the patterns seem far more elusive and unpredictable.

Joanna Shulman and Garry Lloyd, for instance, have worked out a mature and balanced approach to the Jewish and Christian duality in their home, and after twelve years of marriage they're more secure than ever in their arrangement to give their two daughters, ages eleven and nine, meaningful experiences with both Joanna's Jewish faith and Garry's Christian one. It's fitting that they'd have settled on such a plan. They're strong personalities who care equally about their religious and ethnic attachments, and their marriage has always been predicated on equality, mutual respect, and a willingness to accomodate their differences. Handling the issue of religion, however, turned out to be far more touchy and unsettling than they ever expected it to be.

"In the beginning, religion was a snap," Joanna recalled, thinking back over Garry's and her wedding ceremony at the Ethical Culture Society and their early years of marriage. "At our wedding, I read from the 'Song of Solomon.' Garry read from the New Testament. He broke the glass. Everyone said, 'Terrific! How nice!' It was only after that sweet and easy part, when our understanding of our backgrounds started to deepen, that we began to get touchy about religion, and how much we cared about it. The more uncomfortable we got, the more we didn't talk about it."

Indeed, there was lots they could have spoken about, as they chose names for their daughters, celebrated each other's holidays, began to register their unexpected longings for more religious participation, and started to consider the larger questions about how to raise their children. As Garry had once observed, with words that bear repeating, "My theory is that you take a long trip out into the wilderness in your twenties and thirties, and then with parenthood and aging you're brought back home to your childhood memories." Garry and Joanna weren't at all sure what to do about their religious memories that came flooding back, however. They were all too aware of the conventional responses available to them—to go with one faith or another—but channeling their feelings into those narrow alternatives seemed impossible.

Garry wasn't comfortable with a policy that relegated one partner's traditions to a secondary position, which would have been the case, he felt, if they chose to raise their daughters exclusively as Christians or as Jews. "It's a funny thing about self-denial," he said. "Selflessness is only good up to a point. I know it from my wife who'll give of herself enormously until suddenly she's had enough, and then she becomes absolutely furious, usually at me. With self-denial, there's always a kicker. Sooner or later, there's a price to pay."

Joanna was also sensitive to the nuances of power within their marriage and unwilling, as well, to impose her needs at the expense of her husband's. "I was all bottled up and worried that even the smallest thing I did, like buying a challah for Friday night or putting a white cloth on the table for Chanukah, would make Garry feel edgy, as if I were trying to take over and make our kids wholly Jewish."

What ultimately freed both Garry and Joanna to express their religious feelings was simply their agreement to raise their daughters with something of both traditions. Having reached an understanding that their home would support both faiths, they could comfortably nourish their own religious identities and wholeheartedly share Jewish and Christian experiences with each other and their children.

Through a similar process, Jordan and I have also decided to raise our children as "both." For us, as with many couples, the other choices involved a forfeiting we weren't willing to absorb. After years of doing "both" but feeling hesitant about affirming it as a valid and worthy choice, we woke up one day to its being the best alternative for us, one that felt right for our children and ourselves.

Although the commitment to "both" was a liberating decision for us, as for Garry, Joanna and many other couples, the task of working through our personal definition of "both" was only beginning. Without the clear-cut guidelines of a single faith or congregation to follow, we, like other families, had to find our own way to give our children a meaningful religious experience. How we've chosen to combine the vast array of what's Christian and what's Jewish into their lives and ours continues to be an evolving synthesis that's uniquely our own. What we share with all families engaged in doing "both," however, is the hard work and attention that are necessary to assemble this religious patchwork and make it strong and vibrant.

Determining the family's relationship with the church and synagogue is a very important choice. In the case of Garry and Joanna, for instance, he attends the Episcopal church every Sunday for the early Communion service. On holidays, Joanna and their young daughters join him, but otherwise he worships alone. Garry would have liked to be part of the late-morning service when the music and ceremony become more elaborate, but since that scheduling interferes with Sunday's family life, he's willingly opted for a pattern that allows him to be home in time for Sunday breakfast.

Joanna's attendance at the Reform synagogue is less regular but equally meaningful to her. She attends many services during the High Holy Days and often joins a friend—usually an intermarried Christian or Jewish parent—for a Passover service. Periodically on the Sabbath, she'll take her daughters or go alone to the synagogue. For many years, the family's major events together have been the children's services held during Rosh Hashanah and Yom Kippur and, days later, the jubilant ceremony at Simchat Torah.

For Joanna, the celebrations of Jewish tradition at home are equally important endeavors, however. True to Judaism, which honors and relies upon the ceremonies at home to transmit its faith and history, Joanna has gradually enriched the family's way of acknowledging the Sabbath, Chanukah, and Passover. "On Friday nights, we light the candles, and nowadays, the girls join me in saying the blessings," she explained. "We do Chanukah for eight days in a sweet and steady way with games at home and small, personal gifts. Passover is the really demanding holiday, however. We always have at least two seders, one with my Jewish family and another with our friends, most of whom are intermarried with children. I cook, Garry leads the singing, and it's quite a marvelous—and tiring—week for us . . . only equaled by what we do at Christmas!" she added, sighing with mock exhaustion.

It's impossible to pass on the essence of Judaism or Christianity without some meaningful involvement with the church, the synagogue, and each faith's celebrations at home. Families handle those responsibilities in diverse ways, however. Some support membership in both the church and synagogue and feel comfortable within both congregations, while others aren't able to find a church or synagogue that incorporates the ritual and philosophy of their family. Instead, they look to their single-faith relatives and friends to include their children in a variety of religious events that wouldn't be available otherwise. Many interfaith families welcome the opportunities, for instance, to have their children join their Jewish cousins for a Sabbath service in the synagogue once a year, to celebrate Christmas Eve with their grandparents in the Baptist church, to share Passover with their observant neighbors, or to sit securely between both parents for Rosh Hashanah in the Jewish Center nearby.

Interfaith parents who are assertively trying to give their children "both" are always reaching out for new resources that can communicate the best of each faith to their children. The search is a continual one for the individuals, books, trips, courses, conversations, and broad experiences that will reinforce a child's dual identity and give him or her a basic foundation in two faiths to build on as he or she matures. Whether it's researching a sectarian summer camp, planning a trip to Israel, or figuring out how to handle the Christmas/Chanukah season, the initiative is always in the hands of the parents, and, in fact, the responsibility must be theirs if their choice of "both" is to be a responsible and vital one.

Within those interfaith families who have made such a commitment, there's an infectious spirit of pride and enthusiasm about their choice. Because there's no programmed religious life to hand their children, they've had to thoughtfully address and create it themselves, and in that effort, they've been able to grow in their understanding—and acceptance—of their spouse's roots and their own. If they've reached out to other interfaith families to carry out a project, such as an interfaith seder, or if they've simply talked to other members of interfaith families about their questions and discoveries, they've also felt the exhilaration of being part of a growing, confident community, increasingly stimulated by its new ideas and emotions. The necessary involvement in the process of raising their Jewish/Christian children has given mothers *and* fathers, together, a consciousness of religion and its important role in their lives. For many parents, that affirmation alone is an invaluable one to offer their children, one that may not be delivered as meaningfully within single-faith homes where the religious program can sometimes become an assumed and lifeless routine.

Where the confidence falters, however, is the point at which parents consider the *depth* of their children's religious instruction. "We give them both worlds, but are they strong worlds?" asks a Catholic friend of mine, uneasily. She and her Jewish husband offer her interfaith children an abundance of Jewish and Christian experiences yet they wonder how their rich patchwork will hold up without a more formal and long-term religious program woven into it. The choice of religious instruction for parents raising their children as "both" remains a challenge.

"We wanted our son to know more about Judaism, so it seemed sensible to enroll him in an afterschool class at the Reform synagogue in the neighborhood," an intermarried Jewish mother of a sixth-grade son recalled, describing her attempts to fill that instructional gap with a traditional form of religious schooling. "What became clear, unfortunately, was that the program and its teachers couldn't accept the Christian part of my son's identity. They didn't value it. They didn't think it was something for him to be proud of. They wouldn't even acknowledge it, except in a negative way. Only his Jewishness counted in their eyes, and that exclusive message wasn't what we wanted him to hear."

Had she enrolled her child in a Christian program, it's not unlikely that she'd have found the same insensitivity to his Jewish needs. The bias and inexperience with interfaith families, especially with the children, conditions the teaching in many, if not most, Jewish and Christian institutions, and that imbalance and limited perspective dissuade many parents from taking advantage of that ready-made option.

But how can our children acquire the knowledge that formal instruction can facilitate? Judaism is a strange and ancient faith, with a history, calendar, even a language of its own, that requires years of study to appreciate. Christianity might seem easier to comprehend because it's so all-pervasive in American society, but it too has its vocabulary, rituals, cycles of the year, theology, and history that aren't communicated without careful teaching.

In my daughter Rachel's school, Trinity School in Manhattan, an exciting experiment has begun to create an afterschool program for the large number of interfaith offspring in the elementary grades. Its goal is to introduce the children more deeply to the two traditions that are part of their heritage. A Conservative rabbi and Presbyterian minister, affectionately called "our bearded wise men" by the parents, team-teach the classes once a week. The curriculum focuses on each faith's major holidays, as a way to ground the information in the children's concrete experience and provide a way to explore the core of each faith and the rich ways it's observed. The clergy, who are skilled in teaching fifth- and sixth-graders—our first group of twelve students—insist that they're not teaching an impersonal comparative religion course; instead, they're engaging the children in exploring their family's two long histories and helping them understand the compatibility, the differences, and the riches that exist. This year's pilot has been an unqualified success with all the participants.

In planning the children's interfaith education, it became very clear to the parents involved that they also had a great need for information about both religions, and just as importantly, a need to share their feelings and concerns about managing the religious duality in their homes. As a consequence, a second part of the interfaith program has gathered the parents over thirty together (from third, fourth, fifth, and sixth grades) for discussion once a month among themselves. The clergy joins them to share their observations on the children's work, explore religious content, and help them plan further events: for parents and children together, from a seder to a tour of various Sabbath services. Some parents are interested in creating a ceremony for those adolescents who aren't having a confirmation or bar/bat mitzvah; others are eager to arrange a series of lectures for interfaith families throughout the thirteen grades of the school. In its first year, the pilot has been an unqualified success with all its participants—parents, clergy, and children (who think it's fun). This program, which may well be the first of its kind in the country, is likely to expand and inspire others.

No one can predict the outcome of this pilot effort or any other way that families have chosen to support both faiths in their homes. Whether they feel their solution, at least for now, is the Unitarian Church or the Ethical Culture Society, a total reliance on education at home, a mixture of traditional Sunday school with a comfortable Jewish/Christian homelife, or a commitment to designing a new form of interfaith education, the balance will always be a delicate one. Given that unpredictability, I'm always drawn to a statement by Rabbi Edward Feld, the Jewish chaplain at Princeton University, that reminds me what we are, in fact, aiming and preparing for. "You can say there are good things in both religions," he said. "But if it has power, a religion speaks to you and gives order to your life. You have to take a stance within it and hear the special voice of that religious method. One chooses a path to go on."

Rabbi Feld's words remind us that children will ultimately evolve into their own religious identity. The best we can do as parents is to give them a good start on the way.

SECULAR

Some couples, of course, make the decision to raise their children without a religious engagement with either Christianity or Judaism. It's their choice to raise their children in a secular way. They have little interest in, and maybe little respect for, the role of formal religion, and they're comfortable staking out their lives without it.

Often their passions come from their engagement with the world. These secular mixed-marriage couples, for instance, may run the town paper, fight for preservation of the land, dedicate themselves to science or social work, the arts or law, and they involve their children in those vital issues. Some parents choose to sit down on Sunday morning for a family conference and discuss ethics and the Ten Commandments as they review the past week and their expectations for the one to come. They're proud of their passionate sense of responsibility, their community involvement, and their stimulating and cosmopolitan friendships. In these families, you'll find a spirited interest in everything from animals to acting to politics to music. Spirituality may be a part of it.

"My spirituality went into music," said Lucy Simon, the composer and sister of performer Carly Simon, as she sat back in a large white wicker armchair on the wide porch of a Long Island beach house. "When I was being wheeled in for surgery recently, I had my sisters around me, and out of the blue, groggy from medication, I said, 'Let's sing.' And we sang two songs. One was a folk song. The other was the benediction, 'The Lord bless you and keep you,' which we've sung at my mother's birthdays, at weddings, and probably at every occasion since my sister Joanna brought it home from high school and we all learned it. Songs have always been one way of blessing the happy occasions, and in this instance, it was a way of easing the pain and sharing a harmony we all feel."

Lucy's Jewish/Christian parents had no interest whatsoever in organized religion. "We never acknowledged the Jewish holidays," said Lucy, and though Christmas and Easter were more widespread in our house, the celebrations had nothing to do with Jesus Christ. Maybe we were told about Him, but celebrations were about the family getting together with lots of cousins, aunts, and uncles singing at the piano."

In secular families, sometimes, there's nothing at all religious or even spiritual about the family celebrations. Christmas and Chanukah may be either perfunctory events or joyous, yet decidedly secular ones in which the huge family gathers together and duplicates its own traditions year after year.

For other families large and small, the "sacred event" isn't Christmas, the Sabbath, or Yom Kippur. It's really any party at home with creative, interesting, urban friends celebrating life and work. Their relatives, friends, and professional colleagues are their special inspiration, and the love they all feel for each other is what they offer their children.

What is true for these families is true for all of us. We make our choices and guide them as best we can, but we can never predict with certainty the outcome of our decisions.

Our children are special individuals who ultimately make their own choices. Some of their choices will surprise us. Some will delight us, and some will disappoint us. "Children of believers breed unbelievers who breed believers again," said Rabbi David Greenberg from East Hampton. It's a cycle I've found over and over again.

There are my friends the Mandels, who raised their daughter in a secular fashion only to find themselves, thirty years later, attending the bar mitzvah of their grandson. As one woman in an interfaith marriage said to me, "David and I have no interest whatsoever in religion. Occasionally we've said, 'And what should we be doing about the children's religious training?' in the same tone and importance as 'Do you think we should recover the couch?' or 'I think the Maytag is wearing out.' We should have known that we'd end up with a son studying for a bar mitzvah."

What's important to bear in mind is that families have the right to their choices. They have options, many of which they're not even aware of yet. As parents, however, they also have the responsibility to prepare their children for a life that's able to draw freely from the strength and beauty of their roots. It's important, at the very least, to provide children with a fair exposure to both parents' faiths that allow them to be proud, comfortable, and knowledgeable about their duality so that it enhances rather than inhibits their lives.

CHAPTER

9

TALKING ABOUT GOD

One morning when Rachel was six, she slid into her seat at the breakfast table, and between spoonfuls of Cheerios, looked up at Jordan and me. "I know God's a boy and a girl, and He's very nice because He made the world for you to live in," she said, pointing with the spoon. "He's like a person which is air . . . like when you go through a cloud you don't know where God is really."

Jordan and I looked at each other. It had been years since either of us had said more than a sentence or two about God. Until our children came along with their questions and discoveries, we kept those private, unexamined, and very ambivalent feelings about religion to ourselves, and no one asked us to sort them out, least of all ourselves. But now with parenthood, it was time to talk.

We felt totally unprepared for all discussions. Rachel, of course, would chat merrily about how God is her father and my father and "everybody's father in the whole world," while I clutched my coffee cup and worried that any minute she'd press for a far more *definitive* explanation of the *real* nature of God. Until I started talking to interfaith parents who confessed their own awkwardness and confusion when they discussed faith and God with their children, I didn't realize how commonly, how understandably we share the same feelings of self-consciousness.

There are many reasons why we struggle with the subject. Odds are that we weren't raised to talk comfortably about our spiritual life. That was intimate territory, almost like a secret between God and oneself. Marie Sabin, a Catholic educator in New Jersey who has been married for twenty-six years to a Jewish book editor, nodded when I asked her about the tentativeness that parents feel. "It's tough to talk to kids about God when you can barely define for yourself what you believe," she explained. "Remember, many of us have had very little practice with this kind of expression. Our childhood training stressed a private relationship with God, not sharing one's faith with others.

"I see the same embarrassment," continued the mother of five, "during the regular Catholic church service when people are supposed to turn to their neighbors and say, simply, 'The peace of the Lord be with you.' Vatican II added that blessing over twenty years ago, but some Catholics still can't get the words out of their mouths," she said. "The phrase is too personal."

The irony is that sex and religion have swapped places. Whereas we probably can rattle on comfortably about most details of sexual experience, our grandparents couldn't. But they, in turn, could talk freely about God, especially to children full of questions.

Part of our problem is a semantic one. Rabbi Harold Kushner, in his clear, encouraging book *When Children Ask About God*, which he wrote before his best seller *When Bad Things Happen to Good People*, reminds us that "God" is a "convenient time-honored code word for discussing the problems and promises of being alive and human in this world, a term which lends our discussion a great deal of emotional momentum and a continuity with the past." After all, he adds, it's part of "a vocabulary so rich in emotional connotation and evocative power . . . We are not starting a new enterprise."

Nevertheless, many parents hear the word and get scrupulously analytical about whether they *really* believe in God or not and what *is* God? Or they get lost in negative associations with organized religion. They worry that anything they say might conflict with their spouse's supposedly different theology, which is even more fuzzy to them than their own. Or they avoid the word entirely and more readily talk about the Universe, the Force, the Power, cosmic flow, love, universal energy, "The Light Within," which is a Quaker phrase, or Jung's references to the universal religious symbolism in the human consciousness. I've lost count of everyone who's inquired about my book, stuttering, "Are you going to write about . . . ah . . . God?"

The anthropomorphism that comes naturally to children also makes us uncomfortable. "Parents get so antsy when a kid talks about God as an old man in the sky with a long, white beard," said Reverend Daniel Heischman in his study at Trinity School. "The image is so foreign to them now, and they want to get away from what they were brought up with."

But what can replace our childish naivete? The trouble is we're not sure what beliefs we've substituted. Our feelings have evolved dramatically since we were young, and we haven't always kept careful track of them.

James W. Fowler noted in his book, *Stages of Faith*, that adults in their twenties and thirties tend to lose interest in religion and get more deeply involved in the secular aspects of their lives. They stand back from religion and eye it critically, subjecting it to an analysis that continues to influence their thoughts and feelings even after a midlife rapproachment may have begun. Along come our children with their innocent fairytalelike beliefs and their need to know what we believe, but we don't dare say a word lest we'll damage them with our doubts and parochialism.

Not everyone's such an overearnest and confused parent. I've met many sensible adults who take the subject of

God in stride because they've figured out long ago what took me some time to realize. God isn't an unnatural subject, and no one knows that better than our children, who eagerly and very naturally go about creating religious lives for themselves, with or without our help. No matter how jumbled and confused we may be, our children pass through a series of rich and predictable transitions in their understanding of God, and with some self-knowledge, good instincts, and basic information, we can help them even more build a sure spiritual foundation that will prepare them for life.

Religious perceptions begin as early as infancy. The pioneering Unitarian educator, Dr. Sophia Fahs, wrote movingly about the fundamentally spiritual message that a parent communicates to a child from the first moment of birth—that the world is loving and constant and responsive to his needs. A child must develop "a faith in life," says Dr. Fahs, in her classic, *Today's Children and Yesterday's Heritage*. Through all the senses of touch, taste, smell, sight, and sound, the child learns to trust, enjoy, and make sense out of his or her immense and complicated surroundings.

Awe and wonder are a natural part of a child's repertoire of feelings. For what's more mysteriously beautiful and powerful than rain, wind, music, flowers, sunshine, and shadows, especially when they're experienced for the first time? The discoveries can feel overwhelming to a small child. While I've been working on this chapter, I've often thought about an afternoon I spent with Rachel when she was less than a year old. I had wheeled her in a carriage onto the campus of Columbia University, when suddenly we turned a bend, and the huge expanse of the academic quadrangle opened up before us. Rachel's whole body stiffened with excitement. She had never seen such a vast space, and her head rotated slowly as if to comprehend something so unbelievable and awe-inspiring that she had to feast on it for minutes before I could move on.

In England, the Religious Experience Research Unit of Oxford University examined 500 reports by adults of sacred experiences they'd had when they were children, usually age three, four, or five. Edward Robinson, director of the unit, wrote a beautiful little book called *The Original Vision* about these profound impressions that were vivid enough to be remembered decades later. The memories shared certain features—a heightened awareness of surroundings that gave the children moments of absolute joy and an astoundingly clear sense of self and direction, as well as intense feelings of peace, security, gratitude, and connectedness to the larger universe. In the book's preface, the naturalist Edward Muir wrote: "Certain dreams convince me that a child has this vision, in which there is a completer harmony of all things with each other than he will ever know again."

During a child's early years, these simple emotional experiences lay a groundwork for all further religious understanding. Before the child has words, constructs, dogmas, and ceremonies to organize and confirm his sense of the world, before he even knows the words "God" or "Jews" or "Jesus," he can *feel* the love and trust in God, other people, and oneself that's basic to all faiths; he builds from there.

Rabbi Kushner, in his own valuable book about God and children, illuminates a child's stages of religious and emotional growth by comparing them to the levels of spiritual understanding that mankind has also passed through. His thesis is a simple one: "that society's idea of God parallels the individual's idea of authority." The infant, for instance, has an egocentrism and dependency on his caretakers that's like primitive man's reliance on nature. Parents, nature, God are magical extensions of the ego, automatic guarantors of food, water, and warmth as well as harvests, raindrops, and sunshine. When the providers fail, there's surprise, anger, and terror.

But children and civilization mature and learn how to manipulate the authorities in order to get more dependable results. They enter into a second stage in which they figure out the rules and regulations that will win them approval. They learn how to bargain to get their way. And they believe that the authorities are all-powerful, all-wise figures who make decisions for them and demand obedience.

The Bible itself reflects stage-two attitudes. God has a number of personalities. He's an exacting anthropomorphic force who lays down sacred commands and punishes and rewards people according to how they follow His instructions. In the Book of Deuteronomy (11: 13–14), it's written, "And it shall come to pass, if ye shall hearken diligently unto my commandments, which I command you this day, to love the Lord your God, and to serve him with all your heart, and with all your soul, That I will give *you* the rain of your land in his due season, the first rain and the latter rain, that thou mayest gather in thy corn, and thy wine, and thine oil."

But God is also tender, compassionate, fair, and capable of extraordinary miracles such as parting the seas, turning a rib into a woman, talking to men, and making bushes catch fire without burning up.

How do children understand God? God has the looks and feelings of the authorities—living and imagined—that they also know best. When I asked Georgia, at age three, to tell me about God, she shook her head and said, "He doesn't live in my school." But at six, a more experienced Rachel thought a minute and said, "He's very nice except when He makes bad people." By seven, she described God as "like spirits. He's all white with a big white gown floating all over Him. And His voice is very deep."

An eight-year-old from Pleasantville, New York, borrowed her image of God from television commercials featuring Count Chocula, a slightly menacing but harmless ghoul who reminds me of Vincent Price. The cover of the original *My Fair Lady* album supplied an Associated Press reporter with her picture of God when she was small. "George Bernard Shaw was a puppeteer coming out of the clouds and pulling the strings on Rex Harrison who pulled the strings on Julie Andrews who was another puppet," she recalled. "That's what God was for me—someone calling the shots."

God's also a miracle worker, especially for children under nine years old who aren't compelled yet to reconcile reality with their free and magical fantasies. They adore hearing about the divine feats in the Bible; nothing's too impossible for them. And through all of childhood, they love hearing stories about good being rewarded and bad being punished. They're creating for themselves a framework of morality, and God is the wise judge.

Some children get carried away with the idea of God as what Rabbi Kushner calls "a punitive, judgmental bogeyman." But generally, if children are treated fairly in their lives, they think of God as someone who makes legitimate demands on them, like a parent with the right to tell them how to do what's right.

What matters to them is that God, like all the authorities in their lives, is fair. Because of a child's heightened sensitivity to that issue, it's understandable why an interfaith parent turned her back on her Free Methodist church when she was eight-years-old because the minister began raving about how God would punish "heathens" in Africa for not believing in Jesus. "But the little children there were innocent," she said. "I argued that they hadn't even heard about Jesus yet!" It's been remarkable to me how keenly I can recall my own childhood memories of unfairness from the authorities in my life—teachers, my minister and father who reprimanded me without justification. I can still feel the overwhelming sense of confusion and frustration generated by those thirty-year-old incidents.

For many children, especially preteens, God is also a confidant. One of the most popular books for young adults is called *Are You There God? It's Me, Margaret* by Judy Blume, and it's the story of an eleven-year-old named Margaret Simon who's half Jewish and half Christian. When she moves to a new town, she has a number of dilemmas to solve, including which religion to choose and whether to join the YWCA or the Jewish Community Center. She also wants to grow up and get her menstrual period, wear a bra, dance with someone named Philip Leroy, and "be like everybody else." So she chats with God regularly, tells Him whatever's going on, especially what's scary, and asks and bargains for help in a comfortable, sweet way, as if she's communing with the best kind of accepting, appreciative grandfather.

She's on her way toward Kushner's third stage of development when rules, morality, and the concept of God gradually become internalized and abstract. During this final level, God's not a superperson out there calling the shots but inside the individual, guiding him to know right from wrong and how best to live one's life. According to Rabbi Kushner, "God will no longer be thought of as 'our Father in Heaven,' whose approval we seek to earn but will be the divine spark in every human being and in every God-oriented community, which impels people to growth and self-fulfillment. God will be, as the Rabbis of the Talmud anticipated, the 'soul of the world,' with a spark of Him in every mature human soul."

Needless to say, the world is yet to be so enlightened. And the passage for young adults isn't speedy, guaranteed, and direct either. How could it be when teenage emotions are so variable and intense? A teenager's feelings about authority change from moment to moment; a teenager changes from moment to moment, too, and his or her image of God is naturally as multifaceted.

Daniel Heischman observed that his students commonly report two kinds of heightened religious experiences. According to the school chaplain, "The first one is 'the mountaintop experience' and has to do with feeling isolated, free, yet profoundly connected to God and Nature. The second one happens when students go off on a retreat with other kids and feel an overwhelming sense of community."

Teenagers long to feel connected to others and reinforced by a clear-cut set of rules and values, but because of their equally passionate need to feel free and independent, their identification with any community becomes complicated. When she was eleven, the character in Judy Blume's book visited a Catholic church, a Protestant church, and a synagogue in order to decide what religion to be, but she couldn't find God in any space, except at home when she was alone; she decided to postpone making any choices for a while. Older students check out their possible affiliations (which sports team, fraternity or sorority, pack of friends, political organization, and, for many of the "half and half" offspring, which religious identification) with the same earnestness. "This is the time," says Reverend Heischman, "when they're getting very serious about themselves and understanding who they are, and they know it's dangerous to be one thing or another. There's a tension between wanting to commit themselves to an ideology and stand for something yet not being ready. Dr. Erik Erikson calls it a 'moratorium.' "

Their choices are doubly emotional because of their shifting moods, and it's understandable how they project onto God—and onto all their other heroes from Mahatma Gandhi to Michael Jackson—the features that mark their own lives. God becomes deep, complex, wise, and tolerant enough to understand and accept their private, mysteriously emerging selves.

And God also becomes something to contest, challenge, analyze with their developing intellect, and think about at random times when they're playing tennis and looking up at the huge sky, lying in bed and reviewing the last eighteen years, or passing an old man on the street who suddenly reminds them of the way they used to imagine God. By the end of college, if not earlier, God tends to move to the background until marriage and childbirth begin a cycle of life all over again.

So many passages happen inevitably as emotions and intellect develop in their natural course of life, but there are five recommendations to keep in mind that can help our children develop their religious, moral, and ethical foundations with the most ease and least conflict.

1. *Help them trust themselves, the world, and God.* Long before anyone talks intellectually about God and religion, our family environment transmits the essential feelings of love, hope, self-worth, trust, and competence that give our children the inner strength and sureness, down deep, that help them love others and weather whatever life holds for them. It's up to us to enhance those virtues and make sure that nothing undermines them. "Our first responsibility," insists Rabbi Kushner, "is to maintain the child's sense of his own worth. Under no circumstances whatsoever should his religion ever be permitted to condemn him as one who has been judged and found wanting."

A child's understanding of God begins at home, by demonstration. "Sometimes I tell my sons this about God," explained Donald Graff, a popular administrator at Trinity School who was a Catholic priest for nine years before his marriage to a former nun. He turned, as if he were speaking to his seven- and ten-year-old boys, and said, "As I love you everyday by reading to you, buying your clothes, taking care of you, sitting down and trying to understand what you care about, and doing what I can to help you, so God loves all of us. God does all those things and so much more for everyone.

"I was in a restaurant recently with my family," he continued, looking back toward me, "and there was a guy there with six kids. He was screaming at them continually, yelling, 'Don't do this, don't do that.' It was cruel, and everyone was terribly upset. There wasn't a moment that was loving. The relationships seemed so hopeless." Graff scowled, gently shook his head, and added, "No matter what good things that father might say about God, they would never stick."

2. *Respond in a relaxed and honest way.* At one point in this research, I telephoned Rabbi Kushner for my own reassurances because it seemed impossible that I'd ever learn how to make appropriate and supportive comments to my daughters, let alone to the readers of this book.

He was wonderful. He laughed and said, "What makes any discussion about God possible is that kids basically outgrow our mistakes. A consistent, loving attitude covers multiple slips."

I've also felt better since it dawned on me that talking about religion is very much like talking about sex. The same rules of thumb apply, such as to remember that talking gets easier as you go along. And answer only what you're asked, keeping the answers simple and tied to a child's experience. Complexity is for our adult selves only.

I'm reminded of a recent episode with a friend's very bright six-year-old son Zachary who's half Christian and half Jewish. A Jewish book editor visited Zachary's house in Connecticut, and the little boy decided to ask him some questions. Plopping himself down on the couch beside the visitor, he asked, "Are you all Christian or all Jewish?" The bearded adult turned red in the face and looked as if he wanted to crawl away. Zachary was persistent; he hit him with another bombshell. "Do you believe that God was the father of Jesus?" he asked. Seeing he was trapped, the editor said, "Well, I'm just getting to the question of whether I believe in God."

"Well," said Zachary impatiently, "Do you believe in God?"

Once again, the earnest editor knitted his brow and said, as if confessing his deepest thoughts, "Well, I'm getting to the point of considering the question that there's *maybe* a God."

Zachary couldn't stand the delay any longer. Totally exasperated, he blurted out, "I don't understand *what* you're saying. Do you believe *in* God?"

Being honest doesn't have to be so tricky. Zachary would have been satisfied if the editor had said, without much ado, that he is Jewish, doesn't think that Jesus is the Son of God, and doesn't always know what to believe about God either. Children accept a clear and sincere point of view.

And they also adapt to adults who confidently admit that there are questions they can't answer. As parents, we should feel free to say, "I don't know" when it's true. After all, people have been trying to understand the mysteries of God, religion, and the workings of the universe since they first appeared on earth, and as we grow, we'll always have new questions. It's important for our children to understand that their questions, as well as their observations, are equally valid and important. "They need to discover that people have learned all of what we know about God by seeing for themselves what is in his world," wrote Sophia Fahs. Their on-going search to determine their own beliefs, make sense of the world around them, and act on their knowledge is, after all, what life is all about.

3. *Allow children a natural passage through their stages of understanding about God. Don't rush them.* "The lesson I feel most strongly about," said Dan Heischman in his office, one morning, surrounded by all varieties of teenagers coming and going, "is that a person develops in his concept of God, and you have to let that process emerge. At each stage of their thinking you want to encourage them to dream and fantasize and struggle to explore their beliefs. You might be very uncomfortable with a little child's image of an old man with the long, white beard, for instance. But you can't deny her that, and in her heart and mind you can't replace it with an abstraction that she's not ready for."

As parents, we manage a balancing act. The goal is to support a child without fully endorsing a notion she'll eventually outgrow, all the while encouraging her to move toward the next level of comprehension. It's possible to tell a concrete-thinking first-grader who's about to understand the intangibleness of God, for instance, that some people, like her, imagine God as a kind person with a long robe. But others think about God as something within you that helps you grow and know right from wrong and be strong when you need to be. There are many ways to understand God.

Or when you talk to fourth-graders who are overzeal-ously concerned with pleasing God and all the other authority figures in their lives, you can temper their idea of a retributive God by saying, "Maybe God doesn't punish that much."

"You direct a child's image of God toward those things that might appeal to him and draw him to the next stage," explains Heischman. The worry isn't that he'll get stuck forever with a set of primitive notions. "Concepts are outgrown if there's any nurturing theology whatsoever," advises Heischman. The goal is to encourage them to keep looking ahead and probing their concept of God so that it can be counted on to be a reliable, strengthening resource for them.

"Teenagers get religion here around exams," Heischman said, chuckling, as he elaborated on his own philosophy. "They come to chapel, and I say a prayer to God about guiding us, supporting us in the trying days ahead, and giving us courage to meet failure, if necessary. Of course, they don't want to hear this; they want to hear about all As on their tests. But I always add that God speaks to the matters of most concern to us, and results are not always what we expect. I do that a lot—give them something new to think about and sit back and wait. They'll grow into it when they're ready."

Another subject that can't be rushed is the Holocaust. A child's introduction to this very difficult subject also follows a natural timetable. It's not by chance that many of the sons and daughters I interviewed were about ten years old when the story of the Holocaust first touched them in a personal way. At that age, they'd become more empathetic, more aware of the precariousness of their own lives, and emotionally adaptable enough to cope with the frightening implications of those terrible facts. Their feelings may have been triggered by reading Anne Frank's diary, hearing a personal story, or seeing concentration camp numbers tattooed on someone's arm. Suddenly the murder of 6 million Jews became very real to them.

"I'd heard how millions were killed, and I used to think, 'Big deal.' " said John Michaels, a tall fifteen-year old from

Princeton, New Jersey. "But then my uncle's wife told me how she and her brother were her parents' second kids because the first two children were killed in a concentration camp. I remembered how her parents were real old. They had to have two new children!" he said, looking straight at me. "I was a little kid myself, and that really struck me."

What's important to remember is that "each stage has the potential for wholeness, grace, and integrity and for strengths sufficient for either life's blows or blessings . . ." The quote is from James Fowler in *Stages of Faith*, and it reminds us to respect our children's passages and their capacity for a lifelong search for strength, joy, and meaning in their lives.

4. *Discover and honor what we share—one God, our values, and many important elements of our faith.* It amazes me how often people forget that our God is one and the same. I even caught my own husband, a sophisticated man, fantasizing one day about three different Gods lined up in heaven. He imagined the Jewish God, with Moses' dark beard, sitting next to the Protestant God with a white beard, alongside the Catholic God who didn't have a beard—or hair—because he looked like Pope John Paul. He was kidding, but not totally. When I nudged him about how Jews, Protestants, Catholics (and Buddhists, Moslems, and so on) share the same God, he caught himself and mumbled something about how easy it is to forget the obvious facts.

The Ten Commandments are also shared, as well as many of the lessons and prayers from the Torah and Christian Bible that Jews and Christians know by heart.

Jesus, for instance, said, "Thou shalt love the Lord thy God with all thy heart, and with all thy soul, and with all thy mind. This is the first and great commandment. And the second is like unto it: Thou shalt love thy neighbor as thyself. On these two commandments hang all the Law and the Prophets" (Matthew 22:37–40).

In turn, Judaism's most sacred prayer, called the *shema* in Hebrew, reads, "Hear, O Israel, The Lord our God is

One." The entirety of that prayer (Deuteronomy 6:4–9 and 11:13–21) has a slightly different translation, but essentially it's the original passage that Jesus knew well ("And thou shalt love the Lord thy God with all thine heart, and with all thy soul, and with all thy might"). As a measure of its special meaning for Jews, it's the wisdom that's written on parchment and sealed within the *mezuzah* that's traditionally fixed to the doors of a Jewish home.

Jesus's second commandment also echoes well-known Jewish wisdom. Thirty years before Christ, the great scholar Hillel was asked to explain Judaism to an inquiring Gentile. "Do not do unto others that which is hateful unto you," said Hillel. "That is the essence of Judaism. All else is commentary."

I'm drawn toward these connections, and I find myself pointing them out to my children wherever possible. It's meaningful to me that Jesus was a Jew— a rabbi, at that— who never stopped being an observant Jew. He attended the synagogue every Sabbath. The Apostles and Mary were also Jews. When Rachel and Georgia are older, they'll know that The Last Supper was a Passover seder. And they'll hear how the beautiful psalms weave throughout synagogue *and* church liturgies, and how The Lord's Prayer is rooted in the Jewish prayerbook, the *Siddur*.

No matter how deeply they may or may not commit themselves to one of these two faiths, I want them to feel the harmony and the powerful, constructive relationship between both. They'll know about Christian heroes like Swedish Raoul Wallenberg who courageously saved thousands of Jews in Budapest during World War II; and they'll know about the loving and very wise Jewish theologian Abraham Heschel who moved Vatican II to condemn and begin to reverse two thousand years of anti-Semitism. They'll see ceremonies and discussions where rabbis, priests, and ministers sit side by side and talk, argue, and share their feelings. And they'll see their parents, friends, and family around them learning from each other and discovering a strong, human center of agreement.

Most interfaith parents whom I've interviewed feel strongly that, at the very least, their values give them that strong center of agreement. Call them Jewish or Christian values, but basically they're based on trust in one God, respect for the rights and integrity of all people, and a commitment toward improving the world. They translate further into common beliefs in hard work, kindness to others, loyalty to family and friends, truthfulness, courage about doing what's right, and the struggle to keep the world from destroying itself. Those virtues are at the heart of each religion, and if parents do nothing more than invest their children with a sense of those responsibilities, they're still doing justice to their faith—more than most people, I might add.

5. *Don't shy away from the differences between Judaism and Christianity.* Trust your children to recognize them and reconcile them in a way that works for them. God is One, but each of the two religions has taken thousands of years to carve out its own special route to realizing God and bringing a degree of love and order to the world.

I've always been struck by the dramatically different way that each religion handles death. Every Protestant funeral that I've known talked about heaven, peace, and life everlasting, of course. Some of them briefly discussed the person who died; most of them only mentioned the person's name once or twice. During normal Sunday or Easter services, there's usually a warm thanks for the donors of the flowers on behalf of their loved ones. You can find those names in the program.

Weekly Jewish services, on the other hand, are tough going for me. They're so blunt. The *kaddish*, which is the prayer for the dead that everyone stands to recite, is part of the liturgy, but I never get through it without crying—for my late mother-in-law and father-in-law, my grandparents, even my parents who are alive and well, as if anticipating my sorrow in the future. Jewish funerals are also very much to the point, and the ones I've known have been both wise and wrenching. They focus totally on the person who died, his life on earth, and the memories that live on within us.

It's natural to think that death would be especially difficult for interfaith children to cope with, because their grandparents and parents approach it, and comfort themselves, with such different understandings. What belief does a child grab hold of when a fellow student in his class or a member of his family suddenly dies? Wouldn't the comfort he'd receive from the Jews and Christians close to him only hopelessly confuse him and leave him bereft of any comfortable certainty?

"Kids have a wonderful way out of confusion," said Hilde Prinz, who's both the wife of Jordan's rabbi and a wise family counselor from East Orange, New Jersey. The more I talk to parents and interfaith children who've dealt with tragedies close to home, the more her words ring true. Children are able to sort out the most diverse information and miraculously integrate it into a form that makes sense to them.

I'm familiar with a recent funeral for the Jewish father of an interfaith third-grader. A rabbi officiated, but the Catholic mother of the little boy suggested that her son's minister from school, someone who'd been close to the boy, also attend and help plan the ceremony. Many of the boy's friends of both faiths attended. His special request was also honored: All the participants sang his favorite hymn from school, "Holy, Holy, Holy," during the ceremony.

Another moving example of a child's capacity to find comfort through their religious understanding was told me by Catherine Mason, an artist in New York. She'd had to watch her own family, including her daughter Andrea, cope with the death of her twenty-three-year-old brother, Tim, in a water-skiing accident three years ago. When he died, Catherine was in the tow boat with Andrea, who was then four years old.

It surprised Catherine, who's Protestant, that so much of her strength through the ordeal came from the religious convictions she'd had as a child. "My faith was like a cushion that came up when I needed it," she said. Even though she hadn't read the Bible since sixth grade, she found meaningful passages about how God will not test one beyond thy strength, and she incorporated the phrase, "mounting up as eagles," into an image of her brother that comforted her. She shared her thoughts with her very religious Presbyterian parents and her husband Steven, a theater director who's Jewish.

Andrea, meanwhile, had witnessed the accident, and she kept asking about Tim. She talked with her mother about "the good part"—that they have Tim's picture and can still love him—and "the sad part"—that they can't see him. Then one day, Andrea was talking about how God makes rain. And suddenly her face lit up with a wonderful discovery. "I know!" she announced. "God stands on the clouds and throws water down in buckets." At once, she asked, "Is Tim in the clouds?"

"Sort of," her mother answered.

"Then I think Tim's in the clouds, and every raindrop has Tim's smiling face on it," she concluded.

Like all children, Andrea had easy access to the magical thinking that could explain a huge, sad mystery and help her find her own route through her parents' different philosophies. Yet Andrea's resiliency was rooted in more than a child's innate creativity. Her family was strong around her, and Andrea felt the totality of her family's support and love for her and she, in turn, could freely dream about a God who made a beautiful world and helped people be loving and brave.

For those of us who are interested in addressing our children's eagerness to know about God and the faiths within our families, there are many available resources. You can trust your instincts to guide you to them, but to remind you of what you yourself love, what you'd be happy to see at work in your children's lives long after they've become adults, and what can be counted on to give respect to each religion, here are three categories of "gifts" we can share with our children.

6. *Offer them the images you love.* By "images," I mean all the singular, evocative symbols that children respond to so intuitively—the golden glow of the menorah, the primal sound of the *shofar*, a twinkling Christmas tree surrounded with presents, Mother's voice singing a holiday song, fingers lighting a candle—a thousand memories that constitute a spiritual collage of their childhood that they'll call upon through their entire lives and ultimately share with their own children.

Our wonderful opportunity is to remind ourselves which magical pictures and sounds generate those powerful feelings of joy, awe, well-being, deep thanks, clarity, and inner purpose in us. As adults we feel how profoundly we're affected by a glimpse of water, a breeze over our face when we're lying in bed, the opening of the Ark when the Torah is revealed, a gift from our grandparents, all the images that are sacred to us because they connect us to the meaningful layers of our experience—childhood, family, faith, mankind, the universe, and our soul. We should feel free to offer our set of images to our children with the genuineness they were offered us. In turn, our children should feel free to reject the ones that don't have meaning for them, honor their own attachments, and assemble an inspirational inventory that will enrich them, as well as those who know them, for life.

7. *Tell them the stories you value.* Stories also carry other profound messages. They illustrate our values, explain life to our children, feed their imagination, and entertain us at the same time. James Fowler writes reverently about our "master stories," the stories we tell ourselves about what we believe to be true about life, and the topics are as limitless as the lessons we've learned firsthand and those we've heard from generations before us. How to overcome odds. How to treat people. What to expect from others. What joys and blows life hands us. How to keep plugging away. How to trust the cycles of life. How to fight for what you believe in. What it means to fall in love. These and many more are the stories that are as immediate as the events on the nightly news or a discussion at the dinner table about what problems we solved today. They're also our family myths, resonating back through history. Our children pack them away in their minds and recall them, as needed, years later and with their original power. The stories that grandparents tell are seldom forgotten.

Books are also a source of stories, and the Bible is one of the richest. The incantation of the language casts its own spell and creates an indelible effect. The drama is intense, the interpersonal conflicts are compelling, and, though we may be uncomfortable with the blood and gore, children love it. There are many beautiful children's Bibles from all three denominations—Jewish, Catholic, and Protestant. I have many in our library, including: *Signs and Wonders, Tales from the Old Testament*, by Bernard Evslin (Four Winds Press); *A Child's Bible*, rewritten for children by Anne Edwards (Paulist Press); *Brian Wildsmith's Illustrated Bible Stories*, as told by Philip Turner (Oxford University); and *Stories from the Bible*, newly retold by Sipke van der Land (Eerdmans Publishing Company), and there are others. Add the works of Tolkien, I. B. Singer, C. S. Lewis, and the many other jewels of children's literature, and we can rest assured that we're doing our part to expose our children to the finest of characters living out a faith in the fairness and goodness of the world.

8. *Build relationships that are built on frank exchange.* Ultimately, relationships make the strongest impression on our children, however. The religious educator Ronald Goldman, in his classic *Readiness for Religion*, wrote, "The quality of human relationship is the major formative religious influence in childhood and adolescence, and all that is taught stands or falls by the kind of relationship which exists between teachers and their pupils."

Our children want to know where we stand, how we really feel about these moral and religious subjects we're talking about, and what example we demonstrate to them. Children "read" us more than they read books. They want us to be honest, strong and respectful of their thoughts and feelings. They want to see the sources of our strength, and they want to see how we put our faith to use. One of the strongest arguments for the power of Judaism, Christianity, and love for God will always be the trusted adult in a child's life who embodies those beliefs and encourages them to flourish in others. The bottom line is that there's no substitute for parents, grandparents, clergy, and heroes who lovingly share the best of themselves and their religious heritage with their children.

CHAPTER
10

CELEBRATIONS

One spring evening a year ago, I was sitting in the living room of a young mother on West End Avenue in New York City, waiting to begin an interview about her interfaith marriage. She had just tucked her three children into bed and had a pot of tea brewing on the coffee table in front of us.

"Let me get some coasters before I sit down," she said, opening the drawer of an end table on the left of the couch and rummaging through some forty little colorful menorah candles and several small plastic dreidels. Unable to find any coasters, she moved to the end table at the other side of the couch. The drawer was stuck, and when she finally yanked it open, small white cocktail napkins with red and green Christmas trees all over them flew out and floated down around her. We both laughed at the symbolic rendering of the familiar juxtapositions we experience as interfaith families. Then we began talking about the way she, her husband, and their children celebrate the holidays.

Most interfaith families merge two different calendars. Although it's sometimes a strain on the emotions, these celebrations are an invaluable way into the richness of each faith for parents and children. They're also occasions on which to express many wise, authentic, and loving messages about their heritage to the family and to the world. It seems to me that religious holidays are our greatest resource for sharing personal memories, family values, and the history and power of our faiths. Like the major ceremonies of life, they inspire us to grow, to understand ourselves better and feel the fullness of life in a context that's as ancient as it is contemporary.

In order to help families incorporate some or all of these important holidays into their lives with joy and significance, here's a basic introduction to each of them, along with examples of how other interfaith families have adapted and expanded them through their years together with their children.

THE HIGH HOLY DAYS

In Jewish/Christian homes, the calendar begins in the Fall with the most important religious observances of the Jewish year—the High Holy Days, which include Rosh Hashanah and Yom Kippur. This ten-day period that begins in September or October is one of reflection, prayer, joy, and repentance. The moods are mixed during this time. There's both the joy of beginning a new year and reverence for what's taken place in the past. Friends and relatives often remember each other with greeting cards. Parents and children spend quiet and peaceful days together, without work or normal busy activities. What makes these days so special, however, is that they're celebrated primarily in the synagogue where one feels the power and history of the Jewish people, not only in the congregation but through the ancient liturgy.

Rosh Hashanah

Rosh Hashanah is the Jewish New Year. The word *Rosh-Hashanah*, in fact, means "head of the year." For this holiday, as legend has it, Jews pray to God to be entered into the

Book of Life for the coming year. On the eve of Rosh Hashanah, which begins at sundown, there is a special family dinner at home that's complete with prayers, apples, and honey to mark the sweetness of the New Year, and a special round challah (bread). Some interfaith families share dinner together and then attend services at the synagogue, where the New Year is ushered in with the blowing of the shofar, a ram's horn. In some households, however, the Jewish partner goes to synagogue alone that evening and the next day attends a family service. In Conservative and Orthodox households there is often a second day of observance, as well. Realizing that the holiday is a difficult one for children to comprehend, some synagogues conduct a special New Year's service for children and their parents. Usually the entire Jewish community fills the synagogue at Rosh Hashanah services, and there's a solemn but festive quality in the air as Jews greet each other and confirm their unity and interconnectedness.

Yom Kippur

Yom Kippur, which means "day of atonement," is the holiest day in the Jewish calendar. Everything grinds to a halt for this reflective and sacred holiday. The holiday begins the evening before Yom Kippur with a ceremonial dinner at home. After the dinner, Jewish adults will not eat again until after sundown the following day. Observers then go to the synagogue for Kol Nidre night, the powerful and atmospheric service marked by the playing of the passionate, haunting melody called "Kol Nidre," which has an origin as ancient and mysterious as its sound. Yom Kippur itself is a time to take stock of your life, to review what you've done in the past year, to ask forgiveness of God for any wrongdoing, and to think about how you want to improve upon your life in the coming year. Supposedly, the answer to one's prayer for entry into the Book of Life comes down from God that day.

It's important to many Jewish parents that their children

attend at least a part of these services—or special Yom Kippur services for children and their families—in order to begin to feel a sense of belonging to the larger Jewish community, not only at that moment, but over thousands of years. Although these holidays may seem alien to Christian partners, the whole theme and mood of repentance and renewal are resonant with the human cycle known so well from Lent, Good Friday, and Easter. Yom Kippur ends with a single blast of the shofar.

The Festivals of Sukot and Simchat Torah

Sukot and Simchat Torah are less significant holidays, but they're wonderful for children. They take place within days of Yom Kippur, and they're rich with active sensual experiences for the children.

Sukot is a harvest festival that occurs five days after Yom Kippur. It lasts for seven days and commemorates the wilderness experience of Jews wandering in the desert for forty days after their exodus from Israel. It's celebrated with the construction of a *sukah*, which means a "hut" or a "booth" that's filled with naturally scented fruit and the branches of trees; its roof is always open to the stars. Some families construct the sukah and eat their meals in it for the duration of the holiday. Constructing one's own sukah or visiting another in a synagogue or at a neighbor's home is an experience that speaks to a child's senses and spirit of celebration about being Jewish in the New Year.

Simchat Torah, which takes place on the last day of Sukot, is a special celebration marking the reading of both the last section of the Torah, which is in Deuteronomy, and the first section, which is Genesis. *Simchat Torah* means "rejoicing in the Law." At services in the synagogue, the Torah scrolls are taken from the Ark, their holy place, and carried around the synagogue. The congregation, including many children, march around, sing songs, dance, and wave colorful flags. Simchat Torah is a commemoration of the value of learning, the richness of lifelong scholarship, and the wisdom of the ancient books themselves that have formed the foundation of Judaism. This holiday is a time of ethnic pride and revelry, and is a joy for children to attend.

CHANUKAH AND CHRISTMAS; PASSOVER AND EASTER

The winter holidays of Chanukah and Christmas, as well as the spring celebrations of Passover and Easter take more time to explain. These are holidays that have both religious and emotional meaning, and because they happen close together, most interfaith families are aware of the complicated choices they involve, and the deep feelings that are activated by them.

Chanukah

Chanukah begins in early to middle December, and it lasts for eight days. Historically, it's a commemoration of events that took place in Jerusalem around 150 B.C.E. (in other words, "Before the Common Era," formerly known as "Before Christ"). A small contingent of Jews led by Judah Maccabeus banded together and conducted guerilla warfare against the powerful, well-equipped army of ruling Syrians who were cruelly imposing Greek culture and religion on the Land of Israel. Three years to the day before the Maccabees' victory, the Syrians had decreed that Jews couldn't pray, speak their language, honor the Sabbath, become circumcised, keep kosher, or worship in the Temple, and the Temple itself was used for pagan rituals and sacrifices to Zeus. According to the Chanukah story, the Jews triumphantly regained the Temple and relit the sacred lamp which the Syrians had extinguished, and despite the fact that there was only one day's worth of oil, the light miraculously burned for eight days. The menorah, which is a nine-branched candelabra, (with eight candlesticks and a ninth for lighting) has become the symbol of Chanukah, signifying joyous freedom and the dedication of Jews to their belief in One God. *Chanukah*, in fact, means "dedication."

As with all Jewish holidays, Chanukah begins at sundown the day before it's marked in our American calendars. The family gathers together at home to light the menorah, say the *berochot* (blessings), and sing and tell the Chanukah story, and traditionally, there are latkes (potato pancakes) to eat, dreidels (tops) to spin for money or nuts, and presents and Chanukah gelt (money or chocolate coins covered in gold foil) for the children.

According to the Jewish Code, a rabbinical document that answers questions about ritual and rules, Chanukah is to "eat, and be merry, linger over viands and punctuate meals with jest and song and relate miracles." In our house, we've been learning how to do that better each year as the children get older. At first, it was easy enough to polish up the menorah we'd inherited from my mother-in-law, bring home a present for the baby, and light candles for the first two nights. But the holiday was new to me and not particularly important to Jordan growing up. We've had to learn *how* to celebrate it and invest it with meaning, improve it bit by bit, and let its own specialness and form gradually emerge.

For us it's become a small-scale, intimate holiday celebrated quietly at home and protected as much as possible from our normal, rushed busyness and the frenzy of Christmas. It's our time to be together as a family—Mommy, Daddy, Rachel, Georgia, and Alex, if possible—feeling close to each other and connected to the Jewish history and tradition we're celebrating and learning about.

To do that we've had to master the most basic lessons, such as why it's crucial that Jordan and I leave work early and plan ahead, so the night's reasonably calm and focused, or what's the right way to light the nine candles on the menorah. For those who don't know, the tradition is to add new candles nightly, moving right to left, ultimately using forty-four candles for the whole celebration. The *shamash* (the "servant" light) is lit first, then the blessings are said, and moving right to left, the shamash lights the other candles (one for the first night, two for the second, until there are eight on the final evening). The children tend to alternate the lighting, which is a magical and very serious task for them, and after that the song *Ma'oz Tzur* ("Rock of Ages") can be sung, and the presents opened.

The children are also accumulating their own rituals. Rachel loves to pick out the colors of the candles, and this season she insisted on reading the story of Chanukah each night from a children's book that came from the Jewish Museum in New York. She also asked for her own menorah in her bedroom, an electrified one with a golden glow so beautiful that she decided to keep it aglow through large portions of the year, replacing the bulbs as they burned out. At school, she also learned how to read the markings on the dreidel, and Jordan and she huddled over the table on the first night of Chanukah, spinning the colorful tops and piling up their winnings of pennies and nuts. Then she taught me each Hebrew letter: Nun, Gimmel, Heh, and Shin, which stand for the translation, "A great miracle happened there."

Georgia's contribution through all this was her own hearty version of the song, "Dreidel, dreidel, dreidel, I made you out of clay; when you're dry and ready, dreidel, I will play!"

Every interfaith family has its own way of celebrating Chanukah, and it mixes inherited traditions with a variety of very personal adaptations that keep giving the holiday fresh meaning. Interfaith families proudly told me about Gramma's annual Chanukah party or a discovery of Isaac Bashevis Singer's *Chanukah Stories for Children*. Others enjoyed searching the city for a new, beautiful menorah to replace the battered tin one that came from mother, or they found a recipe in the newspaper and learned how to make fresh, crunchy latkes rather than lazily baking frozen ones from the supermarket. One year there was the festive International Latke Festival and a concert of Sephardic music at Ansche Chesed, a Manhattan synagogue that celebrated Chanukah by highlighting the diversity of Jewish culture around the world. For many families Chanukah would be meaningless without the resonance of the Hebrew blessings, the *berachot*, spoken aloud as the candles are lit.

Inevitably, decisions about how to celebrate Chanukah have to involve its relationship to Christmas. Will Chanukah share the season with Christmas or stand alone?

Some intermarried families, especially those in which the Christian partner has converted to Judaism, have decided that Chanukah is their exclusive holiday. They feel that Chanukah is "not only eight days rich" but that the Jewish calendar is sprinkled with so much food, fun, and inspiration that they have no need for anything more.

Families who celebrate both have other decisions to make. How equitable will their Chanukah and Christmas efforts be? When one family realized that their expensive presents, such as the bikes and stereo systems, were part of Christmas and never Chanukah, they evened out the gift giving; another family switched their annual mother-daughter day of cookie baking from Christmas to Chanukah, and rather than cut out bells, trees, five-pointed stars, and angels they specialized in dreidels, Stars of David, and menorahs instead.

But the truth is that parity's almost impossible, especially for an American child living in a family that celebrates Christmas in any way. Rachel noticed the difference this past December when she pulled me over to her bedside and said sadly that she felt "sorry for Daddy because Christmas was so much funner than his holiday." Of course, it's more fun for a eight-year-old! What can compete with Santa Claus, the appealing story of a baby, a shining tree loaded with presents, and the excitement and Christmas hype that dominate mass culture from Thanksgiving through New Year's? Besides, Chanukah is not a holy day invested with sacred ritual, law, and the highest expression of art, music, and liturgy, as are Passover and the High Holy Days. As old and special as it is, the holiday is not essential to Judaism, not recorded in the Torah, and only briefly in the Talmud.

Christmas, however, is and always will be of major religious significance to Catholics and Protestants around the world. It is a day filled with such symbolic and spiritual importance and celebrated by such large numbers of people that it often seems to overshadow Chanukah in an interfaith family.

Accepting that imbalance, I've been more concerned that Chanukah have its own integrity and importance in our house, that it's treated as much more than a preview, a warmup act before Christmas. There's a lot that Chanukah and Christmas have in common: their origins as winter festivals to bring light to the shortest days of the year; their celebration of God's miracles; the geographical closeness of Jerusalem and Bethlehem; and in the children's eyes, the candles, gaiety, family togetherness, and presents. It's natural that they spill over into each other, especially during years when the dates of Chanukah and Christmas overlap.

But I try to guard against an unnecessary blurring of the best of each holiday. We will have the menorah and the tree in the living room, but the Chanukah presents won't serve as Christmas tree decorations. The smells in the kitchen, the music on the stereo, the routines at dinner, the memories we share, the personal and religious stories told, and the events we participate in outside our home will be different for each holiday. In addition, our beginning and ending of Chanukah will be acknowledged so that it doesn't just dribble away and leak into Christmas. These holidays, after all, are our special opportunity to explore our traditions and let them take hold in our hearts and imagination, and we want to allow them to express their distinctive messages.

The most evocative reminder of the power and separateness of each day was expressed in 1970 by Rabbi Jacob J. Petuchowski, professor of Hebrew Union College in Cincinnati, in a publication from The Institute of Judaeo-Christian Studies at Seton Hall University in New Jersey. In it, the rabbi reflected:

These lines are being written on Christmas Day, 1970. It is also the third day of Hanukkah, in the year 5731. Last night, my Christian neighbor lit candles, and I lit candles. His children received gifts, and my children received gifts. This morning, he heard Handel's "Hallelujah Chorus" in his church, and I recited the Hallel *psalms in my morning devotions. But, unless we are willing to commit the "fallacy of primitivism," and regard ourselves as engaged in the observance of the pagan festival of the winter solstice, we shall have to admit that my neighbor and I are not celebrating the same festival. Hanukkah is not Christmas. My neighbor is celebrating the birth of the Christian savior. I am celebrating God's mighty deeds in letting the Maccabees be victorious. But neither my neighbor nor I are engaging in mere reminiscences of the past. We are not, primarily, archeologists or historians. The stable in Bethlehem is a very present reality to him, just as the rededicated Temple in Jerusalem is a very present reality to me. Now, I want him to understand what Jerusalem means to me, just as I am trying to understand what Bethlehem means to him. . . .*

Christmas

Christmas is celebrated on December 25th, and commemorates the birth of Jesus Christ. Christmas also celebrates the beginning of the cycle of life, and reminds us of the bounty and miracle of God's unconditional love. The spirit of Christmas, according to the familiar scripture from Luke, is "Glory to God in the highest, and on earth, peace, good will toward men" (Luke 2:14).

The rituals of Christmas are intended to reinforce the best of our human inclination towards peace, unselfish love, and caring for others. The carols and sacred music are filled with serenity and exaltation. The crèche—typical of traditional religious celebrations—recreates the magic of the humble birth. Traditionally people remember each other with cards and gifts to show appreciation and caring. Most households have a tree which everyone in the family decorates with lights and decorations that have been accumulated over many years. Stockings are set out to be filled by Santa Claus. The lights in the window and the color and spectacle everywhere are expressions of wonder and festivity. Families and friends gather together and kiss under the mistletoe, renew their relationships, and feel close and supportive. Christmas food usually includes turkey, cookies, eggnog, as well as many special ethnic dishes that spread happiness and well-being. All the senses are addressed by Christmas—sight, taste, smell, hearing, and touch, and they're indelibly impressed on a child's memory forever.

Christmas is about love, which is why it stirs and moves us on so many complicated levels. It can be a disappointing reminder that there's no family or loved one to share the holiday with. It can make us long for a childhood that was —or wasn't. Because it falls at the end of the year, it causes us to take stock of ourselves and reflect on successes and failures. And it pressures everyone to run around in a frenzied attempt to remember those they care about and show their love. Memories, loyalties, and a host of obligations surface. Add the buzz and excess of the commercialism to the entire season, and it's not surprising most children and adults become overstimulated and exhausted. It's a feat to maintain a sense of wonder, let alone spiritual inspiration, throughout the weeks of hard work and emotional overload that are frequently part of Christmas.

To some people, it would seem that Christmas has become so secularized and so much part of the American scene that it couldn't possibly be a trying time for Jews, especially those within interfaith marriages. Christmas is a national holiday, after all, and many Jews have, in fact, celebrated it as children, with presents and family gatherings. Indeed, I've interviewed many Jewish parents who have readily adapted to Christmas and feel that the festivities are warm additions to their lives and important to those they love; they're not conflicted about celebrating them.

But many Jews aren't accustomed to Christmas or comfortable with the intrusive aspects of it, especially in the early years of marriage and parenthood when they're suddenly confronted with the Christmas phenomenon. It's not their holiday or their religious story, and if it's to become a harmonious, even meaningful occasion for them, there are decisions and adjustments that have to be made.

The first decision is whether to celebrate Christmas at all. Rabbi Helene Ferris of Stephen Wise Free Synagogue offered her advice on arriving at a choice. According to the Reform rabbi, she says, Christmas is acceptable if the non-Jewish spouse hasn't converted to Judaism. In other words, a Jewish/Christian household has the freedom to celebrate both Chanukah and Christmas; a Jewish household is officially expected to celebrate Jewish holidays only.

In reality, however, interfaith families adapt their seasons in many other ways as well. There are those who decide to honor Chanukah but eliminate Christmas, even though the Christian spouse hasn't converted. But there are also families where there's been a conversion to Judaism, but the agreement between the partners is to honor Christmas as well as Chanukah. Either Christmas will be celebrated within their own home with a tree and festivities, or it will be celebrated with their Christian family in their homes, in order that the couple's house remain exclusively Jewish. Contrary to some Jewish advisers who insist that the child of conversion should *not* experience Christmas with relatives because it will dilute his Judaism and confuse him, these parents wisely believe that nothing should stand in the way of a child's closeness to his extended family at this intimate time.

Once the decision has been made about "doing" Christmas, there's the matter of the tree. Most Jewish partners welcome it into their living rooms easily, but some eye it suspiciously and have to struggle to explain it to themselves. Saul Sheingold, for instance, managed to kick it over and break a few glass balls for fifteen years in a row. Pierre Marcus banished it to the pantry. After ten years of marriage, Roberta Dietrich is still "queasy" about it. For these and other parents, the tree is a classic Christian symbol that's threatening, one that identifies their home as a Christian home, one that may also symbolize too much Christian power within their own marital relationship. In the case of Saul Sheingold, it reminds him of his mother who told him that it was a betrayal of six million Jews. Another husband associates it with childhood feelings of being a lonely outsider during the Christmas celebration in his predominately Italian neighborhood.

Frequently, the feelings of resistance to Christmas change with time. "I used to think the poinsettia was a *goyische* plant, but now I have to admit it's pretty," explained a thirty-six-year-old Jewish mother from Cincinnatti who's delighted by how far she's evolved in her acceptance of her husband's traditions. "The tree used to be entirely representative of an alien faith I couldn't accept. But now I love its beauty. The greenery, lights, the beautiful music create a sense of joy in our house. Christmas comes at the time of the winter solstice when the festiveness is particularly gratifying. I don't relate to the Christmas story, certainly not like my husband. Maybe I will someday, but not now."

What gradually changed her mind were common experiences within interfaith homes. Year by year she found herself enjoying aspects of the holiday with her husband and children. She realized the celebration didn't violate her own Jewish identity, which was growing stronger, in fact, as she got older. Moreover, it became clear that her participation in Christmas only made it possible for her to celebrate the Jewish holidays even more elaborately with her family. Learning to trust that her marriage would respect both the Jewish and Christian traditions equally was the key to her comfortable evolution. "Celebrating holidays is really a marital negotiation, like any other matter, such as where you live, how you'll deal with each other's work, or where you'll take your vacations," she explained. "Once I realized how hard I worked shopping and cooking for two weeks at Christmas, I felt perfectly easy about asking for three days for Rosh Hashanah and Yom Kippur."

The adaptations and negotiations over Christmas may never end, however. In my own home, Jordan is still irritable every year when he begins to sense the quantity of presents being purchased for our extended family and friends. In his eyes, unaccustomed to that pattern of gift giving, my generosity becomes "a feeding frenzy," and we argue annually about what's meaningful and what's excessive and try to arrive at a compromise.

For others, the adaptations can mean deciding to go to Christmas services together, whether or not to enroll a child in a Christmas pageant that demands weeks of rehearsal, or how prominently to display Grandmother's crèche, if at all. Some families decide it's time to stop celebrating Christmas because it no longer expresses the family's loyalties. Others, however, resume Christmas festivities after an old choice to suspend them becomes too great a deprivation for the formerly Christian partner, despite his or her conversion to Judaism. Contrary to the advice often given to interfaith families, Christmas is not a time to worry about "dangerous precedents." Every year is a new one to discuss and negotiate.

To handle these problems, some couples attend interfaith workshops like those sponsored by the Paulist Center in Boston, the Union of American Hebrew Congregations, and many Reform and Conservative synagogues throughout the country. These discussions about "the holiday dilemma" are well-attended during this provocative month. Other couples simply keep communicating their memories, needs, and deep feelings about Christmas and Chanukah to each other, and they listen to their children.

What matters is that the family feels the harmony and renewal of the season, each in his or her own way, and that we allow each other the freedom to give and receive love in the ways we're accustomed. As Rachel, age seven, wrote to Jordan and me on December 22nd almost two winters ago, "Happy Times are wen peope love peopole and joy's are joy's and the world is Happy. By Rachel Gruzen."

Spring is the second miraculous season where major Christian and Jewish holidays converge. Passover and Easter take place in March or April, sometimes overlapping each other or occurring weeks apart, maybe in different order. Since Passover, which is also known as Pesach, preceded the events of Easter by about 1,300 years (and since it plays such an essential role within Christianity), let's begin with it.

Passover

Passover celebrates the exodus of the Jews from Egypt where they had become enslaved until Moses, with God's help, petitioned the cruel Pharaoh to free the Children of Israel. After a series of horrible plagues on the Egyptians, the Jews finally fled and regained their freedom. The story about suffering and liberation is much more elaborate than my summary; anyone with even passing knowledge of the Bible and the Book of Exodus is familiar with the chain of dramatic and revolutionary events: the discovery of baby Moses in the bullrushes; God's revelation to Moses within the burning bush; the ten plagues on Egypt, and the parting of the Red Sea. The name *Passover* refers to the last of God's scourges on Egypt when the Angel of Death killed all first-born Egyptians but "passed over" the Jewish families who had sacrificed the Paschal lamb and marked their doorposts with its blood.

Passover is celebrated for eight days by some Jews, seven days by others. All the rituals and symbols during the week are reminders of the original Passover story. No bread or leavened foods are eaten throughout the week, to memorialize the hasty exit of the Jews before the bread could rise or be baked. Flat matzoh is eaten instead, and traditionally the house is cleansed of all leavened goods, from macaroni to cookie crumbs.

The seder or ceremonial dinner is the highpoint of Pesach, and families and friends gather together at home for the first, sometimes the first and second, nights to read from the order of service, the *Haggadah*, eat well, enjoy each other's company, and sometimes sing. The meaning of the foods and objects on the table are defined and described in the *Haggadah*, as is the mythic story itself with its traditions that have been shaped and repeated for thousands of years.

It's impossible not to enjoy Passover. The food is opulent and exotic, and there's usually course after course drawn from the family's tradition and national origin. The fact that the *Haggadah* insists on four glasses of wine also adds to the spirit, and the Passover story itself is rich enough to inspire new, personal thoughts everytime it's told.

But for me, there are two highlights. The first is the children, who are the reason for the seder, after all. In the Bible it was said three times that the story of Passover must be told when the children ask. So after the blessings over the candles and the wine, the youngest child at the table traditionally asks the Four Questions, beginning with the famous first question that's familiar to all Jews: "Why is this night different from all other nights?" or, *Mah nish-tana ha-lay-lah ha-zeh mekol ha-lay-lot*? And so, the seder unfolds.

I learned about the children's role last year when I called my hostess for the second seder and asked if she wanted me to bring two centerpieces—one for the adults' table and another for the kids'. Besides being uninformed, I'd forgotten about the magic of the children's participation at the same table, and what it offers them *and* us as they sip their wine (or grape juice) in fancy goblets, read better year by year, imagine the boils and frogs and other gory plagues, take their proud place at the table, and rush around to find the *afikoman* (which is half of the middle matzoh hidden by the host from that special Passover plate).

The second highlight is the spirit of the seder which is open, inviting, and very generous. Indeed, I've been told about long and boring seders, and tense and difficult ones because the family members are feuding. But I've only experienced the warm and accessible ones that have included a variety of people within the festive circle, from Jews who never celebrated a Passover to those who haven't missed one in their lives, from Christians for whom it's totally new, to others, like the children of interfaith marriages, who are building on old, fuzzy memories. Some seders are extravagant and full of confident songs and learned elaborations; others are simple, experimental efforts to touch base with the past and introduce it to children. Even though the story and order of events do not change from house to house, country to country, or century to century, the personality and content of every celebration are always different. Passover's message of liberation encourages all Jews, their friends and family, to add their personal touches and perspectives to the night's celebration.

For a number of years Jordan and I had the opportunity to celebrate what we call our annual mixed-marriage seders with three other Jewish/Christian children. It's fun, exhausting, and very meaningful, which is what it's supposed to be. Joanna, who's Jewish, usually organizes the rest of us and runs the seder. We all cook at home, then mill around the kitchen together, while the children bang on the piano and entertain themselves. Since we usually celebrated Passover with our Jewish families the night before, this is a repeat performance, enhanced by our own additions. We use various children's *Haggadahs* which make the service go faster. It was filled with songs like "Dayenu" and "Listen King Pharaoh," which we belt out while Joanna's husband Garry accompanied us on the piano. Joanna's older daughter reads her portions in the Hebrew her mother taught her, while the younger children pride themselves on mastering new words, like *Pesach* or *Elijah*.

One year, Joanna asked the parents to talk to the children about their feelings about the holiday season, since our households celebrate both Easter and Passover. I went first, speaking about how much I love Easter and Passover, because at the end of winter I usually feel sad, tired, and worried that I'll never feel strong and lively again. But when Passover and Easter come, spring does, too, and a miracle happens. I want to run and dance and thank the world for being so wonderful and helping me feel alive and able to work hard. That's what God did for the Jews, too; He helped them feel strong and free after they'd been so weakened by slavery. God gave them courage, and a miracle happened. And another God-given miracle happened at Easter, and it happens in me every year at this time.

We kept talking. Joanna's husband Garry asked the children if they knew that Jesus, many, many years ago, had a Passover celebration very much like this one. He added that all of us are very lucky to be able to learn about both beautiful holidays, since our families from way back have always loved these days and learned from them and enjoyed being together. And Jordan remembered his very best Passover in Israel when he was a teenager, celebrating it with Jews who had come from India and Poland and Africa, and tonight Jewish children and their parents, just like us, are getting together all over the world to have fun together and hear this great story.

Easter

What makes this season so complicated is that there's another great story to be told. And that story engenders more soul-searching, emotion, food, family, and accomodation. Easter Week is Christianity's most sacred series of days that are prefaced by Jesus's triumphant entrance into Jerusalem on Palm Sunday, continuing into the Last Supper on Thursday, the Crucifixion on Good Friday, and the celebration of the Resurrection on Sunday. Unlike Passover which is a holiday for the home, Easter week is a time for church, especially during early afternoon on Good Friday and Easter morning.

Not everyone would agree that church is essential. Many interfaith parents have special Easter memories that are about dressing up in Mary Janes with white socks and a bonnet with a long ribbon down the back, stepping out into warm, sunny weather, and seeing the first robin or flowers sprouting in the backyard. Easter is the smell of lilies and new clothes, the taste of chocolate eggs and Easter ham, and the surprise of the Easter bunny and the candy hidden around the living room. The colors are pink, lavender, and pastel blue, and though it may rain on Easter, the memory is always of sunny days and a fresh spirit in the air that's part of the miracle of spring.

For other adults, the associations aren't the childlike ones, but the sober transformation of the religious events themselves. The solemn, confessional tone of Good Friday followed by the exaltation of Easter is a passage they can only experience fully in church. That cycle of continuity—from darkness to light, death to life—is an Easter theme choreographed with an ancient resonance and command only equalled by Judaism's Yom Kippur.

Easter is not an easy holiday for the Jewish partner to accept. Its glorification of the Son of God is antithetical to the tenets of Judaism. The idea of Christ's rising from the dead is difficult enough for Christians, let alone for Jews who often find it totally incomprehensible. Although Christianity no longer holds the Jews accountable for Christ's death, some Bible passages read during the Easter service are also not flattering to Jews.

Some Jewish spouses have the added strain of having grown up in Polish or Russian families where Easter memories are associated with pograms and violent anti-Semitism.

For most intermarried Jews, however, the service is simply alien until they find their own individual way of relating to it—whether through its spiritual message of forgiveness and love, its pageantry and artistic beauty, its community, or the family experience of sitting closely together and sharing, each in his or her own way, a time of importance.

When considering the Christian and Jewish calendar—one based on the life of Jesus Christ and the other focused on the history of the Jewish people—it's often easy to forget a celebration of equal if not greater importance, one that occurs fifty-two times a year—the Sabbath.

The Sabbath

The Sabbath in Judaism begins at sundown on Friday and ends at sundown on Saturday. It's so central an observance in Jewish life that it's stipulated in the Ten Commandments: "Remember the sabbath day and keep it holy" (Exodus 20:8). Twice, in fact, the commandment appears in the Torah, reminding Jews of the meaning of this day of rest.

In Exodus 20:11, it's a time for remembering God's creation ("For in six days the LORD made heaven and earth and sea, and all that is in them, and He rested on the seventh day"). And in Deuteronomy 5:15, it's also a time for remembering the Jewish people, their culture and history ("Remember that you were a slave in the land of Egypt and the LORD your God freed you from there with a mighty hand and an outstretched arm; therefore the LORD your God has commanded you to observe the Sabbath day").

Although there's enormous variety in the degree with which Jews honor the Sabbath, the tradition calls for communal worship and prayer in the synagogue on Friday evening or Saturday morning and private observances with the family during festive meals that take place on Friday night, Saturday midday, and Saturday at dusk. Children especially love the lighting of the candles, special blessings and singing that are part of a traditional Friday dinner. *Havdalah*, the ceremony with spices and a candle that marks the end of the Sabbath, is less frequently observed but also enjoyable for children.

Many parents start taking their children to the Friday or Saturday service in the synagogue as soon as the youngsters can sit still, observe, and feel the importance of the occasion. At the very least, their children learn "how to do it"—meaning how to say the prayers, know the participants and the religious objects, and settle into the rhythms and mood of the event itself.

"The Sabbath is a major way of expressing one's Jewishness," reminded Rabbi Lavey Derby, Associate Director of Education at the 92nd Street YMHA in New York. "There isn't any Jewish education that can ignore it."

The Sabbath in Christianity takes place on Sunday, in honor of the Resurrection. It, too, is a critical day of observance ordained by the Ten Commandments. The church, however, plays a far more ceremonial role in the Christian's Sabbath tradition than the home does. Commonly, Catholics and Protestants attend weekly services in the morning, and depending on the denomination, their children join them for all of the worship or, if there's a Sunday school, part of it.

"Basically, praise and prayer are the main things that Catholics and Protestants have in common with respect to their responsibilities on Sunday," said Richard Spalding, a Presbyterian minister in New York. "By praise, I mean the hymns and spoken passages in thanks to God. The prayers are for forgiveness."

It's hard to talk about "an average Sunday in church" since the liturgy, architecture, music, and mood of every Christian denomination—from Catholic to Congregational to Unitarian to Episcopal—appear so dramatically different. What's shared, however, is what Reverend Spalding calls "a wonderful rhythm pattern to a Sunday service when it's rightly conceived." The confession, the assurances from God, the Bible passages, sermon, communion, and, sprinkled throughout, the hymns and prayers are the substance of the experience. When it's enhanced by the family rhythm of a Sunday that's spent in a special way together, the day assumes even deeper meaning in the mind of a child.

Certainly our gatherings are enriched and informed by the larger Christian and Jewish tradition that helps bind us together through the repetition of these ceremonies and events. Nevertheless, whether it's a Sabbath in which parents and children share prayer and thanksgiving, conversation, or simply a good meal together, or whether it's a large celebration such as Christmas, Chanukah, Passover, or Easter, the moments of understanding, the laughter, stories, warmth, and sense of renewal are what give these traditions a richness and meaning that leave an indelible emotional impression on our children's lives.

CHAPTER
11

CEREMONIES

Will the choice be a baptism, bris, bar mitzvah, or confirmation? The options are classic ones, fused over centuries into an elaborate choreography of belief, ritual, symbol, and theatre. They can be moving, reassuring, and resonant with ancient and personal meanings. Most of all, they're benchmarks for important transitions from one stage of life to another. They're expressions of a people's and a family's goals, values, and vision for the future.

Because these ceremonies are so classic, however, they're a thorny issue within many Jewish/Christian homes. Classic, after all, means traditional, rooted in one faith or another. Christian. Or Jewish. Not Jewish/Christian or any fusion that's been practiced long enough to have acquired authority, richness, and acceptance from family and religious officials. As a result, interfaith couples interested in blending traditions in a manner that feels right to them have often been discouraged from participating in these and other ceremonies. For Jordan and me, for instance, the task of choosing a birth rite for our daughters required more formalized religious commitment on our part, more enlightenment on the part of our families, and, overall, more hard work, knowledge, and emotional risk than we were prepared to muster at that time. The standard models didn't reflect us; the possibilities for originality seemed too formidable to consider. Since we have yet to resolve the issue of whether or not our daughters mark their adolescence with a religious ceremony, this subject continues to be a provocative and unresolved one for us.

For many Jewish/Christian couples pressed to find their way through the same seemingly limited range of choices, there's a need for basic information about these rituals, not only from the religious authorities but also from interfaith families who've sensitively handled these events. For me, an additional resource that's been helpful in making the topic less formidable and rigid has been returning, with an appreciative eye, to the one ceremony I know best and have indeed, like most Jewish/Christian couples, managed to handle successfully—the interfaith wedding. Not only does that special event reflect a couple's early instincts and attitudes about religion, family, and the role that both heritages assume in their lives, but it serves to remind parents how satisfying a well-considered, personal ceremony can be. By remembering the features in the wedding that were meaningful and natural, parents may find a similarly sure and intimate route through the other ceremonies commemorating life's passages, from birth through adulthood to the death of a loved one.

The wedding serves another purpose, however. It's an encouraging preview of what's possible once the interfaith population begins to make its mark on the significant events in a family's development. Up until now, the burst of energy and creativity from the rapidly increasing number of Jewish/Christian couples has been turned toward the wedding ceremony. As a result, their families and clergy (or officials) have been able to work together and adapt tradition to their own unique needs with a new confidence and freedom. As the population of interfaith children continues to expand— and grow older—I think it's likely that the same experimentation and knowledge will begin to shape their own celebrations, inspiring a wider, fresher variety of ways to give them power and meaning.

THE WEDDING

It's been ten years since Jordan and I planned ours on Block Island. It was a homemade affair in a modern glass house overlooking the island's brilliant blue harbor and stone lighthouse. A retired businessman who'd become the island's justice of the peace officiated, reading our vows from a booklet he'd made out of folded red construction paper. The reception for our fourteen guests was a clambake catered by a theatrical Italian who toasted me with Elizabeth Barrett Browning ("How do I love thee?") and served lobsters and fresh corn from a box on the back of a Vespa scooter.

What I remember most of all were the small touches, both planned and unplanned: Vivaldi's "Gloria" on the record player, the journey by boat through the fog for our family and friends arriving the day before, and my cousin, a stewardess, wobbling on high heels through the cow pasture, dragging her suitcase with tiny rear wheels because the taxi driver, a local fellow named Omar Littlefield, couldn't maneuver his old black Cadillac up the sandy driveway. In addition, a CBS-TV news crew unexpectedly asked to film that day for a documentary they were making about the island itself, adding three more guests and a fat, black camera to our intimate group assembled in the living room.

I doubt Jordan's and my mother, both elegant women, would have designed our wedding in the same way, if given half a chance, but it was exactly as we'd wanted it to be—casual, nonsectarian, small, and empowered by its beautiful surroundings. All of those features felt right.

When I compare our marriage ceremony to the others I've attended or heard about in the course of writing this book, I'm struck by the extraordinary variety that's represented. Each one is its own special blend of concerns for religious affiliation, family ties, balance of power within the relationship itself, and each partner's individual style and spirit.

Anyone scanning the wedding announcements in the newspaper will encounter a wide assortment of today's common models. There's the balanced ecumenical wedding with the rabbi alongside the priest or minister. There's the wedding exclusively celebrated in a dominant faith—Protestant, Catholic, or Jewish, with its clergy present. There are many officiated by a justice of the peace, judge, or nonreligious figure (half of them, as a matter of fact, according to Egon Mayer's recent findings). On occasion, there's also the sequential choice involving two weddings; the first ceremony is a Jewish one with rabbi and Jewish relatives, and hours or days later there's a Christian one with its clergy and complement of relatives. The order can be reversed. Or to vary the program slightly, there can be two different receptions for the families, but only one ceremony, a nonsectarian, private one attended by a chosen few.

Within those basic structures, however, there are infinite ways in which a couple expresses its traditions and feelings more fully, and these, of course, are seldom recorded in the routine newspaper coverage. For all appearances, Susan Toland and Eli Mayer's wedding five years ago was a standard ecumenical ceremony in her parents' backyard in Connecticut; the priest and rabbi stood side by side during an event witnessed by fifty friends and relatives. For me, however, it's the richest, most integrated model I've found for merging two distinct personalities, faiths, families, and personal histories. Any Jewish/Christian couple having difficulty thinking about how to blend two backgrounds and interests into a ceremony, whether it be a christening or a bar mitzvah, can look to this wedding as the ultimate example of how to do it.

There were few aspects of this wedding that did not reflect the couple's blended approach. When the bride and groom first addressed their guests, Susan had said, "We hope that through this ceremony you will also share in the deep and enriching qualities that Eli and I bring to one another through our individual backgrounds."

In his words of welcome, the groom had said, "We respect and encourage one another's unique development as we know that our individual experiences strengthen our mutual love and growth."

With that philosophy at its heart, the forty-five-minute ceremony proceeded. There was something from her side, something from his side in all phases of the event, from the traditional Jewish wedding canopy, the *chupah*, which the bride's Catholic mother had designed out of lattice and boxwood to the pattern of interwoven daisies added to the bower by each of their guests, both Christian and Jewish. Susan's Catholic grandmother placed the Sign of the Cross on her granddaughter's forehead as a blessing. Susan's Protestant father read a passage aloud from Walt Whitman. Eli's Jewish daughter, age fourteen, joined Susan and her father under the chupah where Eli said warmly, "Our home is your home."

The clergy were also a special balance. The rabbi had fought alongside the groom's father in Egypt during the battles for Palestine in the 1940s; the priest had known the bride since her childhood days at the Convent of the Sacred Heart. Both rabbi and priest were also close friends themselves and fully prepared to share responsibility for each of the rituals, which they explained carefully to the guests. Using goblets the bride's Catholic grandmother had brought from Germany, the rabbi performed the wine ceremony in Hebrew as the priest recited the English version. The priest introduced and offered blessings for the ring ceremony which the rabbi completed. Together they wove an elaborate history of each individual and family and the events, both personal and international, that ultimately brought Susan and Eli together on July 4th, their wedding day.

To enrich the event further, the couple borrowed the Sign of Peace from the Catholic Mass and repeated the words "Peace be with you" to each of the guests, moving among them, she to her friends and family, he to his. When the rabbi sang the final benediction in Hebrew, like a cantor

(*"Y'bharekh'khagh Adonoy w'yishm'rekhah"*), the priest chanted antiphonally in English ("May the Lord bless thee and keep thee"). Consistent with the Jewish tradition, the groom broke the glass, and the couple embraced and exited to the folk song, "Tis a Gift."

Susan and Eli were married *not* "in the name of the Father, and of the Son, and of the Holy Spirit," which is the Christian confirmation, *not* "according to the law of God and the faith of Israel," which is the Jewish affirmation, but rather, "according to the laws of God," an acknowledgement often used for interfaith celebrations.

Not everyone works as hard as Susan, Eli, and their clergy to create an event with as many layers of meaning. For many couples I've met, a touch here or there is enough to reflect their uniqueness, and they wouldn't be interested in anything more elaborate. An Armenian bride wore a floral wreath on her head during an interfaith wedding at Columbia University. A Baptist/Jewish couple was delighted by the bluegrass band that played at their reception, their only personal amendment to an otherwise routine appearance at City Hall. For many couples, five minutes of an exuberant hora is a satisfying Jewish statement. During a Long Island, New York, wedding televised as part of a series on interfaith marriage, the priest relaxed the guests gathered together in the Catholic church with a joke about the wine being a blend of Christian Brothers and Manischewitz. Each of these couples, with the help of their officiants, created a wedding in their image, filled with things they loved.

Spiritually, the Jewish and Christian ceremonies that mark the major transitions in life bear many similarities. They're times of celebration and nurturance when God's love is communicated. They're times of identification when an individual enters into a new relationship with the Christian community or the Jewish community. And they're times of instruction when the responsibilities of a Christian or Jew are spelled out so the faith continues from generation to generation.

In Christianity, these events are called *sacraments*, and they're inspired by the important occurrences in Christ's life. Catholics, Episcopalians, and Eastern Orthodox have seven sacraments: Baptism, Confirmation, Holy Eucharist (or Holy Communion), Matrimony, Ordination (or Holy Orders), Reconciliation (or Penance, better known as Confession), and Anointing of the sick (or Extreme Unction). Generally, the other Protestant denominations emphasize two of them: Baptism and Holy Communion.

Judaism doesn't have sacraments. It has life-cycle events: birth, adolescence, marriage, and death, with certain religious rituals and traditions associated with each. Although both faiths acknowledge many of the same emotions and highlight similar themes, the detailed way they handle each transition may differ significantly, as interfaith parents discover when they confront each other's accepted method of celebrating life's passages.

B IS FOR BABY, BAPTISM, OR BRIS

It's rare to find an intermarried Christian parent who hasn't been baptized. I have my Certificate of Baptism from Hancock Church, Lexington, Massachusetts "in the year of our Lord 1946." A clear-eyed Jesus with a glow around his head and a lamb on his shoulder tends his sheep, and below him are written the words, "He that believeth and is baptized shall be saved" (St. Mark 16:16).

The baptism is the ceremony that introduces a child into the circle of Christianity. It's the first and most important step in the process of being a Christian. Though it's usually done within the first year of birth (and during adolescence in the Baptist Church), it's a rite that's possible at any stage of life. Adults who convert to Christianity, for instance, are initiated into the Church through baptism.

The ritual varies among denominations, but there's always a purification with water, either by a sprinkling or an immersion. A member of clergy marks the Sign of the Cross on the child's forehead. Parents and godparents promise to raise the child in the Christian faith and help him or her love and live with the knowledge of God and Christ.

For many Christian parents, there's a romance about a christening. The parents stand by the baptismal font in the front of the church, cradling the baby in the crook of an arm before watching the minister or priest drop water on a fuzzy little head. There may be a white christening dress with seed pearls, handed down from a parent or a grandparent. In some families, the event is an occasion for a large, jubilant celebration.

The decision to have a christening, often a routine one for Christian families, is anything but that for interfaith families. Many aren't prepared to make such an exclusive and public commitment in a church. Although there are no conclusive statistics, it seems as if only a small percentage of Jewish/Christian parents choose to have a baptism performed.

The Resniks, a family from Detroit, Michigan, made the firm decision to raise their three children as Catholics, so baptism became standard operating procedure. Marie Resnik, the oldest child in a large Italian family accustomed to splendid baptisms on the scale of a wedding, kept her Jewish in-laws in mind when she carefully arranged a private ceremony in the quiet of the church with a favorite priest officiating; both sets of grandparents attended each of the three low-key events.

Jewish/Christian families make many other accommodations, however. When he was a baby, Father Gary Gelfenbien was given two birth rites—one in the church and another in the synagogue where he was presented to his father's congregation and given his Hebrew name, Schlomo, meaning Solomon.

In Syracuse, New York, a Catholic mother with eight grown children couldn't bear the idea that all six of her grandchildren—the interfaith ones, as well as the children of Catholic parents—hadn't been baptized. "When I was brought up, the child who wasn't baptized wouldn't go to heaven," the widow explained to me over the telephone while her parakeet cheeped in the background. "Now that I'm an adult, I don't believe we have an unjust God who'd take a baby and do such a thing. But it's kind of ticklish for me because in my heart that idea is still part of my doctrine.

"I was talking to my priest about my grandchildren," continued the sixty-four-year-old who still teaches weekly Sunday School classes to the eighth-graders in her parish. "I'll tell you what he said," she confided. "He told me, 'Go to the kitchen. Turn on the water. Dip your hand in, make the Sign of the Cross, and say the basic words: I baptize you in the Name of the Father, and of the Son, and of the Holy Spirit.'

"Enough said?" the cagey grandmother asked me, chuckling over the implication that she'd made a number of such trips to the kitchen sink with her young grandchildren over the past few years.

For Susan Tolland and Eli Mayer, the birth of their first child, a daughter, two years after their elaborate interfaith wedding gave them another opportunity to be ecumenically creative. "With my family history you couldn't slide through it. My mother has a lot at stake in having events recognized," Susan explained. Since Eli wasn't willing to raise his daughter exclusively as a Catholic and since Susan wasn't ready to give up her Catholicism for an exclusively Jewish home, they opted once again for a mixed affair—"another home-made thing."

"This is truly a religious home," said their priest from the wedding, casting a reassuring glance at Susan's eighty-one-year-old Catholic grandmother who was skeptical, at best, about yet another untraditional chain of events outside a church. The twenty friends and family members held candles in the Mayer living room while passages from the Jewish Reform prayerbook *Gates of the House* were read aloud. References were made to deceased loved ones and to the rabbi from their wedding who was unable to break an engagement to join them. He would be a source of inspiration and support for the baby as she grew up, they said. Holding her six-week-old daughter dressed in her 1950s Christening gown, the twenty-nine-year-old mother announced her name—Elizabeth Eleanor. "May she bear this name with dignity and honor through a long, healthy and useful life," said the twenty-nine-year-old mother. "As Elizabeth grows in body and mind, may the law of truth be found on her lips, and justice and love in her heart. Amen."

Eli blessed the wine with a Hebrew prayer, and they all toasted their happiness and sat down for a festive meal.

When Samuel Carroll Mayer was born three years later, however, Susan and Eli sighed with exhaustion at the idea of another homespun, ecumenical affair. The last one had been hard work, and they had felt tense, trying to please so many relatives who missed the rituals and sacred phrases they knew so well. Elizabeth's naming ceremony had been "a little forced, a little too self-conscious," Susan realized. The couple was ready for another approach.

Besides, their baby son needed a circumcision, an essential sign of Jewish identity that Susan and Eli were committed to honor. Given their predisposition toward acknowledging events in a spiritual way, the idea of a simple procedure in the hospital seemed too sterile. As Susan describes the evolution of her plans, "I did such soul searching about a bris. But one day it suddenly seemed so right for us. Whatever feelings of rejection I had about it dissolved. I was in the hospital and I remember sitting up and thinking, 'Ah! We're going to have a bris! I'd better get busy making some calls.' The first person I phoned was a Jewish friend who knew a rabbi who was also a mohel."

Bris is the Yiddish word for *Berit Milah* (also referred to as a *Berit*), the oldest religious rite in Judaism. Almost 4,000 years ago, Jewish males adopted circumcision, the surgical removal of the foreskin from the penis, as a sign of their membership among Jews and their covenant with God. As early as Genesis 17, the Torah records God's words to Abraham, spelling out the rules that have been practiced for approximately forty centuries: "Every male among you shall be circumcised. You shall circumcise the flesh of your foreskin, and that shall be the sign of the covenant between Me and you. And throughout the generations, every male among you shall be circumcised at the age of eight days. . . . And if any male who is uncircumcised fails to circumcise the flesh of his foreskin, that person shall be cut off from his kin; he has broken My covenant."

The *mohel* is the person trained and licensed to perform the surgery. Three adults are chosen to be godparents, and one of them, a man, assists the mohel during the ceremony, which takes about five to ten minutes. The hope expressed through prayers and readings is that the child grows up to have a life of study, marriage, and good deeds. During the service which can take place at a home, hospital, synagogue (which is rare), or even a country club, the child is also given his Hebrew name, which is a second name used for religious purposes only. During baby Sam's bris, for instance, the rabbi said, "Let him by known in the household of Israel by the name Shmuel Kalman," in honor of his late grandfather and great-grandmother.

What Susan and Eli liked best about their ceremony was its authenticity. Paradoxically, Susan also felt she'd done right by her parents and grandmother by not telling them about the bris until a month after it had happened. When she did break the news to her mother, the woman seemed genuinely pleased that "something religious had been done for the baby," as well as relieved that she didn't have to participate in it. For Susan, a practicing Catholic, the knowledge that Jesus himself had the same rite of circumcision on January 1st, when he was eight days old, gave her son's ceremony added personal meaning.

For Barbara Radin, however, the idea of a bris for her baby Edward was out of the question. "It's too gruesome!" she declared. "Who needs twenty-seven grinning relatives standing around my living room watching my naked baby cry? We had a doctor do the circumcision in the hospital, and the rabbi came by the house a few days later."

Indeed, there are many ways to handle Jewish traditions, officially and unofficially. A circumcision can be religious or secular, attended by a rabbi, mohel, and assemblage of relatives or simply by a doctor and nurse. According to the Torah it should take place on the eighth day (or later if necessary for health reasons), but many parents who aren't observant arrange it for a day better suited to the baby and the hospital's scheduling.

For baby girls, there's a relatively new service called *Berit Hachayim*, with its blessings modeled after a bris, but without an accompanying surgical procedure, of course; it appears in the prayerbook *Gates of the House*. A more common practice, however, calls for the father (and mother in Reform synagogues) to read from the Torah in the temple a month or more after the child is born. Her Hebrew name is announced and recorded in the census of the synagogue, and her birth is celebrated by the congregation. Boys are often honored in the same way.

My Jewish friends and the rabbis I've talked with insist that these options are far less complicated than they may appear. When I asked Rabbi Greenberg from East Hampton about the tradition of Hebrew names, he said, helpfully, "There's nothing mysterious about it. If a child enters Hebrew school and doesn't have a Hebrew name, the rabbi can give the child one. A rabbi can always help a family arrive at a name. It serves two purposes. It's a name for religious affairs such as a bris, a wedding contract, a tombstone, or being called up to the Torah. It's also a way to keep a person in the family alive and remembered."

To help me identify with the tradition further, he explained how Jesus's Apostles had two sets of names. "Paul was Saul of Tarsis," he said. "He gave himself the name Paul to do business in the non-Jewish world. Simon was a Hebrew name, but Peter was his other name, meaning 'rock.' "

When planning birth rites, it can be assuring to know that circumcision is the only choice that really can't be delayed without serious implications for the child. While the other rituals and traditions have a classic timetable, they're not once-in-a-lifetime opportunities that must be satisfied or else a child will never have a religious identity. Baptism is available throughout a person's life. A bris, covenantal naming, presentation in the temple, or any other Jewish commemorative event is advised by the religious authorities, of course, but they can be celebrated at any point during the child's life.

These rites are not fixed in stone either. If the child grows up and chooses to adopt another religion, the fact of having had a baptism or circumcision will never stand in the way of a person's choosing and finding acceptance within another faith. In other words, the fear that a baptized child can never become a Jew because he or she has been permanently stamped as a Christian is unfounded. And likewise there are no grounds for alarm among Christians who might fear that a child with a Hebrew name or a bris in his history will be disqualified forever from growing up and choosing Christianity.

What matters to Christianity is the baptism, and anything Jewish is not the issue. In Judaism, the answer to the question, "Who is a Jew?," is what matters, and baptism is not the issue. What affects the Jewish status of the children of interfaith marriage is the point of view of each branch of Judaism, not the Christian influences. Reform Judaism, for instance, honors patrilineal descent so it welcomes the children of Jewish mothers and/or Jewish fathers into the temple, its education program, and ceremonies if there's a sincere desire to identify with the Jewish faith and people. Conservative Judaism upholds matrilineal descent, so it requires the children with non-Jewish mothers to have a Jewish education and immerse themselves in a purification ceremony, a *mikvah*, before they have a bar or bat mitsvah. If they have been raised as Christians or become practicing Christians and decide to convert to Judaism as adults they're asked, as are all converts, to give up their former faith and sever other religious affiliations.

Interfaith parents have the freedom to make a choice that works for them and allows them the satisfaction of getting their child off on the right footing. Irreverent Barbara

Radin said she had a brief naming ceremony with the rabbi at their apartment in order to pacify her mother. "It's like all other rituals; you do them and no one ever thinks about them again."

Another Jewish intermarried daughter, however, felt compelled to present her son at the temple and carefully plan his names in order to express her love for her deceased father. "No one told me what I *had* to do; I *had* to do it for me, and my husband was wonderfully supportive." They made their choice together, which is how all ceremonies should proceed.

BAR MITZVAH, BAT MITZVAH, AND CONFIRMATION

"When I was young and going to my friends' bar mitzvahs, I thought they were a joke," an interfaith parent told me recently. "All those little boys' voices were cracking, and parents were spending $20,000. Now that I'm a mother I still hate those big parties, but I'm beginning to see how wonderful it is for kids to have milestones in their lives. My poor Protestant stepson turned thirteen recently, and he was so excited about being a teenager. But all he got was a birthday cake. I'd have loved to celebrate a bar mitzvah with him and make him really feel he'd crossed a threshhold. Teenagers need a time to shine."

Rabbi David Greenberg added another interpretation of the event that's at least 1,500 years old for boys (and sixty years old for girls). "It's the world's most civilized puberty rite," he said. "The only thing a thirteen-year-old has to do is pass a literacy test."

Bar and *Bat Mitzvah*, literally, mean "Son" and "Daughter of the Commandment." Or "Son" and "Daughter Worthy of the Law." On a day close to a Jewish child's thirteenth birthday (or nearest a girl's twelfth birthday within some Conservative congregations), the young person stands before family, friends, and the congregation to recite the bene-

dictions and read the weekly portions from the Torah and/
or *Haftarah* (the prophetic writings) in Hebrew and usually
offers a short and personal interpretation of the chosen passage. The child has studied Jewish history and Hebrew for
an average of four years, intensively for several months,
before the great event, and the solo performance (sometimes
shared with another) marks his or her symbolic entrance into
Jewish adulthood.

"When a child becomes a bar mitzvah," Rabbi Greenberg explained, "a father is commanded to free his son and
allow him to grow. It's the time for parents to begin to let
go. What Judaism is also saying to the adolescent, however,
is 'Here's a book, the Torah, to help you on your way.' "

When teenagers (and others like my husband Jordan)
reflect on their bar mitzvah ceremony, many of them talk
about how proud they were to stand "on stage" as the center
of attention, display their skills and hard work by reading a
foreign language, open the Ark and carry a Torah scroll like
a member of the congregation, and say something of meaning to adults who offered their praise, congratulations, and
gifts. "I did it myself!" they often tell me confidently, as if
by crossing a difficult hurdle on their own they had earned
the right to feel grown-up and responsible.

Jimmy Mitchell is a fourteen-year-old child of an interfaith marriage who adored his bar mitzvah for a number of
illuminating reasons. He loved doing a good job without
mistakes. He had pals in his Hebrew school who made the
preparation fun. At his party after the service, he celebrated
with forty-four of his other friends, along with all his aunts,
uncles, and cousins—Catholic, Protestant, and Jewish.

"My little Catholic cousin from Swarthmore, Pennsyl-
vania, thought it was great to be Jewish," Jimmy said. "After
it was over, he went up to the disc jockey and asked for his
card."

Jimmy loved having his family close around him, "all
warm and friendly."

"They build a little wall and comfort and protect you,"

he said. "Especially my Gram. She was there with banners flying.

"She's not Jewish. She's Protestant. But, the freckled dark-eyed boy with braces continued, "my Gram likes to learn. She was always asking to see my Torah portion and help me with my speech. All the time during my bar mitzvah I knew she was there in front rooting and praying for me, like she did when I was in the musical *Joseph and the Amazing Technicolor Dreamcoat*. When I look at her, we don't even have to talk. It all goes through her eyes. I think Gram's got ESP. It's like God is close with her."

Jimmy Reddick's mother converted to Judaism before her son was born, and the pattern of raising Jimmy and his younger brother as Jews was established early and maintained consistently. Jimmy's family was well prepared for the bar mitzvah and ready to enjoy it. But that's not the case for many other interfaith families who can't imagine such an ecumenical, family-supported ceremony. Tom Johnson, for instance, a Catholic father of a twelve-year-old son and nine-year-old daughter, reflected a point of view often held by interfaith couples when he said, "I'd love to have my son learn Hebrew and the Old Testament, but I'm not wild about a bar mitzvah. It's not part of my tradition. I think I'd find it difficult to go through. I know I wouldn't be able to prod, drill, praise, and create incentives, which is what parents have to do for children in order to help them get through it. It would be hard on my parents, too, and I don't want to do something to hurt them. A bar mitzvah wouldn't bring our family close together."

Indeed, a bar mitzvah can be a touchy subject for all three generations. Jewish parents and grandparents often feel moved by their memories of their own bar mitzvah or their need to perpetuate a tradition that's been an important part of their family for generations. Some feel it's their last chance to give a child a Jewish identity and fulfill their obligations as a responsible Jew. A bar/bat mitzvah would give them peace of mind, they feel, and a comfortable sense of resolution that would end the ambiguity that may have accompanied the child's growing up. Sometimes there's an almost desperate urgency, as if the child will never learn Hebrew, the prayers, or have knowledge of Jewish history and customs unless he or she is forced to study the basics of the faith at this opportune time. For some grandmothers or grandfathers, having the bar mitzvah means so much because it's proof of their power and control over children and grandchildren. The pressure to conform socially may be a factor as well.

For interfaith children, approaching age thirteen can be an especially confusing time because of so many mixed messages and unspoken feelings—their own, their parents, their grandparents—that swirl like a maelstrom around this provocative subject. They see many of their Jewish friends celebrating this rite of passage, and some of them have to deal with the peer pressure to conform and be one of the crowd. Others feel that maybe they'd like a ceremony for themselves, but they sense it's too controversial for their parents to accept, so it's dismissed before their feelings are properly discussed. When they sit in the synagogue or eat and dance at the party afterwards, many teens also feel awkward and unsure how to react. They're confused about what they don't understand in the service. They feel disconnected, jealous, maybe guilty that their disapproval for whatever lavishness they find is really anti-Semitic on their part. What could be an opportunity to learn more about their family's strong beliefs and their own roots is passed up, for want of preparation and support.

I'm incredulous when I hear how poorly some parents handle this subject. They wait too long to think and talk about it, hoping their child will initiate it totally. Whatever talks they do have with their children last about a minute, and, if longer, the conversation often focuses almost exclusively on how elaborate it would be, how much it would cost, and how many presents the child will get.

The way a family deals with a bar mitzvah is often a good index of how they've dealt with the other aspects of their dual heritage at home. A bar/bat mitzvah is a reckoning of sorts, a deadline that puts a child's religious identity into relief and reflects on how much the parent has done—or not done—to enrich it. It shows how comfortably parents, grand-parents, and children have learned to talk honestly with each other about religion and their personal differences. It also calls attention to the Christian parent's feelings about a child's becoming Jewish.

I feel like I've been preparing for the possibility of my children having a bat mitzvah ever since I met and fell in love with Jordan. A bar or bat mitzvah was too unsettling to me *not* to feel compelled to learn about it and find ways to feel more comfortable with its procedures and meaning. So much about it is totally foreign to my experience. The liturgy, the long service with the arcane Bible readings, the exaltation of a single child rather than a group of children, and the sexist glorification of the bar mitzvah boy were some of the features I had to reconcile and understand. I'm still getting used to them.

The deeper problem has been something else, however. Because that event in the life cycle is a very definite stage in the process of a child's separating from parents, it's become associated in my mind with losing my daughters. When I met with Edwin Friedman in Bethesda, I remember men-tioning my image of a bat mitzvah as a waving goodbye to Rachel and Georgia as if we were going to be estranged forever. He leaned back in his rickety black chair, nodded, and without a moment's hesitation said, "Yes, after every bar mitzvah and bat mitzvah I've noticed how sad it is when parents and children kiss good-bye and never see each other again."

Naturally, my expectation was irrational, as his tongue-in-cheek remark quickly reminded me. Nevertheless that fear of separation, heightened by an exaggerated sense of reli-gious differences and ignorance about what it really means for a teenager to make a commitment to a faith and people different from a parent's, is one I've heard expressed re-peatedly by parents and grandparents, Christian and Jew, who, like me, have yet to deal with that important choice. Knowing well how intimidating it can be for many interfaith families to consider whether to have a bar/bat mitzvah, let alone carry out their first one, I've been interested in the varied ways that other families, further along in their experiences with interfaith children, have chosen to handle this stage of life.

Many families personalize a bar/bat mitzvah by making it a small and/or participatory event. Parents learn or relearn the material along with the child. Maybe they create their own service, with or without a rabbi present, within the sanctuary of the temple or outside it. In addition, the teenager or family members can enrich almost every element in the ritual if they wish. They can make the tallis, decorate and print a copy of the Torah and Haftahrah portions, or play music. Adults, both Jew and Christian, can read from the Torah, as well as toast the child afterward with a rich recall of memories and impressions.

Many families follow a classic ceremony in the synagogue but the reception reflects their uniqueness. In Rockville Centre, New York, for instance, Paul Steinman's bar mitzvah feast was prepared by his Vietnamese mother and grandmother, so the menu included, in part, fried wontons, crispy noodles with beef and vegetables, potato pancakes, and chopped liver. According to *The New York Times* (June 29, 1983), "Tung Tu, age 9, thought it was the best bar mitzvah he'd ever been to."

Rose Epstein, an old friend of the family said, "It's a new world, isn't it? I can't get over how nice it is when people accept."

When planning a bar/bat mitzvah the goal is to give the child a rooting section of loved ones and a sense of connection to the rich resources from his or her heritage. It's a challenge to draw from both families in expressing that strength. Although I've yet to hear about a bar/bat mitzvah in which the rabbi is assisted and supported by a Christian clergyman in order to affirm a child's bi-religious richness, I expect that it won't be long before the integration that's become so common within interfaith weddings is introduced into adolescent ceremonies, as well.

A Jewish confirmation is another established option, however. Originated by the Reform branch of Judaism, it's primarily a group ceremony that takes place in the temple during late spring on the holiday Shavuot, the time when Moses received the Torah at Mount Sinai. Traditionally, teenagers are fifteen years old when they declare their commitment to Judaism by completing a course of study and participating in a service that varies in its elaborateness. The preparation can involve anything from years of after-school work to the research and writing of a paper or a community-action project. Some synagogues prefer their students to be older than fifteen; some students prefer a private ceremony with a rabbi. A confirmation can be a flexible and personal event.

Because a bat mitzvah was celebrated rarely in the 1950s and, in the 1960s and 1970s, less commonly than a bar mitzvah, many intermarried Jewish mothers had a confirmation when they were growing up and consider it a pivotal time in their religious development. Writing a complex paper and carrying on challenging discussions with rabbis who treated them as adults were especially important experiences they frequently want to incorporate into their own children's religious education. I've met a number of interfaith youngsters who've also decided, on their own, to have a confirmation. It's a ceremony that's more accessible than a bar/bat mitzvah and one well suited to a fifteen-year-old who's beginning to explore his or her religious identity and prepare for a thoughtful commitment to a faith. As with all the other rites of passage, this one is readily available to Jewish adults, as well.

What many interfaith families feel more comfortable supporting, however, are not ceremonies at age thirteen or age fifteen, but alternate ways to help their children establish a religious identity in the late teens and early twenties when a deeper commitment can be more natural and needed. At thirteen, a child is strengthened by his feelings of mastery of the group identity and conformity. By seventeen, eighteen, or nineteen, however, the period of time when so many interfaith parents have experienced their own meaningful rush of religious consciousness, he often shifts his focus toward spirituality and intellectual questioning rarely possible at an earlier age. A bar mitzvah and confirmation can play an important role, families feel, but the ceremonies are not essential to a child's religious identity; they're a warmup for more important growth that's possible later.

James Fowler helped me look at my responsibilities as an interfaith parent from a broader point of view when, during a telephone conversation from his office in Atlanta, he said, "A bar mitzvah or confirmation can be a significant step toward shaping a religious identity. But there should be no expectation that it's a final decision or that it resolves a religious identity. It should be looked at as a time of *quest*," he emphasized, "with the culmination to come later. It will anticipate the later teens and young adulthood when the independent choices are made."

It was Dr. Fowler, in fact, who first suggested to me the possibility of a religious ceremony for adolescents that could affirm both religious pasts as part of the preparation for a more considered choice and commitment later.

When I discussed the bar mitzvah and confirmation with Rabbi Greenberg in East Hampton, he supplied yet another way of looking at the contributions that interfaith parents can make, no matter how they choose to handle the traditional ceremonies. "To the extent that daily life becomes empty of religious content, the rites of passage become a bigger deal," he said. In other words, interfaith parents have good reason and countless ways to invest their children's lives with religious content that can enhance their ceremonies or supplement them.

A trip to Israel, a summer on a kibbutz, volunteer work on behalf of Soviet Jews, a course on the Talmud, carpentry work to rebuild an old synagogue, and close relationships with special individuals (often grandparents) are some of the important experiences that interfaith teens have mentioned to me.

The equivalent Christian experiences are very similar and equally meaningful. Nothing is ever more instructive than a loving relationship with wise old friends or relatives. Big family events with the cousins, trips to "the old country" or to the part of America where a parent grew up, singing in a choir, studying ethics, lobbying with the Church against racism in South Africa, or teaching poor children in a Catholic parish are additional memories that can make an impression on interfaith teens. Those expressions of Jewish and Christian values can inspire their search for meaning in their daily lives and teach them about the hard work and rewards that are part of their committing themselves to something they believe in, affiliating with others, feeling one's inwardness and being of use in the world.

CHRISTIAN CONFIRMATION

When I move to the subject of a Christian confirmation, I feel as if I'm writing about Chanukah after dealing elaborately with Christmas. A bar mitzvah, like Christmas, usually overshadows the alternate celebration. It's full-blown and intrusive and, more often than not, a big deal among family and friends. A Christian confirmation, like Chanukah, is low-key, sober, and far less intensive. That's not to say that Chanukah or a Christian confirmation is any less meaningful to those who celebrate it. My sense, however, is that interfaith families who choose a Christian confirmation for their adolescents have more often than not prepared for it in advance by agreeing to raise their children as Christians, and most of them have already celebrated a baptism and, if they're Catholic, a First Communion. There's less of a last-minute, surprise effort to squeeze in a Christian confirmation before it's too late, as often happens with a bar mitzvah in interfaith families who haven't planned for a Jewish education for their children at an earlier time.

There are other characteristics that are different, however. A Christian confirmation is usually a group affair that doesn't single out the confirmee. It's seldom attended by more than the immediate family, and it's not marked with elaborate gifts and a big party. The thirteen- or fourteen-year-old stands in front of the church, answers questions about the faith and spiritual beliefs, in a chorus or individually, and then receives the blessings of the bishop. He or she is congratulated for becoming a complete member of the church with the responsibility to protect and carry out its beliefs.

To prepare for the event, teenagers have been to religious classes after school and learned the prayers and creeds that are standard elements in their denomination's liturgy. They've learned how to take Communion, which is the sacrament involving bread and wine in remembrance of Christ's sacrifice and God's love. Catholic students have already had their first formal introduction to the church through their First Communion at age eight, when they put on their white dresses and fancy suits and were celebrated, more royally than at Confirmation, for their entry into the pattern of church life, from Sunday school to weekly Mass. Protestants and Catholics have all been baptised, as well, if not years before the confirmation then at the start of the ceremony itself.

As with Jewish education, there's no prescribed length of time necessary to prepare for these ceremonies. Some interfaith children are products of many years of parochial school. Others studied once a week for three or more years. An interfaith son from my daughter's school decided to be baptised and confirmed on his sixteenth birthday after a few intense months of discovering and familiarizing himself with church worship and information.

Some churches require parents to attend a course that dovetails with the children's preparation for confirmation, so both generations can discuss the material and share what they're learning or remembering. When a parent is Jewish, however, there's even greater need for learning about the ceremony, at least enough to be comfortable with it. When seen through the eyes of an adult who wasn't raised with those traditions, a confirmation, just like a bar mitzvah, can be dramatically strange and threatening. The pageantry, crucifix, references to "Our Lord Jesus Christ," the stained-glass windows, and, in Catholic churches, the unfamiliar statuary, the kneeling, and maybe the background musk of incense are some of the aspects of Christian confirmation that can be unsettling. The initiation rites of both faiths have their special mysteries and vocabulary that take time to accept, let alone comprehend and appreciate for the universal messages they communicate.

As Edwin Friedman once wrote in an essay on ceremonies, "The more one prepares the soil before the celebration, the richer the harvest will be at the event itself."

When it comes to planning a particular ceremony, the following suggestions may be useful:

1. *Search hard for compatible advisers.* The stories that many interfaith couples tell about finding clergy to perform their weddings are often tributes to their own perseverence and talent for detective work. They'll all agree the labor was worth it, however, if they were able to create an event that was loving and memorable. The ceremonies for children require the same special touch, so seek assistance once again from the advisers who are open to helping parents explore the right solution for themselves. The clergy should be a generous source of information, a bridge to the rest of the family, a genuine supporter of the parent and grandparents of the opposite faith, and a flexible and enthusiastic presence who's willing to adapt the old ceremonial models when necessary. Best of all, they're friends and examples to the children, and they can become very important role models and confidants to adolescents.

Since they're often the first members of the clergy that the family of the other faith has ever met, they're also important representatives who can make strong first impressions. Be aware that not all clergy have a warm, open-minded interest in dealing with interfaith issues, so search for those who are genuinely supportive and encouraging. Remember, however, that they are religious officials with civil and sectarian obligations. Even the most innovative, responsive clergy that I've met complain about interfaith couples who treat them irreverently. "I won't appear at any ceremonies as a good-luck charm," said one of the more liberal clergy I've met. "Couples can put a mezuzah around their necks for that."

2. *The best way to learn about ceremonies is to attend them* —lots of them over many years. They're an opportunity to feel part of one's family and community, a way to keep learning about each faith, and models to celebrate the cycles of life. To deprive Jewish/Christian children of their cousin's christening or bat mitzvah, an uncle's ordination or an aunt's wedding because the dual exposure will supposedly confuse them is nonsense. Ceremonies aren't a substitute for religious instruction, but they're occasions when parents and children (and grandparents) can have first-hand experiences with the tangible ingredients of each religion—the vocabulary, objects used, the rituals, clergy, and worshippers—and hear and respond to the beliefs that are expressed. Ceremonies are a chance for parents and children to talk about what they see, feel, and don't understand about the events. With preparation, some selectivity, and sensitivity to the children and one's spouse who can easily think of ceremonies as penance rather than something meaningful, they can become an important, shared experience in a family. No matter how children grow up and choose to celebrate ceremonies for themselves, they'll always have a familiarity that will help them share a life of special occasions with others.

3. *Read about ceremonies and talk to friends, interfaith and otherwise, who've been through them or are planning for them.* I've been helped a great deal by the official manuals used by ministers, rabbis, and priests; these are available in religious bookstores or the libraries in churches and synagogues. I also think *The Jewish Home*, a series of pamphlets about Jewish

traditions and ceremonies published by the Union of American Hebrew Congregations, is invaluable. *Handbook of the Mass*, a paperback written by George Fitzgerald, C.S.P. became my Catholic guide. The newspaper and magazines are also filled with references to ceremonies, and there will be more attention to interfaith ceremonies as the Jewish/Christian population keeps growing. Read what's available and adapt it to one's needs.

The best source of information is always peers, however. The books tell you about the official way to conduct ceremonies and what they mean to a faith and its history. But friends share their personal experiences and practical advice.Of course, the clergy can also be helpful, but they're not as available for the nitty-gritty details and questions that come up day to day. Friends inspire the imagination. And they help you out with such equally essential things as what to serve and wear, how to be diplomatic with the touchy relatives, and ways to really make an event special for children.

4. *Solicit the family's concerns and dreams before any plans go into action.* I'm aware of two stunning instances where this was not the case.

The first involved a bris, which the mother, who was a convert to Judaism, had always said she hated. In fact, she and her husband had negotiated an agreement to raise their children as Jews, and in it she had stipulated that a bris would not take place. Nevertheless, when she was recuperating in the hospital after the birth of her first son, her husband went into action and invited fifty guests, including his Jewish family and her Protestant one, to a bris at their home. The young woman learned about it when her mother called her to find out what a bris was, exactly, and how she could be of help.

In another case, a Catholic wife made an appointment with her Jewish husband for a luncheon. When she stopped by his office that day to pick him up, she was carrying their three-month-old daughter in her arms. When he asked why, she mustered an excuse and, without further explanation, led him across the street to the Catholic cathedral where a priest waited at the door to greet them. The plan, unannounced or ever discussed, was a baptism for the little child. The husband was incredulous and angry, and he stormed out of the church. After many years, the first couple is still very much together, although the mother talks bitterly about her experience; the second couple separated a year later for this and a number of other deceits.

It's essential that parents support each other and make an effort to reach a compromise if one is needed. Although grandparents really don't have the right to interfere, most Jewish/Christian couples try to be sensitive to their feelings as well in order to keep peace and make it easy for the grandchildren. For some grandparents, it's enough merely to air their concerns and feel confident that their wishes are being listened to and taken seriously. Others, however, have very specific requests that, when met, help them feel more at ease about a ceremony. Maybe they want the couple to talk to a priest or rabbi before they act. Maybe they prefer to have the ceremony in a hometown institution or they want an invitation extended to all their cousins. Couples can be alert to the thoughtful gestures that draw grandparents into the occasion.

There are some grandparents that are impossibly demanding. "Sometimes I want to tell couples to tell their parents to shut the hell up," said Father Gary Gelfenbein adamantly, echoing a minister and rabbi who voiced the same complaint.

"I tell couples to make up their own minds," the priest reiterated. "Everyone will adjust."

More often, however, I hear tributes to the grandparents who surprised everyone with their adaptability and warmth. When Barbara Radin's baby son Edward was given the Hebrew name of Moishe Fischl, her Italian father-in-law joined them for the ceremony at home with the rabbi. Barbara looked over at the seventy-three-year-old gentleman at one point before the blessings began. Noticing that he looked a little sad, she asked if anything were on his mind. He paused a bit, then shrugged and asked gently, "Does this mean we can't call him Ed?"

Couples often forget that what's customary for one side of the family is new and strange to the other. They can help clear up misunderstandings and show their appreciation to grandparents who make an effort to learn and accept.

5. *Do as much as you can to plan and anticipate the ceremony you're comfortable with, but remember that it's always the unexpected human touches that make it work.* When I've asked people what they've loved about ceremonies they've attended, they always talk about the brief, personal images that caught them off guard and made them gulp or blink away the tears. At a bar mitzvah, a grandfather handed the Torah to his son who, in turn, handed it down to his son. At a baptism, a mother looked at her baby with adoration as if nothing else in the world were going on in the world except the blessings over that child. A touch of hands, a toast, an acknowledgement of a life well lived or another one about to begin, laughter, a look exchanged between two people—these are what give families a sense of renewal and the connections they have to each other and to the process of life.

When wedding guests circle around the priest and rabbi to compliment them on how wonderful the service felt to them or when the Jewish groom's mother exults in dancing the hora with her Christian daughter-in-law, embracing her and welcoming her to the family, I feel the power of yet another level of connectedness. It's an ecumenical harmony of Christian and Jew expressing their compatibility, their mutual acceptance, and their love for each other. Having seen that magic in many interfaith weddings, I look forward to seeing it even more often in the ceremonies that we celebrate for our interfaith children as they grow.

CHAPTER
12

DAY BY DAY

"Now, tell me the truth. People don't really get upset about intermarriage anymore, do they?" the lawyer asked me, leaning across the dining room table while the ten other guests seated around us listened to our party conversation. "It's not really that important, is it?"

He was a vital, very warm, and successful Jewish lawyer, and his wife, on his right, was a composed, equally warm presence with the added distinction of being a member of the board for a number of large American corporations. They had two intelligent, loved Jewish/Christian sons in their twenties who'd been raised in their stable home.

"Not too many people sit shiva for an intermarried child or ban the grandchild from their lives, if that's what you mean. If there's a real problem in the home, it's not the mixed marriage that caused it," I said, eager to wave the flag another time for how wonderful and diverse I found interfaith children to be and how outmoded the myths about sad, confused children had become.

But once having offered that exemption, I had a strong sense of how inadequate my words had been. All night and later into the day, the image of one of the guests at the table haunted me, and I was reminded repeatedly of what I should have said that would have been much more fitting and useful. The woman who brought the truth home to me was a Jewish grandmother whose son I'd interviewed at length one evening. At the time, I was struck by how obliquely he and his wife, a Catholic, made decisions about raising their three teenage children. The subject was never really discussed in their home. What they offered their children were bits and pieces of each heritage—a bagel here or there, some unfinished conversations, and, on occasion, a sneaked trip to the Catholic church with the children's other grandmother. But mostly, I felt, they passed on their ambivalence, their longing, their static relationship to both backgrounds that left their sons and daughters on their own to patch together their identities out of their parents' confused messages. If the children's grandmother had not sat quietly through my dinner conversation, what would she have liked to express about the joys and sadness, the hopes and concerns that accompany her feelings about her grandchildren's engagement with their Jewish and Christian legacies?

What's true is that the way parents handle their religious heritage and deal with the decisions affecting their children's lives *is* "that important." The feelings generated by this experience *are* "that important." It's not easy or smooth to find one's way through the information and emotions that are as contradictory as they are compatible. But it's essential to face up to those realities and make choices that will benefit the children and ring true for each of our families.

There are questions for all of us. The grandmother at the table wonders how her grandchildren will feel part of the continuum of history and belief that have strengthened her own life as a Jew, and she wonders what her role should be in generating that love and respect.

The newlyweds are just beginning to understand what

each other's religious experiences mean, and they bring their unsureness about how to juggle their responsibilities to family, faith, themselves, let alone the unknown factor of children.

The adults whose parents intermarried many years ago raise other questions, sometimes for the first time, about the meaning of their dual heritage and their own worthy approach to resolving it and allowing it to enhance rather than diminish their lives.

The young children ask where they belong and what they should believe about God and religion.

Interfaith parents, meanwhile, weigh all the above considerations and demands and stake out, as securely as possible, the route that makes the most sense for them and their children. There's no perfect solution, no simple plan, no allowance for coercion or duplicity, and definitely no program that doesn't require adaptations and reevaluation as families change. It's an active, unpredictable, very personal process of making choices, day by day. No doubt the job of raising Jewish/Christian children will become less of a pioneering effort as more families mark the way. But for now it's an exploration with a destination that's unclear. "Be patient toward all that is unsolved in your heart. Try to love the questions themselves," said the poet Rilke.

While we keep asking the questions and testing the solutions, however, we can't forget to congratulate ourselves on an astounding process of growth and learning. If you're wondering just how to congratulate yourself, start with being proud. Appreciate what you've accomplished when you:

- enjoy the distance you've covered since you first met your spouse.

- enjoy discovering the differences and similarities between your family and his.

- cook one new recipe from each side of the family with your child's knowledge or participation.

- open the Christian Bible and the Hebrew Bible at least

to familiarize yourself with each book's character and emphasis.

- assemble a collection of friends, allies, and "consultants" from Catholicism, all branches of Judaism, and a sampling of Protestant denominations.

- take your children to church and the synagogue for services, ceremonies, and cultural events or tours.

- become comfortable talking about God once again.

- begin a library (with basic texts and histories, stories and guidebooks for the holidays, and biographies of Christians, Jews, and interfaith offspring like your own).

- talk with your children about the meaning of Rosh Hashanah, Yom Kippur, Chanukah, Christmas, Passover, and Easter.

- enjoy a conversation with a rabbi, priest, and minister.

- have a dialogue with other interfaith couples—in a workshop or over dinner—about your religious identities and sense of your children's religious needs and behavior.

- share a holiday with an intermarried friend of the other faith, either by preparing an elaborate seder or attending a religious service, lecture, or festive party together.

- encourage grandparents to share stories with your child about what they love and remember about growing up.

- make sure the children see their grandparents and have enough time together.

- encourage grandparents to talk about their thoughts and feelings with their peers whose children also intermarried.

- point out to your children other Jewish/Christian offspring, famous or otherwise, and the choices they've made about religion and professions and their way to make a contribution in the world.

- answer your children's questions about religion as best you can, sharing your own experiences where it's been natural to do so.

- keep tabs on your children's evolving thoughts about God, their religious identity, and the puzzles they're solving.

With all or some of these accomplishments behind you, you can look forward to more joy and wisdom, deeper commitments and the miracle of watching your children evolve and create rich, authentic lives for themselves. Being part of a Jewish/Christian family is a profound opportunity for everyone who's open to its challenges and unexpected rewards. Trust the way it compels you to build even stronger foundations for your understanding of life and your own experience.

BIBLIOGRAPHY

Adler, David A. *A Picture Book of Jewish Holidays*. New York: Holiday House, 1981.

———. *A Picture Book of Passover*. New York: Holiday House, 1982.

Alexander, Ron. "Bar Mitzvah with a Vietnamese Flavor." *The New York Times*, June 29, 1983.

Allen, Woody. *Four Films of Woody Allen*. New York: Random House, 1982.

Anonymous. *I Married a Jew*. New York: Dodd, Mead & Company, 1939.

Archdiocese of Newark, New Jersey, Commission on Ecumenical and Interreligious Affairs. "Guidelines for Jewish-Catholic Marriages Committee Report (Draft)." February, 1983.

Authorized King James Version. *The Holy Bible*. Massachusetts Bible Society, 1953.

Axelrad, Albert S. "Mixed Marriage and the Rabbi: A Rational Alternative to Company Policy." *Reconstructionist*, December 1983–January 1984.

Berger, Joseph. "Who Is a Jew? The Debate Continues." *Newsday*, September 1, 1982.

Blume, Judy. *Are You There God? It's Me, Margaret*. New York: Dell Publishing Co., Inc., 1970.

Bossard, James H.S. and Boll, Eleanor Stoker. *One Marriage, Two Faiths*. New York: The Ronald Press Co., 1957.

Brothers, Dr. Joyce. *What Every Woman Ought to Know about Love and Marriage*. New York: Simon and Schuster, 1984.

Central Conference of American Rabbis. *A Shabbat Manual*. New York: 1972.

———. *Gates of Prayer. The New Union Prayerbook. Weekdays, Sabbaths, and Festivals, Services and Prayers for Synagogue and Home*. New York: 1975.

———. *Gates of the House*. The New Union Home Prayerbook. New York: 1983.

———. *Rabbi's Manual. Revised Edition*. New York: 1961.

Coles, Robert. *Erik H. Erikson. The Growth of His Work*. Boston: Little, Brown and Company, 1970.

Cowan, Paul. *An Orphan in History. Retrieving a Jewish Legacy*. New York: Doubleday, 1982.

Crohn, Joel. *Ethnic Identity and Marital Conflict*. New York: The American Jewish Committee, 1986.

Croner, Helga, compiled by. *More Stepping Stones to Jewish-Christian Relations, An Unabridged Collection of Christian Documents, 1975–1983*. New York: Paulist Press, 1985.

Darton, Longman & Todd, Ltd., based on the text of The Jerusalem Bible. *The Taize Picture Bible*. Philadelphia: Fortress Press, 1978.

Dawidowicz, Lucy S. *A Holocaust Reader*. New York: Behrman House, 1976.

Eban, Abba. *Civilization and the Jews*. New York: Summit, 1985.

Edwards, Anne. *A Child's Bible. The Old Testament*. New York: Paulist Press, 1978.

Efron, Marshall & Olsen, Alfa-Betty, *Bible Stories You Can't Forget No Matter How Hard You Try*. New York: E.P. Dutton & Co., 1976.

Elliott, Laurence. *Little Flower. The Life and Times of Fiorello La-Guardia*. New York: William Morrow, 1983.

Evslin, Bernard. *Signs and Wonders. Tales from the Old Testament*. New York: Four Winds Press, 1981.

Fahs, Sophia. *Today's Children and Yesterday's Heritage*. Boston: The Beacon Press, 1952.

Fitzgerald, George, C.S.P. *Handbook of the Mass*. New York: Paulist Press, 1982.

Fleischner, Eva, ed. *Auschwitz: Beginning of a New Era? Reflections on the Holocaust*. New York: The Cathedral Church of St. John the Divine, 1977.

Fowler, James W. *Stages of Faith. The Psychology of Human Development and the Quest for Meaning*. San Francisco: Harper & Row, 1981.

Goldberg, Vicki. *Margaret Bourke-White*. New York: Harper & Row, 1986.

Goldman, Ronald. *Readiness for Religion. A Basis for Developmental Religious Education*. New York: The Seabury Press, 1965.

Gordis, Robert, ed. "Children of Intermarriage: Are They Really Jewish? Symposium." *Judaism Quarterly*, Winter 1984–1985.

Greenfield, Howard. *Passover*. New York: Holt, Rinehart and Winston, 1978.

———. *Rosh Hashanah and Yom Kippur*. New York: Holt, Rinehart and Winston, 1979.

Harlow, Jules, ed. *Lessons from our Living Past*. New York: Behrman House, 1972.

Haskell, Molly. "We Don't Match the Way Couples Do on Wedding Cakes." *New Woman*, December 1982.

Herberg, Will. *Protestant, Catholic, Jew*. New York: Doubleday & Company, 1955.

Heschel, Abraham Joshua. *God in Search of Man: A Philosophy of Judaism*. New York: Farrar, Straus and Giroux, 1955.

Isaac, Jules. *Teaching of Contempt*. New York: Holt, Rinehart and Winston, 1964.

Isaacson, Dr. Ben. *Dictionary of the Jewish Religion*. New York: Bantam Books, Inc., 1979.

Jacoby, Susan. "I am a Half-Jew, American born." *Present Tense*, Fall, 1983.

Kaye, Evelyn. *Crosscurrents: Children, Families and Religion*. New York: Clarkson N. Potter, Inc., 1980.

Kleiman, Nancy. "The Language of Mixed Marriage: One Couple's Religious Struggle." *Reform Judaism*, Spring 1985.

Klenicki, Rabbi Leon, ed. *The Passover Celebration. A Haggadah for the Seder*. Chicago: The Liturgy Training Program of the Archdiocese of Chicago, 1980.

Kohn, Judith. "Reaching Out to the Children of Mixed Marriages." *The Jewish Week, Inc.*, November 29, 1985.

Kukoff, Lydia. *Choosing Judaism*. New York: Union of American Hebrew Congregations, 1981.

Kushner, Harold S. *When Bad Things Happen to Good People*. New York: Avon Books, 1981.

―――. *When Children Ask About God*. New York: Schocken Books, 1976.

Lawless, Richard M. *When Love Unites the Church*. St. Meinrad, Indiana: Abbey Press, 1982.

Lewis, C.S. *Mere Christianity*. New York: Macmillan Publishing Co., Inc., 1943.

Lewis, Linda. "Half Jewish Half Something Else." *Boston Sunday Globe*, May 6, 1979.

Luka, Ronald, C.M.F. *When a Christian and a Jew Marry*. New York: Paulist Press, 1973.

Malamud, Bernard. "Pleasures of the Fast Payoff." *The New York Times Book Review*, August 28, 1983.

Mayer, Egon. *Children of Intermarriage. A Study in Patterns of Identification and Family Life*. New York: The American Jewish Committee, 1983.

―――. *Intermarriage and Conversion. A Study of Identities in Transition*. New York: The American Jewish Committee, 1986.

―――. *Love and Tradition. Marriage between Jews and Christians*. New York and London: Plenum Press, 1985.

Mayer, Egon and Sheingold, Carl. *Intermarriage and the Jewish Future. A National Study in Summary*. New York: The American Jewish Committee, 1976.

McGoldrick, Monica, Pearce, John K. and Giordano, Joseph, eds. *Ethnicity and Family Therapy*. New York and London: The Guilford Press, 1982.

Mead, Margaret. *Blackberry Winter*. New York: Pocket Books, 1972.

Morton, Leah. *I Am a Woman—and a Jew*. New York: Marcus Wiener Publishing, 1986.

Naiman, Arthur. *Every Goy's Guide to Common Jewish Expressions*. Boston: Houghton Mifflin Company, 1981.

Nichols, Anne. *Abie's Irish Rose*. New York: Samuel French, Inc., 1924.

Oesterreicher, John M. *The Brotherhood of Christians and Jews*. Newark: Institute of Judaeo-Christian Studies, 1964.

———. *The Rediscovery of Judaism*. Newark: The Institute of Judaeo-Christian Studies, 1971.

Perlmutter, Nathan and Perlmutter, Ruth Ann. *The Real Anti-Semitism in America*. New York: Arbor House, 1982.

Pike, James A. *If You Marry Outside Your Faith. Counsel on Mixed Marriages*. New York: Harper & Row, 1954.

Plaut, W. Gunther. *The Torah. A Modern Commentary*. New York: Union of American Hebrew Congregations, 1981.

Prinz, Joachim. *The Dilemma of the Modern Jew*. Boston: Little, Brown and Company, 1962.

Rawson, Christopher and Lloyd, Reverend R.H. *The Children's Picture Bible. The Childhood of Jesus*. London: Usborne Publishing Ltd., 1981.

———. *The Children's Picture Bible. The Easter Story*. London: Usborne Publishing Ltd., 1981.

———. *The Children's Picture Bible. The Miracles of Jesus*. London: Usborne Publishing Ltd., 1981.

———. *The Children's Picture Bible. Stories Jesus Told*. London: Usborne Publishing Ltd., 1981.

Renberg, Dalia Hardof. *The Complete Family Guide to Jewish Holidays*. New York: Adama Books, 1985.

Robinson, Edward. *The Original Vision. A Study of the Religious Experience of Childhood*. New York: The Seabury Press, 1983.

Rossel, Seymour. *When a Jew Prays*. New York: Behrman House, Inc., 1973.

Rosten, Leo, ed. *Religions of America. Ferment and Faith in an Age of Crisis*. New York: Simon and Schuster, 1975.

Rosten, Philip. "The *Mischling*: Child of the Jewish-Gentile Marriage," an honors paper submitted to the Dept. of Social Relations, Harvard University, April 1960.

Roth, Philip. *Portnoy's Complaint*. New York: Random House, 1969.

Sandmel, Samuel. *When a Jew & Christian Marry*. Philadelphia: Fortress Press, 1977.

Schumacher, E.F. *Small Is Beautiful*. New York: Harper & Row, 1975.

Scopus Films. *Haggadah. A Text for Children*. London, 1985.

Seltzer, Rabbi Sanford. *Jews & Non-Jews Getting Married*. New York: Union of American Hebrew Congregations, 1984.

Silberman, Charles E. *A Certain People: American Jews and Their Lives Today*. New York: Summit Books, 1985.

Singer, Isaac Bashevis. *Chanukah Stories for Children*. New York: Farrar, Straus & Giroux, 1984.

Sklar, Marshall. "Intermarriage and Jewish Survival." *Commentary*, March 1970.

Spann, Paula. "Half-Jews." *Present Tense*, Summer 1979.

Steen, Shirley. *A Child's Bible. New Testament*. New York: Paulist Press, 1978.

Stein, Joseph. *Fiddler on the Roof*. New York: Pocket Books, 1964.

Strassfeld, Sharon and Green, Kathy. *The Jewish Family Book. A Creative Approach to Raising Kids*. New York: Bantam Books, 1981.

The Episcopal Church. *The Book of Common Prayer and Administration of the Sacraments and Other Rites and Ceremonies of the Church*. New York: The Church Hymnal Corporation, 1979.

Turner, Philip. *Brian Wildsmith's Illustrated Bible Stories*. Oxford: Oxford University Press, 1968.

Union of American Hebrew Congregations. *The Jewish Home*, Books 1–8. Reprinted from *Reform Judaism*, 1977.

Van Buren, Paul. *Discerning the Way. A Theology of Jewish-Christian Reality*. New York: The Seabury Press, 1980.

Van der Land, Sipke. *Stories from the Bible*. Grand Rapids, Michigan: William B. Eerdmans Publishing Company, 1979.

Waskow, Arthur. *Seasons of Our Joy. A Celebration of Modern Jewish Renewal. A New Age Guide to the Jewish Holidays*. New York: Bantam Books, 1982.

Weber, Bruce. "The Myth Maker. The Creative Mind of Novelist E.L. Doctorow." *The New York Times Magazine*, October 20, 1985.

Weiss-Rosmarin, Trude. *Judaism and Christianity. The Differences.* New York: Jonathan David, 1943.

Zborowski, Mark and Herzog, Elizabeth. *Life Is With People. The Culture of the Shtetl.* New York: Schocken Books, 1952.

INDEX